1|8²

Palo Alto City Library

The individual borrower is responsible for all library material borrowed on their card.

Charges as determined by the CITY OF PALO ALTO will be assessed for each overdue item.

Damaged or non-returned property will be billed to the individual borrower by the CITY OF PALO ALTO.

OPERATION LUCY

Most Secret Spy Ring of the Second World War

OPERATION LUCY

Most Secret Spy Ring of the
Second World War

Anthony Read and
David Fisher

Coward, McCann & Geoghegan, Inc.
New York

First American Edition 1981

Library of Congress Cataloging in Publication Data

Read, Anthony.
Operation Lucy.

1. World War, 1939-1945—Secret service—Russia.
2. World War, 1939-1945—Secret service—Great
Britain. 3. Espionage—Switzerland. 4. Roessler,
Rudolf. I. Fisher, David, joint author. II. Title.
D810.S7R39   1981   940.54'86'47   80-25242
ISBN 0-698-11079-X

PRINTED IN THE UNITED STATES OF AMERICA

Acknowledgements

We would like to thank the following individuals for their help in the preparation of this book: Dr Reuben Aiynsteyn; M. Drago Arsenijevic; Mr Cecil Barclay; Mr Andrew Boyle; Mr Peter Calvocoressi; Mr Victor Cavendish-Bentinck; Mr Fred Copeman; Mr James Cross; Lord Dacre (Professor Hugh Trevor-Roper); Professor Alexander Dallin; Mrs Leila Dallin; Professor John Erickson; Colonel Hans Fischer; M. Edmond Hamel; Dr H. Gauye; Dr Victor Hofer; Dr Willi Guggenheim; M. Charles Knecht; Herr Jürgen Kuczynski; Dr Hans Rudolf Kurz; Mr Ronald Lewin; Dr August Lindt; Herr Alphons Matt; Dr Bernhard Mayr von Baldegg; Mr Malcolm Muggeridge; Dr Marc Payot; M. Jaques Ponget; Mrs Margaret Powell; Herr Otto Pünter and Frau Isabelle Pünter; Professor Sándor Radó; Colonel K. Reichel; Major Pat Reid; Dr Werner Rings; Dr Xaver Schnieper; Mr Antony Terry; Professor Hugh Thomas; Dr H. Urner; Herr S. Wechsler; Air Commodore F. West; Group Captain F. W. Winterbotham; Dr Zbidek Zeman; our wives, Rosemary Read and Olive Fisher; our research assistant and principal translator, Jonathan Wickham; our translators, Victoria Fisher, Mrs Klein, Jonathan Kydd and David Harris; and last but not least, Barbara F. Weller.

We would also like to thank: Jacques Laplaine and the staff of *Le Canard Enchaîné*, Paris; the direction and staff of: the British Embassy, Berne; the West German Embassy, London; the Swiss Embassy, London; the Imperial War Museum, London; the Institute of International Affairs, London; Department of Defence Studies, Edinburgh University; Ministry of Defence, London; the Home Office, London; Communist Party of Great Britain; the Beecham Group, London; Cantonal Police, Lausanne; Cantonal Police, Geneva; West German Bundesarchiv, Militärarchiv; Swiss Bundesarchiv; Swiss Militärarchiv; the London Library; New York Public Library; Berkshire County Library, Maidenhead; Buckinghamshire County Library, Burnham; Norwich Public Library;

Gazette de Lausanne; *Tribune du Matin*, Lausanne; *Tribune de Genève*.

And finally, our thanks to the staff of the Café du Nord and the Café Kondor, Berne, who kept us supplied with beer and refreshments during our stay in their city.

To our children

Contents

Espionage is an odd profession: for some it is a vocation, with an unscrupulous purity, untouched by mercenary or even patriotic considerations . . .

GRAHAM GREENE *A Sort Of Life*

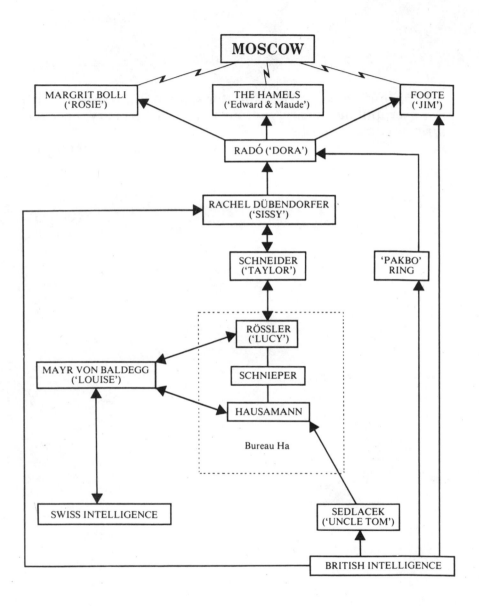

Prologue

The Russian ambassador refused to believe what he was told. As he sat in the British Foreign Secretary's room on 12th June 1941, faced by Anthony Eden and Victor Cavendish-Bentinck, head of Britain's Joint Intelligence Committee, he could only maintain Stalin's view: the devious British were trying to take the heat off themselves by provoking trouble between Russia and her strange ally, Nazi Germany.

'You see,' Stalin said to Marshal Zhukov in Moscow, 'how they are trying to scare us by using the Germans, but also frighten the Germans with the bogey of the Soviet Union, and so goad us one against the other?' To Stalin it was unthinkable that Germany should try to wage war on two fronts at the same time. He was utterly convinced that Russia would not be attacked until Britain had been disposed of, and in Moscow what Stalin said had to be true.

So it was in vain that Cavendish-Bentinck pleaded with Ivan Maisky for a solid twenty minutes, telling him that the information was absolutely reliable, coming from the highest possible source. The Germans were about to invade the Soviet Union. Hitler had already given orders for Operation Barbarossa to begin. There were, said Cavendish-Bentinck, two possible dates for the invasion – but if he were a gambling man he would put his money on 22nd June.

Maisky listened courteously, but remained unconvinced. The British, and various other sources no doubt inspired by them, had been predicting a German attack on that date since April. Certainly there had been troop movements by Germany and Poland, but these had been satisfactorily explained by Hitler, who said that Eastern Poland offered his armies a very good site for training exercises, out of the reach of the RAF's long arm.

When Churchill was informed of Stalin's disbelief, he gave instructions that efforts to convince him of the truth, without disclosing its ultra-secret source, must go on. Even on the afternoon of 21st June,

Sir Stafford Cripps, the British ambassador in Moscow, was still trying to persuade the Russians that they were to be invaded next day. But it was no use. Churchill himself wrote later, 'Nothing that any of us could do pierced the purblind prejudice and fixed ideas that Stalin had raised between himself and the terrible truth.' Indeed, the Russian dictator even went so far as ordering that those who predicted the German attack should be punished! One agent who made his way across the frontier to bring the awful news was actually shot.

Churchill knew that he had to find other ways of passing the information which Britain would continue to obtain about the war in the east. Russia had to be told, had to be helped to defend herself, if the Nazi menace were to be crushed. He sent for Stewart Menzies, who had become Chief of the Secret Intelligence Service in 1939. Menzies listened to the Prime Minister's assessment of the problem: information from Britain's most secret source had to be passed to Moscow by some method which would conceal and protect the source but still convince the ever-doubting Stalin that it was completely reliable.

Menzies considered the problem carefully. There were several possible solutions, but he decided that the best lay in Europe, in neutral Switzerland. He called the Assistant Chief of the Secret Service, Claude Dansey, who had always regarded Switzerland as his private domain. It so happened that Dansey had the perfect instrument to hand.

Part One

CHAPTER ONE

The Making of a Secret Agent

The telephone rang in Fred Copeman's ground-floor flat in Clarendon Rise, Lewisham. It was late on a warm August evening in the long, hot summer of 1947. When Copeman answered it, and identified himself, the voice on the other end was brusque.

'I am speaking from Berlin,' it said. 'Do you know a man called Allan Foote?'

'Yes, of course I know him,' Copeman replied. 'How is he?'

But there was no answer. The line had already gone dead. A few hours later the telephone rang again, and the same male voice spoke once more. 'We are in London now. I'm bringing Allan Foote round to see you, right away.'

'What, now? In the middle of the night?' asked Copeman. 'I'd love to see old Allan, but . . .' He found himself talking into a dead phone again, so he shrugged and replaced the receiver, then made a cup of tea and got dressed.

An hour later there was a knock at Copeman's door on the side of the house. When Fred opened it he saw his old friend flanked by two large men from MI5, the Security Service. The first man stepped forward and spoke, the same voice that Fred had heard on the telephone.

'Mr Fred Copeman? Do you recognise this man?'

'Yes, of course I do. It's Allan Foote. Come in, Allan, and have a drink, or a cup of tea, and tell me what this is all about.'

Foote, six feet two inches tall, his fair, wavy hair beginning to thin on top, smiled at his old friend and stepped forward. But the man from MI5 spoke first.

'You can have half an hour to talk,' he informed Copeman, 'then you must say goodbye.'

Copeman recalls that there was no doubt about the man's meaning. When he said 'goodbye' he meant exactly that. He was to be allowed to talk for thirty minutes, and then could not expect to contact or be contacted by Foote again. Was Foote in trouble? Was he under arrest? If so, why had he been brought here, at this ungodly hour of the morning, instead of being simply locked in a cell? And what had he been doing in Berlin? He looked tired, but quite calm and confident, perfectly sure of himself and not at all like a man under any sort of threat.

The last time Fred Copeman had seen Allan Foote had been in 1938. Since then he had neither seen nor heard anything of his former companion, though in 1942 he had recommended him when asked to suggest someone for dangerous secret operations work in Yugoslavia. It had been an inspired suggestion, but it was a few years too late, for Allan Foote was already occupied, as he proceeded to tell Copeman in the quiet flat in Lewisham.

Fred Copeman had also led an exciting and eventful life. Born in a Suffolk workhouse, he was a Dr Barnardo's boy during and immediately after the first world war. Joining the Royal Navy as a boy sailor, he soon became something of a celebrity when he won the cruiser-weight boxing championship of the Navy. Later he was to be even better known as one of the leaders of the Invergordon Mutiny. After he was discharged the Service, he worked as a dockyard rigger, then as a steel erector, becoming prominent in the Construction Engineers' Union, and then southern organiser for the National Union of Unemployed Workers, arranging and leading hunger marches, for which he was arrested five times. In 1936, at the request of Harry Pollit, Secretary of the Communist Party, he travelled all over the United Kingdom gathering recruits to fight in the Spanish civil war. He collected some five hundred men, helped ship them to France, and led them over the Pyrenees into the conflict, where he became commander of the British battalion. During the second world war he was an active Civil Defence organiser, and now, in 1947, he was once again working for the Construction Engineers' Union, and preparing to stand for Parliament at the next general election. It had been an eventful life, certainly, but Foote's had been even more so.

Alexander Allan Foote was born on 13th April 1905, at 7 Rockley Street, Kirkdale, a suburb of Liverpool. In fact, he might well have been born in Ireland, for the family had only just returned to England after yet another chicken farm had failed under his father, William. The Footes already had a daughter, and later had three more girls, the youngest of whom was born a full seventeen years after Allan. It was not a happy family. Business was always fluctuating wildly, and its uncertainties were reflected in William Foote's temper, which could flare violently with little warning.

Shortly after Allan was born, the family moved to a poultry farm at Armthorpe, near Doncaster in South Yorkshire, and there they stayed. There was never very much money, and the children went to the local school, leaving at the age of fourteen with no academic qualifications. William considered he had married beneath himself, and tended to belittle his wife, May, allowing his children to make fun of her and to mimic her accent. The unhappy family atmosphere was not improved by William's attitude to his children – he only liked his daughters when they were very small. With his son, however, it was a dislike from the very beginning. He never liked Allan, even as a baby – perhaps he recognised too much of his own stubborn determination in the boy's character, and the same violent temper, though Allan was able to control his much better and could remain patient in the face of provocation for a long time before finally exploding.

Allan's best friend as a boy was the local vicar's son. Growing up during the first world war naturally influenced them. Perhaps this was the reason why Allan Foote's favourite boyhood game was pretending to be a spy, and why he always said his ambition was to become one!

It was an ambition that was not to be fulfilled until very much later. He left home for good at the age of fifteen and went to work for a corn merchant in Manchester, where he stayed for the next fifteen years – eventually taking over when the manager left. Allan Foote kept the business afloat through the worst of the Depression, until 1935, when it finally collapsed. For the first time in his life he was out of work.

He looked around for something that would offer both security and the chance of adventure. On 21st July he joined the Royal Air Force, and after basic training was selected to become an airframe fitter.

Allan Foote's career in the RAF was very brief. He was posted to Manston, in Kent, and reached the rank of aircraftsman first class. But his qualities of energy, quickness of mind and resourcefulness were soon noticed. Perhaps he volunteered for special duties, or perhaps he was approached, very privately, and asked if he would be interested in other work, elsewhere. At any rate in the autumn of 1936 he left the RAF, and prepared to go abroad.

Before his departure he visited his sister, Margaret, and told her he was going away to France, and might not see her for a little while. Margaret was aghast.

'You can't just walk out of the Air Force,' she told him. 'You'll be a deserter. You'll never be free again. If you go abroad as a deserter you'll never be able to come back to this country. They'll arrest you and put you in prison.'

Foote smiled confidently. 'Don't worry. It's all been taken care of. I'm quite safe. They can't touch me or do anything to me.'

True to his word, Foote showed no sign that there was any need for concern. He made no attempt to hide from the police, either civil or military, and went about openly under his own name. No one came for him. No one sought him. As he had told his sister, it had all been taken care of. After a few mysterious trips to London, which he never explained to her, he set out for France. On 23rd December 1936, Foote's RAF file was closed, with the enigmatic and unusual phrase 'Illegally absent and discharged the service'. There was no mention of desertion, and nothing to indicate that the RAF might be glad to be rid of him. His conduct had always been exemplary, he had never been in trouble, and he had been expensively trained to do a skilled and valuable job. Normally, when a serviceman becomes a deserter his file is kept open until he is caught, tried and sentenced, even if it takes a lifetime. Occasionally, to mark some special event like a coronation or jubilee, the sovereign will grant an amnesty to deserters, otherwise they must live in fear of arrest and imprisonment in peacetime, and perhaps worse in war.

Allan Foote, however, walked free. Someone, high up, had taken care of everything, as he had said. But was he free – or had he merely moved into something more binding than the RAF?

The organisation into which Foote had been recruited was not the British Secret Intelligence Service as such, then under the control of the legendary Admiral Hugh 'Quex' Sinclair, but a strange, semi-official, semi-private affair known by the melodramatic name of the 'Z Organisation'. This was being built up to operate throughout Europe in parallel with the official Secret Service network. Most of its work is still a mystery, and there are no records of those who were employed by it. Our investigations show that SIS files have nothing in them concerning Allan Foote.

The founder and chief of this strange outfit was Lieutenant-Colonel Claude Edward Marjoribanks Dansey, one of the most controversial figures ever to work for the Secret Service. Born in 1876, Dansey was a veteran of the Matabele wars, and served as a Territorial officer in the first world war, when he was seconded to Intelligence in France. For a short time after the war, he ran a British-style country club in America, where rich Americans could be served in what passed for the manner of English gentlemen. The club failed – but it provided Dansey with many influential contacts for the future, when he returned to England and the SIS.

Dansey was not a popular man. He was violently anti-intellectual, and swore that he would never knowingly employ a university graduate, an antipathy which was heartily reciprocated by the academics who came into the service during the second world war. One of the most distinguished of them describes him now with pungent if un-academic brevity as 'an utter shit and totally incompetent'. This opinion is shared by the majority of people who came into contact with him professionally. But the other side of the coin is expressed by Victor Cavendish-Bentinck, who describes him as 'a shrewd old bird who was very good at his job'.

Certainly, Dansey must have had charm, for he did have many friends in high places. He always believed in operating at the highest levels, and numbered statesmen and powerful businessmen among his friends. One of his closest associates was the film producer Alexander Korda, whom he may have met during the country club phase in America, since it coincided with Korda's own period in Hollywood. Korda's film work brought him into contact with all manner of men and women – he was proud and amused that at one time he had the sons of three British prime ministers working for him (Anthony Asquith, Randolph Churchill and Oliver Baldwin) and actually employed Winston Churchill as a scriptwriter in 1935. He was also able to travel anywhere in the world at will, without attracting suspicion – a perfect cover for the Intelligence work he undertook for Dansey in addition to his legitimate business activities. In view of his fame as a film producer, it is ironic that it was mainly his work for Dansey and British Intelligence which earned him a knighthood.

Dansey, for his part, was made a director of Korda's company, London Films.

One of the places which Korda visited most often and most regularly was Zurich, in Switzerland, which also happened to be Dansey's base in Europe. In Switzerland, too, was Dansey's right-hand man, Frederick 'Fanny' Vanden Heuvel, a papal count who had been managing director of Eno's Fruit Salts until it was taken over by a Canadian company, Harold F. Ritchie Ltd., in the early 1930s. Vanden Heuvel, tall, slim and immensely courteous, looked like everyone's ideal of the perfect old-style diplomat, always impeccably dressed and impeccably mannered, though Malcolm and Kitty Muggeridge recall, with some amusement, that he overdid it slightly by wearing mauve spats with his elegant morning suits. He was another survivor from Intelligence in the first world war. In spite of his name, derived from his Flemish ancestry, he was British with strong Swiss connections. He was educated in Berne and at an English public school, and could speak pure Bernese, the Swiss German dialect which sounds so strange to German ears that during the height of the Nazi regime at least one Swiss youth was able to enjoy travelling on crowded trams in Berlin vigorously expressing his opinions about Hitler at the top of his voice!

Two possible reasons have been suggested for Dansey going to Switzerland in the 1930s, both advanced by former senior SIS men. In one version, having wormed his way back into the Secret Service, he was involved in a scandal over money, banished from London by Admiral Sinclair and sent into exile in Europe, where he set about establishing his own private network of agents with SIS funds but without official SIS approval, sensing the opportunity of building himself a personal power base for the future. In the other, he was brought into the SIS by Sinclair with the specific task of setting up a quite separate Intelligence organisation in Europe, with no visible links to the official Secret Service, to operate in case Britain should ever fall or be overrun, or should the official network be blown. In this case, it would obviously be desirable for Dansey to be discredited by some scandal, to give an excuse for his being sent to Europe.

Whatever the true reason, Dansey set up his Z Organisation. In its early days, the main enemy appeared to be the 'red threat' from international communism and bolshevism, and much of the organisation was concerned with combating this. It was not long before National

Socialism and fascism ranked equal in importance, but communism remained high on the list, even after 1941, when Soviet Russia became Britain's reluctant ally. The official British reaction to the new alliance was put succinctly, as always, by Winston Churchill, who said to his private secretary, 'If Hitler invaded hell, I would make at least a favourable reference to the Devil in the House of Commons.'

It was this organisation, trying to look both left and right at the same time, which saw a potential recruit in the thirty-one-year-old airframe fitter at RAF Manston in 1936. To Foote, Dansey's offer was a wonderful opportunity to make his boyhood dreams come true. Now more than thirty, he was aware of the passing of valuable time. If he was to find adventure it would have to be soon. But where, and how? The RAF was proving a grave disappointment. In Spain a conflict had begun which offered the chance of excitement and action, yet he had signed on as a regular airman.

To the Z Organisation Allan Foote was ideal. He was 'clean'. That is to say, he had never worked for the Secret Service in any capacity. He was apolitical, though he had attended a few left-wing public meetings in Manchester. He was neither an officer nor an intellectual, and he had a North Country accent. There was nothing in his background which could work against him. It only remained to give him something which would work in his favour. What could be better than the Spanish civil war? This would provide him with the excitement he sought, while at the same time establishing him in the eyes of the left as being genuine – he would, after all, be risking his life – and giving him the opportunity to meet, or be brought to the attention of, the appropriate political commissars from Britain and from Russia. And to complete the picture he would be seen as a deserter from the RAF.

There are two time-honoured ways of controlling other countries' espionage networks. One is to find their agents and 'turn' them. The other is to insert one's own men into the network. The second is the more satisfactory, since a turned agent can never be trusted completely, but the problems involved are immense. The agent must be provided with credentials that will stand the closest scrutiny. The Z Organisation now had such a man.

Fred Copeman first met Allan Foote in Spain late in 1936. By this time, Copeman had progressed from being in charge of a machine gun company to the command of the British battalion in the 15th International Brigade. The battalion was fighting at this time on the ill-fated Jarama front, and was suffering not only heavy casualties but also a chronic shortage of supplies.

Copeman was travelling along a road behind the front, trying to organise supplies of arms, ammunition and food for his men, when he came upon an ox-cart at a crossroads. On it, he recalls, were a large quantity of wine, about a dozen very drunken Frenchmen, and a sober, well-built Englishman with fair hair and blue eyes – Allan Foote. Foote informed him that he had been posted to join the British battalion, to serve on the headquarters staff, and that he had deserted from the RAF, in which he had been a corporal.

To Copeman, the news that this bright young man had actually been in the British armed services was welcome, since it indicated that at least he might have some idea of military discipline, a quality sadly lacking in most of the other recruits. That he had been, or so he said, a non-commissioned officer, was a godsend. He happily took him back to the unit, and found him work there.

Shortly after this, Foote demonstrated another quality which impressed Copeman even more – his courage. When Copeman and a wounded comrade were pinned down in a shallow trench by enemy fire, Foote stayed nearby to watch the enemy positions and to do what he could to help, despite the danger to himself. Eventually, with his help, Copeman was able to get out of the trench in safety, and says that he decided there and then that this was a good man to have near him. He therefore appointed him to be his driver. Foote's own account is that he performed the services of battalion transport officer, but was not given officer status because he was not one of the proven 'politically reliable'. Either way, the job amounted to the same thing – ferrying supplies and people – though Foote made it something much bigger.

For the next eighteen months, wherever Copeman went, Foote went too. He became unofficial supply officer, an expert at 'finding' things, including an excellent bed for the battalion commander to sleep on, which always arrived when it was needed, wherever Copeman might be, even under heavy fire. Copeman regards this as a considerable achievement, and one which was particularly valuable as it enabled him to run the unit without having to worry about his own needs.

It was Allan Foote, too, who made a splendid battalion headquarters, carved from the sandstone of a hillside, with seats and tables inside also carved from the rock, and a well-protected, sandbagged entrance. When the battalion ran short of food, or drink, Foote would disappear for a while, invariably returning with a lorry loaded with supplies, and even, on occasions, decent ammunition. No one asked where he had 'found' the stuff, or how he managed to get it back to the battalion. They were content to be able to eat or drink, or defend themselves, and if there happened to be blood on the driving seat, who cared?

On one occasion, when meat had become impossibly hard to find, Foote disappeared for a while and returned with an entire flock of sheep which he had bought from a Spanish peasant. The unit lived on mutton for weeks, until they were heartily sick of it. But they did not go hungry.

His most famous acquisition was a large, black Dodge car, with bullet-proof glass windows, which looked for all the world like something out of Al Capone's Chicago. On the back was a brass plaque which announced that it had been presented by undergraduates of Oxford University. When questioned by Copeman, Foote said he had 'found' it abandoned in a Madrid side street, and decided it would be just the thing for Fred, since it would enable him to go to and from the many conferences at brigade and divisional headquarters more quickly and safely. Copeman refrained from asking more – or even what Foote had been doing in Madrid at all, for by this time he had realised that the fair-haired giant was a law completely to himself.

Foote decided that the big black car was perhaps a little vulnerable. He disappeared again that night, and when morning came Copeman found him in the process of fitting four Lewis machine guns, two fore and two aft, each pair fired by a single button on the steering wheel, like the guns on a fighter aircraft. As soon as the job was completed he insisted on taking Copeman for a demonstration drive behind the lines. With suitable ceremony he pressed the firing button, and the machine guns burst into violent action, hurtling a deadly stream of bullets in the required directions. There was only one drawback – quick-firing machine guns use large quantities of ammunition, and eject an equivalent amount of brass cartridge cases. Within seconds, the interior of the car was a mass of flying brass, as cartridge cases bounced off everything and everybody, and began to pile up on the floor and seats. The demonstration was quickly abandoned, but Foote was quite unabashed, and within twenty-four hours had managed to devise and fit metal chutes to each gun, to channel the cases out of the car.

Copeman, however, cannot recall the splendid guns ever being used in anger. Indeed, only once was there an opportunity for their use, when Foote and he were returning from a visit to Valencia, picking up men along the way. Halfway back to the battalion, Foote declared that there was something he wanted to get for Copeman, and that it would entail a slight detour. They left the main road, and travelled for a few miles, until Copeman noticed that a building they had just passed was flying a red and yellow flag. Franco's flag! Somehow they were behind the enemy lines. Foote turned the car and headed back, but they had been spotted. As they rounded a bend, they saw to their horror a barrier being placed across the road.

Without a moment's hesitation, Foote swung off the road and began weaving the big car through an olive grove, while Moorish soldiers appeared from all directions, firing at them. Somehow, they escaped through the trees, and proceeded at full throttle across open fields.

'That was the only car I've ever known that could actually jump irrigation ditches,' Copeman says. 'How Allan did it I shall never know, but somehow we managed to get back on the road.'

As they headed back for the comparative safety of the main road, Copeman turned to his driver, and asked what had happened to the machine guns, and why had he not used them. Foote replied with his usual good humour that he couldn't do everything at once.

This was the man Fred Copeman remembered from Spain. A man of great courage, able to think on his feet and translate thought into immediate action, always resourceful, who never panicked, and was always cheerful. A man who was capable of wading into four violently drunk soldiers and beating them unconscious with his fists. A man who understood radio and who had the reputation of being able to make practically anything out of a few bits of wire and an old tin can. It is hard to imagine how the Z Organisation could have chosen a better man as a recruit.

In 1938, shortly before the battle of Teruel was about to begin, Copeman was rushed into hospital for an emergency operation on a gangrenous appendix. The surgeons found other troubles, including shell fragments lodged in his abdomen from a narrow escape earlier in the war, and when the operation was complete he was ordered home. For him, the Spanish civil war was over.

Foote stayed in Spain, where he was almost killed by a shell which exploded in front of his car. He was wounded in and around the eyes. Pieces of shrapnel lodged in his face, but after an operation he was sent back on leave to the United Kingdom.

His two years' service had been as exciting and eventful as anyone could wish. They had also served their purpose in other ways, for Foote had been noticed by the party hierarchy, particularly the political commissar and Red Army contact man, Douglas Springhall. He had come into close touch with only one actual Red Army officer while in Spain – a captain who went under the name of Max, following the established practice of Russian officers of concealing their identities behind single first names. Although only a captain, and officially just an observer, the man seemed to wield great authority. He came into Foote's life again in Moscow, when he endorsed his suitability for Red Army Intelligence work, helping to establish him in the confidence of the Director there.

When he left Spain in September 1938, Foote was ready to begin his real work.

CHAPTER TWO

Double Agent in Position

'You will proceed to Geneva. There you will be contacted and further instructions will be given to you.' Foote's orders came from an apparently respectable housewife with a slight foreign accent, in a quiet house in the Central London suburb of St John's Wood. She went on to give him further details of his rendezvous in Switzerland, telling him to stand on the steps outside the busy general post office in Geneva at noon precisely on the appointed day, wearing a white scarf and holding a leather belt in his right hand. As the clock struck twelve he would be approached by a woman carrying in her left hand a string shopping bag containing a green parcel, and in her right hand an orange. She would ask him where he bought the belt, and he was to reply that he had bought it in an ironmonger's in Paris. Then he was to ask where he could buy an orange like hers, and she would reply that he could have hers for an English penny.

The arrangements for the meeting sound bizarre, but they were, in fact, typical of Russian Intelligence procedures.

Foote had been sent back to England from Spain after being wounded, ostensibly to attend the Communist Party Congress in Birmingham that September, though he was not a party member.

To have been selected for such an honour proved how well he was regarded by the political commissariat of the International Brigade. The fact that he had no official connections with the party was most important, for Soviet spies recruited in other countries are never normally allowed to have any recorded affiliations which could draw attention to them.

Foote had been told that he was to drive a Red Cross truck between England and Spain at regular intervals, ferrying medical supplies and comforts. These were provided through the non-political Red Cross with funds raised openly by public subscription. The job therefore sounded highly respectable. But it was also a cover for another job – which was to act as courier between the British Communist Party's London headquarters in King Street, Covent Garden, and the communist command of the British battalion in Spain. Besides messages and medical supplies, he was also to smuggle unauthorised personnel and goods through the Franco-Spanish frontier where controls had been tightened as part of the French policy of non-intervention. He was to make sure that the lion's share of the goods went to the politically enlightened.

Foote said later that he was never sure whether the job he was offered actually existed. If it did, it would seem to have fallen through. But the offer served its purpose in sounding out his reaction to undertaking secret and illegal work. The fact that he jumped at the chance – quite naturally in the circumstances – proved to the people in command that he was the right man for the job they really had in mind for him. But who approached Foote? In his own account, which was highly edited by MI5, Foote himself names Fred Copeman, but Copeman says he has no recollection of being asked to do any such thing, and is sure he never saw Foote after Spain until the night of 2nd August 1947. Yet another account suggests that Foote was recruited through a German or Austrian comrade who had known him in Spain.

The rendezvous in Geneva was duly kept by an attractive woman in her early thirties with 'a good figure and even better legs' (according to Foote), demurely dressed black hair, an orange in her right hand and a string bag containing the stipulated green parcel in her left. She could have passed for the wife of a minor French consular official. Over coffee, she told him her code name was Sonia, which was how he was to address her.

Sonia and Foote continued to meet for several days in various public places in Geneva, while she probed him about his background but told him nothing about herself. Later, he was to learn that she went by the name of Ursula-Maria Hamburger or Schultz – the name of her supposed husband, Alfred, who was said to be serving a prison sentence in China for activities as a Russian spy. Her real name, however, was Ruth Kuczynski. She was the daughter of a well-known German Jewish economist, Professor René Kuczynski, who had fled from Berlin to England in 1935. We will use her code name here, and refer to her as Sonia for the sake of simplicity. At that time, she was living in a modest chalet at Caux-sur-Montreux with her two children and her old German nurse. She had inherited control of the spy ring in Switzerland from another attractive young woman known as Vera, who had gone on to other jobs (maybe even in St John's Wood, London?) before returning to Centre, the Russian Intelligence head-quarters in Moscow, to run the network from there.

Foote was to come into direct contact with Vera later, but at the time he knew nothing of her, or even, amazingly, for whom he was supposed to be working. Having discarded the thought that it could be the British Communist Party, he had at first considered that it might be the German CP or perhaps the Comintern. Now, it was becoming clear that his masters were the Russians themselves, though he was still in the dark as to which particular part of the Russian system, the political KGB or the military GRU. However, as a British penetration agent with no specific brief it did not much matter which Russian organisation he penetrated. All he had to do was remain calm, patient and for the time being passive, doing nothing which might spoil his chances of being accepted into the Russian camp. His role was essentially a waiting one.

Sonia appeared to be well satisfied and gave him his first orders: he was to go to Munich posing as a tourist, learn to speak German, make as many friends as possible, and generally keep his eyes and ears open. She then gave him two thousand Swiss francs to cover his expenses, and told him to meet her again in three months time in Lausanne, on the steps of the general post office there. Until then, he was on his own.

After a brief return trip to London to collect his things and no doubt make his report to the Z Organisation, Foote made his way to Munich. He found a pleasant pension on the Elizabethstrasse in which to stay, where he was taught German by one of the other guests, who also happened to be a local member of the SS. Professionally, he passed his time preparing political reports on the German scene as he observed it.

Looking for a convenient and cheap place to eat, he came across a restaurant called the Osteria Bavaria which served an excellent lunch for the equivalent forty years later of 3p. It turned out to be Hitler's regular eating place, too. The proprietor had been a friend of Hitler's during the first world war, and the Nazi leader had been visiting the restaurant for over fifteen years, sometimes as often as three times a week when he was in Munich. Foote, too, made a habit of eating there, and soon grew accustomed to seeing Hitler and his entourage sweeping through the busy restaurant to the private room that was reserved for them at the rear.

Foote was a sociable man who soon made friends. Before long he had acquired a circle of acquaintances in Munich, among them an attractive young woman called Agnes Zimmermann, tall, slim, bright-eyed, with long auburn hair. She worked at that time for the central fashion bureau in Munich, which organised fashion shows both locally and in other European cities. She moved in artistic and literary circles where there was a general dislike of the Nazi regime and its destruction of German cultural values.

The friendship developed, and Agnes took Foote home to meet her family. It was an intelligent, happy household. Her widowed mother made a living by teaching languages, and her younger sister worked as a secretary at the university. The two girls had been strictly brought up, and educated at a convent school. Frau Zimmermann had taken great pains to keep her daughters away from politics during their youth, though she herself had been a German secret agent in Switzerland. She had little love for the Nazis, making no attempt to hide her feelings from her children when they were more grown up. She liked the blond Englishman, and he was always welcome in her home.

As friendship turned to love, Foote began thinking of the future. He wanted to marry Agnes, but before he could propose he had to tell her the truth about himself. Since at that stage of his career as an agent there was precious little he could tell her that would endanger anyone, he can have had little hesitation in taking her into his confidence. In any case, he soon found he had no cause to fear – she was eager to help. They became engaged to be married, and when he settled in Switzerland she visited him regularly, until the war made such travel impossible. Then, they had to make do with writing letters, though even that became difficult when Agnes was drafted first into the post office censorship bureau, because of her knowledge of English and Italian, and later into a job in military administration. All that, however, was in the future as Foote settled into Munich, learned German and watched Hitler eating his lunches at the Osteria Bavaria.

At the end of his first three months in Munich, Foote returned to Switzerland to keep his rendezvous with Sonia, when he presented his report on life in Germany. This was obviously satisfactory, for she told him at last the identity of his mysterious employers. It was then that he discovered that he had been working for Red Army Intelligence, the GRU. He had been screened by the Russian Director of Military Intelligence and accepted as an agent, with a monthly salary of $150 (all Russian spy payments and all accounts were in US dollars, even though it was often almost impossible for the networks to obtain this currency) plus all reasonable expenses.

Now that he was officially a Russian agent, Foote was given a code name – 'Jim'. He was also told how to contact Moscow in emergency, should he lose contact with Sonia for any reason. He was to go to the Russian embassy in any country other than his own or the one he was working in, and speak to the military attaché alone. Under no circumstances was he to give his name or show his passport to any official. If he had difficulty getting to see the military attaché alone, he was to use any device he chose to persuade the embassy officials, even to threatening them with punishment by the NKVD. When alone with the attaché, he was not to give his name, only a message which the attaché would send immediately to Moscow. In Foote's case the message would read: 'Jim operating in Jersey and a native of Brazil has lost contact with Sonia, who lives in Sicily, where she has a musical box, and wishes to re-establish contact with the Director.' This, translated from the simple code, meant: 'Foote, operating in Germany and a native of Britain, has lost contact with Ruth Kuczynski, who lives in Switzerland where she has a radio transmitter, and wishes to re-establish contact with the Director of Centre.' Only if permission were given in the Director's reply was he to tell the military attaché his name.

The instructions for emergencies when a suitable military attaché could not be found were more bizarre. He was in such a case to take a ticket for the Far East via the Trans-Siberian Railway, leave the train at Moscow, and call at the headquarters of the Red Army itself, where he would be put on to the correct department. He should not travel on an Intourist ticket or have an Intourist visa stamped in his passport, since this would indicate to other governments that he was favourably inclined to the Soviet Union, and might therefore be suspect.

Thus suitably instructed in at least some of the professional secrets of the spy, Foote returned to Munich to continue to keep his eyes and ears open. In particular, he was told, Centre was interested in his report about Hitler's lunch sessions at the Osteria Bavaria. More information was required.

Sonia also told Foote that he might be visited by another agent, and that they might together be called on to carry out some sabotage mission which the Director could check up on in the newspapers – presumably to make sure that the agents were active. In the meantime, he should continue as before, and was given $900 to cover salary and expenses for a further three months.

For a while, the routine of his life in Munich continued as before. It was a pleasant enough existence, with Agnes to keep him happy, and acquaintances in the SS, made through his language tutor, to provide useful information. The information, however, all pointed to the inevitability of war, casting a shadow over his personal happiness.

In April 1939, Foote received a caller, whom he described as an old friend from the Spanish civil war. To his surprise, he said, the man turned out to be the other agent about whom Sonia had spoken in Lausanne, another Englishman working for the network and based in Frankfurt am Main. In his *Handbook for Spies*, Foote gave the man's name as Bill Philips. The Swiss police knew him as Leon Charles Beurton.

But we know now that his real name was Len Brewer.

Brewer came from a working class background. Orphaned during the first world war (he never saw his father) he was soon to be abandoned by his mother, who fostered him with a railway worker's family, whom she paid for his upkeep. At first she visited him regularly, then, telling the little boy that she would return in the holidays, her visits abruptly ceased. The boy counted the days. When the holidays began, he used to wait every morning in front of his foster parents' cottage, listening to the trains arriving at the railway station nearby, convinced that his mother was on one of them. But she never came again. The payments for his upkeep also ceased.

Not surprisingly young Len felt betrayed. As a result, in later life he tended to be withdrawn, hypersensitive, and subject to frequent fits of depression.

Brewer left school at the age of fourteen and went to work as a farm labourer. During the next few years he worked at a variety of heavy manual jobs. But somewhere he must have acquired some technical training, because in his twenties he became a lorry driver and a car mechanic.

It was while he was working as a quarryman in Jersey that he met the man who was to have a great influence on his life – an elderly Irish ex-seaman, named Moriarty. He had for many years lived in Seattle on the West Coast of America, where he had been a member of the revolutionary anarchist group, Industrial Workers of the World. Moriarty regaled the young Brewer with stories about Joe Hill, the legendary bard of the American labour movement who was executed for a murder he may not have committed, about strikes and lock-outs and demonstrations in Seattle. The heroic myths of the international labour struggle inflamed the imagination of the young man. It was inevitable therefore that when the Spanish civil war began Brewer volunteered for the International Brigade, where, according to his wife, he earned a reputation for reckless bravery.

He was an attractive, well-liked man, of much the same height as Foote though not quite as well built, and together the two tall Englishmen made an impressive pair. They got on extremely well together, and seemed to be enjoying life both in Germany and in Switzerland.

Brewer's assignment in Germany at that time was as vague as Foote's. He had been told to keep an eye on the giant I. G. Farben chemical factory in Frankfurt, and to help Foote with what was euphemistically called 'the Hitler scheme'. It seemed that someone high up in Centre was under the impression that Foote was preparing a plan to assassinate the Führer. Neither Foote nor Brewer much fancied the idea of martyrdom, even for such a worthwhile prize as Hitler's life, at that stage in history. Later, when the war was under way, it might have been a different story, but for now all that the two conspirators were prepared to do was examine the possibilities.

To their surprise, they discovered that an assassination might not be as difficult as they had imagined. Together they ate their 3p lunches and watched Hitler coming and going. As the Führer proceeded through the restaurant, all the diners would stand, as was proper in the presence of a head of state. There did not seem to be very tight security, and the Englishmen decided to test it. One day, Foote stood on one side of the restaurant watching for reactions as Brewer, at a gangway table, slipped his hand furtively into his inside pocket as though reaching for a gun, and swiftly pulled out a cigarette case. None of the Gestapo security men batted an eyelid.

Brewer could have shot Hitler at point-blank range, and no one could have prevented it. However, he would never have escaped from the restaurant. There had to be another way. The room where Hitler ate was divided from the remainder of the restaurant only by a thin plywood partition, on which coats and hats were hung. It would be a simple matter to place a briefcase full of explosives against the partition in the corridor, and since the walls of the restaurant itself were stone, all the blast would be concentrated through the thin plywood. It was a simple plan, which could very easily have succeeded, but Sonia was unable to provide a suitcase full of explosives, the plan was shelved, and history went inexorably onward.

The last days of peace passed quietly. A kind of hush had descended over Europe, though the Germans, the French and the Poles had all mobilised their armies. In mid-August, Foote visited Sonia at her pretty, bourgeois chalet above Montreux, to discuss a plan he and Brewer had conceived to blow up the *Graf Zeppelin*. Again, there were difficulties in obtaining the right materials, and after various experiments trying to set fire to Sonia's sofa cushions, the plan was abandoned. On 23rd August, Foote caught the train back to Germany.

Before it could leave Lausanne station, however, Sonia appeared. She had been listening to the latest news bulletins, and was convinced that Britain, although it had not mobilised its forces yet, was about to declare war on Germany. If Foote were caught there when war was declared, he would be interned. It would be better for him to stay in neutral Switzerland. They swiftly arranged a series of rendezvous in Berne on alternate days, then left the train.

Britain did not declare war on that day – but it proved fateful for another reason. It was the day on which Russia and Germany surprised the world and shocked their supporters by signing the infamous Pact of Non-Aggression. Suddenly, the two arch-enemies were officially friends.

While Sonia, as a life-long communist and long-time Soviet agent was trying to digest Stalin's incredible about-turn, Foote faced the problem of extracting Brewer from Germany, where he was enjoying a short holiday on the shores of the Titisee. It took several hours of impatient telephoning to reach him. He had heard nothing of the events of the past few days – he had been enjoying a peaceful break, free of all cares. However, on hearing what Foote had to say he packed his bags, managed to collect his things from Frankfurt, then crossed into Switzerland and safety.

A few days later, on 29th August, the Swiss Federal Council decided to mobilise Switzerland's frontier troops. Some eighty thousand men, all part-time soldiers, were ordered to fortify positions usually only a few kilometres from their homes. On 30th August both houses of the Swiss parliament met and elected Henri Guisan as *Oberstkorpskommandant*, General Commanding Swiss Forces, a position only occupied during time of war. Guisan was sixty-five, a gentleman farmer from the Vaud, a member of an upper-middle-class family. Slim, ramrod straight, with a small greying moustache and cold eyes, he looked very much the picture of the professional officer. He was to prove a most professional politician, too, in the trying years of wartime. One of his first moves was to appoint a new head of Swiss Military Intelligence, Colonel Roger Masson. That evening, the foreign ministers of some forty nations were reminded that in the event of war Switzerland intended to remain strictly neutral.

At 12.30 p.m. on 31st August, Hitler issued Directive Number 1 for the conduct of the war. At 8.00 p.m. a squad of SS soldiers wearing Polish uniforms carried out a mock attack on the German radio station at Gleiwitz, just inside the German-Polish border. The 'raid' produced a number of casualties on both sides. In reality the dead bodies were those of concentration camp victims dressed up in German and Polish uniforms. It is ironic that the first casualties of the second world war should be the inmates of a concentration camp. The 'provocation' of Gleiwitz provided Hitler with the excuse to invade Poland.

The German advance was rapid, demonstrating the effectiveness of the *blitzkrieg*, particularly against outnumbered, under-equipped and poorly-deployed armies, encouraging the German belief in the total invincibility of the Wehrmacht. Britain delivered an ultimatum demanding the withdrawal of German troops from Poland. Hitler contemptuously ignored it. The ultimatum expired at 11.00 a.m. on 3rd September. The British declared war. The French followed suit at 5.00 p.m. Russia mobilised on 8th September, and on 17th invaded

Poland from the east. The Polish government and high command fled to Romania, and on 27th September, Warsaw fell.

The Swiss stayed on the sidelines. They had officially declared their intention of remaining neutral and had mobilised their forces to make their determination clear to the world. In true 'looking-glass' fashion, they were prepared to go to war in order not to have to do so.

In the safety of Switzerland, Foote had to face an agonising personal decision: should he stay there, ostensibly working for the Russians, who were now allied with his country's enemies? Or should he return home to fight with his countrymen against Nazi Germany? The answer from Dansey, who had himself hurried back to London to take advantage of the internal upheavals in the SIS caused by the imminent death from cancer of the Chief, Admiral Sinclair, was unequivocal. Foote must stay where he was. He was already serving his country.

With the Nazi-Soviet Non-Aggression Pact, resident directors of Soviet spy rings were ordered to withdraw all their foreign agents from Germany, and to break off contact with all those who lived there. To Foote and Brewer this meant being held in Switzerland with nothing to do but practise their radio and coding techniques. It was a nuisance, but little else. To those like Sonia, who had spent their lives fighting fascism, the pact came as an appalling shock. It was as though the Pope had ordered the Jesuits to join in Devil-worship and to celebrate the black mass. According to Foote's own *Handbook for Spies*, Sonia never recovered. Her faith was shattered, and she began to look for a way out.

To Foote, this was a splendid opportunity. If Sonia went, he was ideally placed to take over as resident director of her network, perhaps of all operations in Switzerland since there was no official Russian presence in the country, an excellent achievement for a British penetration agent. He began working actively towards that end, encouraging Sonia to think of leaving. Meanwhile he and Brewer installed themselves in a small *pension* in Montreux, just below Sonia's chalet, which they visited regularly for their lessons in Soviet espionage techniques.

Only two major complications disturbed the peace of Foote's existence during those early days of the 'phoney war'. The first was a shortage of money, for with the closing of the frontiers couriers were no longer able to bring cash into Switzerland. Sonia was supposed to have an income from Moscow of $460 a month. Foote also had an income from the British, but none of the others could be allowed to know or even to suspect this. However, by using her reserve funds, Sonia was able to keep going until Moscow could make new arrangements. In fact, the shortage of money did have one beneficial result for Foote and Brewer. It prevented them being transferred by Centre to Romania, in which event it is doubtful whether they would have survived.

The second complication was much more dangerous. Centre sent a new recruit to work with Sonia as an additional radio operator. His code name was Alex, and he had a Finnish passport issued in Canada, where he was supposed to have lived before coming to Switzerland. In reality, the passport was a forgery. Alex was actually a German called Franz Abelmann, who had been recruited, like Foote and Brewer, from the International Brigades in Spain. He should have been a useful member of the ring, particularly later when radio traffic became intense, though as things turned out that would have been inconvenient for Foote and the British Secret Service. However, they were spared that inconvenience, for Centre had been even more inefficient than usual – Abelmann could speak not a word of either Finnish or English.

The Swiss police soon discovered this – it is tempting to speculate on how they came by the information, but we have no definite indication that it was from Foote or the British. They raided his room, where they found the components for the radio transmitter he was building, and his short career in espionage came to an abrupt end. He was arrested and interned for the rest of the war.

Sonia waited in fear, for the Swiss police had seen Abelmann at her house during one of their routine check-up visits. She took her radio set, which she usually left lying carelessly about the house, and buried it in her garden in a biscuit tin. However, the police never followed up the matter, and Abelmann remained simply a nuisance first to Sonia and then to Foote, as they were ordered by Moscow to make sure that he was looked after and kept comfortable in his internment.

Being buried in the garden did not improve the radio set's performance, and Foote was constantly having to attend to it. Nevertheless, Sonia managed to keep in touch with Centre, calling once a month to pass political and economic reports and to ask about money.

In December 1939 she received an order which came as a shock to Foote, poised as he was to take over from her. For the first time, Foote realised that they were not the only Soviet espionage ring operating in Switzerland. There was another, with its own resident director based in Geneva, a Hungarian called Sándor Radó. If Radó was an experienced, trusted agent – which he must be as a resident director – then it might be he and not Foote who would take overall control. It would not be long before he knew the nature of the competition, for Sonia's orders were to contact Radó and put her transmitter at his disposal.

CHAPTER THREE

The Marxist Mapmaker

Sándor 'Alex' Radó, the only apparent threat to Foote's hopes of controlling the Soviet espionage organisation in Switzerland, was a Hungarian geographer who had been an exile in various parts of Europe since his youth. Both he and his wife were long-established communists, known and respected in Moscow. Radó was a professional, and to Foote he seemed a formidable rival.

He had been born in Ujpest, an industrial suburb of Budapest, in 1899. On his mother's side the family was well-connected, with relatives who included the first Hungarian professor at the Sorbonne University in Paris, a famous doctor and a general who later became Minister of Defence. Radó has always tried to play down his bourgeois ancestry, preferring to stress that his father was born and raised in Budapest's gypsy ghetto. But although he has tried to prove that he had a tough childhood, it could hardly be described as deprived.

His father had a commercial business which was sufficiently prosperous to pay for summer holidays in Italy or Austria or on the Adriatic coast, and for Alex and his younger brother and sister to attend high school. Alex was a bright pupil, always top of his class. He excelled in English, French, German and Latin and was a keen musician. But his real passion was for geography. He was fascinated by maps and the idea of foreign travel from the age of six, when he encountered his first map in a weekly magazine. Significantly, the map was of Russia, and Radó says it became engraved on his memory, a powerful influence on his later life.

The cosy existence of families such as the Radós was shattered by the first world war, and afterwards by the collapse and dissolution of the Austro-Hungarian empire. Radó was called up at the age of seventeen, and served as an officer on the general staff of the artillery in Budapest, having been saved from a posting to the front by the influence of his relative, the general.

While still serving in the army, Radó studied law and politics at the University of Budapest, coming into contact for the first time with the works of Marx and Engels. They were a revelation to him, and, coupled with reports brought back by returning prisoners of war of the events taking place in Russia, they made a deep and lasting impression. By the time of the Hungarian revolution of 1918, Radó was a convinced communist. He joined the Hungarian Red Army and was appointed a political commissar at the tender age of nineteen.

The revolution collapsed within a year. Radó was forced to flee for his life from the 'white terror' instituted by Admiral Horthy and his counter-revolutionary forces. In fact, he managed to escape under fire, on the only train to make it out of the capital, and, after spending some time in hiding with relatives, made his way, by train again, to the Austrian frontier. There, he narrowly escaped being hanged by the Hungarian border guards, who mistook him for another wanted man for whom they had a death warrant. They even made him choose the tree he was to swing from, and he was only saved at the last minute when recognised by another passenger who vouched for him. With no passport and no papers, he managed to bluff his way past the Austrian frontier guards with a season ticket for the Budapest tramways, and so began his long exile from his native land. It would be thirty-six years before he set foot in Hungary again.

The young Radó made his way to Vienna, where he enrolled at the university to read geography. In Vienna, together with a group of fellow exiles, he started a German-language periodical called *Kommunismus*, which he described as the first 'scientifically edited' communist review outside Russia. It brought them to the attention of Lenin himself, but it did not provide much of an income, and the penniless young Radó had to earn money by taking a job as secretary to a Transylvanian merchant, a job which entailed not only the checking of cargoes on board Danube river barges bound for Romania, but also giving liberal bribes to officials in order to obtain export-import licences.

His experience in this area proved useful shortly afterwards, when he came to establish himself in business. The way in which he seized his opportunity, using the same methods, illustrates perfectly how he was able to reconcile a quick commercial brain with his communist beliefs.

Through a café friend, he discovered that the Austrian government's wireless telegraphy office was picking up daily radio transmissions from Moscow giving news of events in the Soviet Union. Western newspapers at that time carried little news of what was going on in Russia, which was cut off from the world by its civil war, and these broadcasts seemed to be the only regular source of information. They were certainly the only source of news that was consistently favourable to the Soviet regime – a propaganda service which naturally appealed to totally committed souls such as the young Radó. After a little investigation he found that the director of the wireless telegraphy office could be bribed for fifty dollars a month to provide copies of the radio messages. With these and a little capital, Radó would be equipped to set up a news agency dealing in information about Russia, a unique service which must surely provide him with a decent living.

The 'little capital' was the only problem, but Radó managed to persuade the Soviet government to back him to the tune of 10,000 Swedish crowns – an enormous sum for those days – and he set about establishing his agency. It started work under the name Rosta-Wien, the Russian Telegraphic Agency, Vienna, with a staff of Hungarian communist émigrés, at the end of July 1920, just as the Red Army invaded Poland and advanced on Warsaw. Radó visited the Austrian foreign ministry every day, to receive his information directly from the head of the wireless telegraphy office. He had arranged for the head of the ministry press office, who was also in his pay, to give instruction to the doormen that he was to be allowed in at all times, as he was the diplomatic representative of Ethiopia!

Rosta sent out a daily bulletin in German, French and English to newspapers and left-wing organisations throughout Europe. As the business flourished, Radó extended his activities by setting up a telegraphic agency, Intel, as a counterpart to Rosta, dealing in more urgent news for international distribution. He began, too, to collect material from left-wing sources outside the Soviet Union, employing the leading communist journalists of the day as correspondents, and telegraphing western news into Moscow from Vienna.

Radó was still only twenty-two years of age, but he was already establishing himself as a person of some importance in international communism. As a mark of Moscow's recognition, he was invited to attend the Third International in May 1921. Travelling on a Russian passport he made the long, tortuous journey to Moscow via Germany, Lithuania and Latvia. Spy fever was in the air, and at the German-Lithuanian frontier post the German police took him off the train, stripped him, put him into a bath and proceeded to rub his back with some sort of liquid. He discovered later that secret information was often written on an agent's back in invisible ink – but at that time he was only concerned with public information and not with secrets.

Moscow, the city he had dreamed about for so long, came as something of a shock to him. It was in the grip of famine and ravaged by a typhoid epidemic, but the terrible conditions did nothing to lessen his youthful enthusiasm for the cause. In October 1921 he visited the city again, for a conference on the co-ordination and extension of information services. However, his career in this area was to be short-lived. Early in 1922, diplomatic relations were established between Austria and the Soviet Union. This meant that information from Russia could be distributed and controlled on an official basis through the embassy, and there was no longer any need for the Rosta agency.

With Rosta and Intel closed down, the Russians suggested that Radó might continue working in Vienna, as a Soviet press correspondent. But this did not appeal to him. He chose instead to pursue his studies, and persuaded the Soviet government to help him out with a modest grant, so that he could go to Berlin.

The vitality of the German capital had impressed him when he had passed through on his way to Moscow, in contrast to the fading position of Vienna, which he considered was fast becoming a backwater in the international scene. There was another reason, too, why Berlin appealed. He had fallen in love with a girl from there called Hélène Jansen, who had been working in Vienna for the Communist International's bureau for the Balkans, but who had finished her work and was returning to her native city.

Lène, as she was known, was a bright, attractive girl, with the slim good looks, the caustic humour and the quick wit of the typical *Berlinerin*. Radó says he was instantly struck by 'her resolution, her political knowledge, the spirit of her words, the vigour of her artistic style and her self-control'. She had been brought up by her mother after her father, a master shoemaker, had deserted his wife and three young daughters. She grew up in a tiny tenement flat, consisting of one room and kitchen, which in spite of its size was a refuge for German deserters and escaped Russian soldiers during the first world war, and a regular meeting place for messengers from the Bolshevik Party after the Russian revolution.

The family was closely involved with the formation of the German Communist Party, and Lène worked in the newly-established Soviet embassy in 1918. When the ambassador was expelled from Germany in the October of that year she went with him as a mark of protest, under the pseudonym 'Tchistyakova'. The journey to Moscow was arduous and often hazardous, but eventually they arrived safely, only for Lène to be sent back to Berlin carrying a message from Lenin which she was to give to the first congress of the German Communist Party. The image of the frail seventeen-year-old girl mounting the presidential rostrum of the congress, tearing open the lining of her worn old coat and taking from it a piece of material bearing the message from Lenin became one of the legends of the party.

This was the girl Radó followed to Berlin. But there were snags to be overcome. First, his application for a place at Berlin University was rejected, as he was considered to be a suspect person. Then Lène was sent by the party to work in Leipzig. Undeterred, Radó applied for a place at Leipzig University, and managed to get himself accepted. The two lovers could be together, and were soon planning to get married. They were then faced with yet another hitch; in Hungary at that time the age of majority was twenty-four and below that age parents' consent or that of the Hungarian authorities was needed for marriage. Radó was only twenty-three, and although living in Germany, his national law still applied. As an exile, however, he could not obtain permission. The stalemate was broken with the aid of friends in the local party, who managed to persuade the Saxon government to make an exception. The official permit was brought to Radó and Lène personally by the Saxon Minister of the Interior, a communist named Paul Böttcher, who was to re-enter their lives nearly twenty years later in very different circumstances.

The newly-married couple settled first in Leipzig, where Radó took up his studies at the university and started work on his political atlas of the Soviet Union. But they were soon involved in other activities. The year 1923 was one of upheaval and unrest in Germany – it marked the beginning of the financial collapse into hyper-inflation which was to throw the country into turmoil. Extreme political movements thrived, and with them the possibility of revolution. The Radós, naturally, were heavily concerned with the forces of the extreme left. Under the pseudonym 'Weser', Alex became chief of staff of the 'workers' companies' which had some fifteen thousand armed men in organised groups throughout central and northern Germany. In the south, and particularly in Bavaria, other movements held sway, led by a young agitator just beginning to emerge as a potent political figure, called Adolf Hitler.

In 1924, Radó successfully completed his studies at Leipzig and published his atlas, the first of the USSR, which instantly established him as an expert on that country. Lène continued to work for the party, and for the next few years they shuttled backwards and forwards between Moscow and Berlin. In 1927, Alex began work on the world's first aerial maps, which involved flying all over Europe, Asia and Africa, often in the most primitive aircraft. He had several hair-raising escapes from disaster, but continued to build his reputation as a geographer, becoming a corresponding member of the Royal Geographical Society in London, and chalking up still more 'firsts' to add to his already impressive list of achievements. He wrote the first guidebook to the new Russia. He made the first political atlas of workers' movements, the *Arbeiter-Atlas*, which was published in many countries, including Britain, where it appeared under the title *Atlas of Today and Tomorrow*. In 1932 he published the first world aerial guide. He also claims to have been the first to coin the phrase 'Soviet Union' as an acceptable shorthand for the Union of Soviet Socialist Republics.

For us, however, the most significant 'first' of this period was his creation of the world's first press agency dealing in maps and geographic diagrams, which he called *Pressegéographie*, as an additional source of income. He was by then supporting a family which consisted of himself and Lène, their two sons and his mother-in-law, so he needed every extra penny he could get. As a foreigner and a communist, he was unable to obtain an appointment in any public institution, which could have given him a regular income, though he did teach at the Marxist school in Berlin. The agency proved successful, and the Radós were soon able to afford a small house at Brintz, on the outskirts of the city.

Life for a while was pleasant for the Radós, but it was not to last for long. On 30th January 1933, they and many of their friends met in the brasserie of the Europa-Haus. They had a great deal to talk about, for earlier that day the aging President Hindenburg had named Hitler as Chancellor of Germany. Suddenly, the door burst open and the new Minister of the Interior, Wilhelm Frick, marched in at the head of a squad of SA storm troopers, half-drunk and screaming at the tops of their voices. Within moments, they had smashed up the whole place – a foretaste of what was to come in the years that followed.

A few days later, Radó was called to the office of the new chief of police, Admiral Levetzow, and questioned about his political activities. The danger signs were becoming too clear to be ignored. While he tried to carry on his business, Radó sent Lène away to friends in Austria, and the two boys and their grandmother to his parents in Hungary.

Lène returned on 27th February. As she stepped from the train at Anhalt railway station, the sky was lit by the flames from the blazing Reichstag building, which had been deliberately set on fire by the Nazis with the aim of discrediting the communists and providing an excuse for attacking the party. Already the mob in the streets was falling upon anyone suspected of having communist sympathies and tearing them apart with animal ferocity.

The Radós decided not to go home. Instead they fled, first to Belgium and then to Paris, where they suffered the irony of being unable to rent an apartment because no one wanted to let rooms to Germans! From Paris they moved on to Vienna, which held happy memories for them both, hoping to set up in business there. But the shadow of the Nazis already hung over the ancient city, and it was soon obvious that there could be no future for them there.

Among the old friends whom they met in Vienna was the former Minister of Justice in Prussia, Kurt Rosenfeld, a communist lawyer for whom Lène had once worked as secretary. Between them, Radó and Rosenfeld came up with the idea of starting a news agency with the sole aim of distributing uncensored news and information about Nazi Germany, untainted by Dr Goebbels' propaganda. It was almost exactly the reverse of Radó's first venture, but the aims were very similar. However, Vienna could not be the base. Paris would be far more suitable.

So, in May 1933, the Radó ménage, complete with mother-in-law and large Alsatian dog, moved into their new home, a pretty cottage at Bellevue, halfway between Paris and Versailles. With Rosenfeld as editor-in-chief, the new agency, Inpress (Agence de Presse Inde-pendente), was set up in a small and smelly office in the Rue Mondetour, near Les Halles, the markets of Paris, but was quickly prosperous enough to move to one of the finest office blocks in Paris, the Elysée Building in the Faubourg St Honoré, opposite the British embassy.

Both the agency and the Radós' home soon became established as the centre of left-wing émigré affairs. Other exiles were always glad to receive an invitation to the little house among the hills of Bellevue, for unlike most of the others Alex and Lène had a real home, in a house, not an hotel or an apartment block. It seemed a haven of peace.

But the peace was not to last. The degenerating political situation brought strong hostility to Inpress from the French authorities and the government now led by Pierre Laval. It became obvious to Radó that the agency was doomed. He would soon be forced to rely for his living on his geographical activities, which he kept alive by magazine work, preparing maps for the French press, and editing the volume on foreign countries for the *Great Soviet World Atlas*.

It was work on the atlas which took Radó to Moscow in October 1935. In Moscow a proposition was put to him which was to change the whole direction of his life.

CHAPTER FOUR

Dora, Alias Albert

Radó had many friends in Moscow. One of them, a Hungarian journalist whom he had known for many years, said he had some useful contacts on the general staff of the Red Army. Perhaps Alex could be given an income and at the same time work more effectively against fascism. If Radó was interested, his friend said, he would introduce him to the right people. 'The right people' turned out to be the chief of the Red Army Intelligence Service, Semyon Petrovitch Ourisky.

'I know that you are no novice in secret work,' he told Radó, 'but secrecy is not the only thing for an Intelligence service. You must be able to take stock quickly of changing political situations, because the work of an Intelligence agent lies in the political field. We must first define those who, in the coming times, will certainly be our military enemies, and on that basis our Intelligence operations can be put into action. You know yourself that the Soviet Union has several potential enemies in Europe. The most important are Germany and Italy.'

He asked Radó where he would like to work, and what cover he could use for his espionage activities. For Radó, the question of a cover was easy, particularly if the Red Army were backing him financially. He would revive his Geopress mapmaking agency, a field in which he was already established in the eyes of the world. It was, for him, a golden opportunity. The choice of country was slightly more difficult. Since France was already covered by an existing network he reasoned that there were two main possibilities, Belgium and Switzerland.

Switzerland looked the safer prospect, being less likely to join in any war, but it was difficult to get permission to establish a business there. The Swiss had no objection to allowing anyone with enough

50

money to live in their country, but they were less welcoming to anyone who wanted to work there and make money from them. Belgium was more open, and was also at that time the least expensive country in Western Europe.

So Radó was given his first orders as a spy. He was to close down his Inpress agency, leave Paris and set up a new Geopress agency in Brussels, where he would also continue to pursue his scientific work as a geographer and cartographer. His contact with Centre, the Intelligence headquarters in Moscow, would be through the existing apparat in Paris, using invisible ink messages carried by hand or sent through the post written between the lines of apparently innocent letters or cards. He was to be known by two code names – to other agents he would be 'Albert', but when dealing with Centre he would use the name 'Dora'.

All seemed set fair, and Radó left Paris in December 1935, heading for Brussels. But for some unaccountable reason the chief of police in the Belgian capital refused point blank even to consider Radó's application for permission to set up his agency there. It was not an auspicious beginning to his new career.

However, there was still Switzerland. Undeterred by his failure in Brussels, Radó journeyed to Geneva, and after some difficulty managed to get the necessary authorisation from the Swiss. As required by the local laws, he took two nominal Swiss partners, one of whom was professor of geography at Geneva University. The professor demanded seventy-five per cent of the shares in the agency, and a large monthly salary, before he would give his recommendation to the police. But he had forgotten he was dealing with a Hungarian: Radó beat the man down to a one per cent holding and a nominal 100 francs a month! With the Geopress agency thus established, he was ready to begin his new career.

In the heat of summer, 1936, as Allan Foote in England was being recruited into the Z Organisation, the Radó household set out for Geneva: Alex, Lène, the two boys, Frau Jansen and the dog. They had a *permis de séjour* for three years. Radó had found an excellent apartment on the fifth floor of a large six-storey block in the Secheron district of the city, Number 113, Rue de Lausanne. It had two bedrooms – one for the two boys and their grandmother, the other for Alex and Lène – a living room, a study, and a small room for the maid. By now the Radós had become sufficiently bourgeois to employ a servant.

The flat had marvellous views across Lake Geneva. In good weather they could even see Mont Blanc. Across the road from the building was the pleasant park of Mon Repos, leading down to the lake itself. The Palais des Nations, headquarters of the League of Nations, the International Labour Office and the International Red Cross headquarters, were all close by. It was the same district in which Lenin had lived during his first Swiss exile.

The Spanish civil war was just beginning, and there was a great demand from many different quarters for maps illustrating the progress of the fighting. Soon, Radó was supplying maps to newspapers and journals throughout Western Europe, to libraries and academic institutions all over the world, to embassies, consulates, ministries, military establishments and even private individuals with an interest in international affairs – such as the deposed German Kaiser. Radó did most of the work himself, with Lène running the office, and a draughtsman to do finished artwork. The only other employee was an official of the League of Nations who came in from time to time to look after the accounts. Radó became accredited to the League press office, which gave him the right to use its libraries and other facilities, and – more important for his real purpose in Geneva – to make many highly-placed and useful contacts.

The information he obtained from these contacts and from his own observation, he passed to Paris. He also prepared maps for the network and a particularly detailed map for Centre showing the locations of all munitions factories in Germany and Italy.

Simple information could, of course, be posted to Centre's liaison men and couriers in Paris, in invisible writing. But maps and diagrams had to be taken by hand. This posed problems for Radó, since one of the conditions of his residency in Switzerland was that he should deposit his passport with the police. Every time he wanted to travel abroad he had to ask for police permission – hardly an ideal state of affairs for a spy. However, Geneva's unique situation came to the rescue. Thanks to its dependence on the surrounding area, a free zone had been created in 1814 where goods and services were under Swiss customs control, although the area was actually part of France. The frontier post was therefore well inside French territory. Radó discovered that he could catch a tram or local train into the free zone and then board a steamer on the lake which would take him to Evian. Since he had joined the boat in France there was no passport control when he left it at Evian, and he could walk from the landing stage and board an express train for Paris without hindrance.

This was the route he took in 1937, on receiving orders to go to Paris and meet a representative from Centre. The instructions were, as usual, precise. He was to sit on a certain bench on one of the boulevards, polish his glasses, open a German newspaper and place a book on the bench beside him. The other agent would join him there.

Precisely on time, a tall, gaunt man appeared beside the bench. He gave his name as 'Kolia'. He had a car nearby, and drove Radó out of Paris. They left the road, and walked into the woods, where they could talk privately. Kolia, remarking approvingly that Radó looked more like a prosperous and highly respectable businessman than a communist spy, went on to inform him he was resident director of the network and that from now on Radó was to work directly with him. They would meet regularly in Paris, at pre-arranged rendezvous, and Radó would give his reports to Kolia alone, who would arrange for them to be sent to Moscow. In addition to the general intelligence information, Radó was now instructed to concern himself specifically with obtaining information about Italian aid to Franco's army in Spain.

Travelling in Italy presented no problem for Radó. He had legitimate business there for Geopress, which had many Italian subscribers, including the fascist newspaper *Il Tempo*. Also as an expert on aerial cartography, he had dealings with the Italian state airline, ALI, and with the Air Ministry. This brought him into contact with many prominent and useful men in the Italian government. Travelling all over the country, he could put his time to good effect by reporting on the secret routes used to ship German troops to Spain via Sicily. He even succeeded in getting himself shown over Italian warships which were about to sail to the Balearics to conduct a blockade.

While carrying on his clandestine work, Radó was also continuing to run his business and pursuing his scientific activities, each sufficient to occupy one man's entire time. It is small wonder that those who knew him in Switzerland remember him always being in a hurry!

One day in April 1938 Kolia arrived unexpectedly in Radó's Geneva office with news that he was leaving Paris and that the Director in Moscow had ordered him to hand over his network to

Radó. The Hungarian was to be Centre's resident director in Switzerland.

'Tomorrow in Berne,' Kolia told him, 'I shall introduce you to a certain Otto Pünter, whose code name is "Pakbo". He has people we can use. Pakbo is reliable, we have put him to the test. He will be your closest collaborator.'

Otto Pünter was born in Berne on 4th April 1900, the son of a respectable local family, and has lived there all his life. A beautifully decorated family tree complete with coat of arms hangs on his living room wall, tracing the Pünter lineage through several centuries. He is a social democrat in the classical European tradition, but not a communist. He became the first socialist newspaperman to be accredited to the Swiss federal chancellory, an achievement which brought him many useful and influential contacts in Swiss political life.

At the age of twenty-seven, when Mussolini came to power in neighbouring Italy, Pünter founded a small press agency which he called INSA (International Socialist Agency), to provide newspapers in Switzerland with uncensored reports of developments in the fascist dictatorship, in exactly the same way as Radó was to do six years later, when Hitler took control in Germany.

It seems inevitable that the paths of Radó and Pünter should have crossed, since they were working in such similar fields. Of the two, it was actually Pünter who entered the world of espionage first, though initially he had no connection with Moscow. Through his political contacts, he was introduced to an Italian exile, Randolfo Pacciardi, one of the founders of the illegal Italian Republican Party and leader of the anti-fascist organisation *Giustizia e Libertà* (Justice and Liberty). The organisation had members spread throughout Italy, including men who held positions in the highest regions of industry, commerce, politics, law, the universities, even in the immediate entourage of Mussolini himself. From these varied sources, Pacciardi received a continual flow of information. It was essential that this be put to good use, so that the world would not be blinded by Mussolini's propaganda. Pünter's agency was ideal for this purpose, and the young journalist gladly accepted the task.

Although the job appeared to be a simple news gathering and distribution operation, it had much deeper implications. Pünter was at the end of a long chain of agents stretching throughout Italy, with contacts among anti-fascist movements in many other countries. He found himself involved in organising protest demonstrations, such as a great leaflet raid over Milan from a borrowed aircraft – which crash-landed in Switzerland. This daring exploit captured the world's headlines. As the 1930s progressed, so Pünter became more and more deeply concerned with the fight against fascism. When the Nazis took power it was natural for him to add Germany as one of the targets of his agency, and to develop excellent contacts there.

His principal adversary in Germany at this time was Goebbels, and his propaganda ministry. To this twisted genius, the Swiss fear of communism was easy meat for exploitation, and he spared neither money nor effort in his campaign to swamp the press with Nazi propaganda. The Swiss are bankers, and bankers believe with holy fervour in the sanctity of money and property. Consequently, even in normal times most Swiss news reports tend to be written from a right-wing point of view, but under Nazi influence the slant became a perilously steep slope, on which truth was liable to be swept away in an avalanche of lies. Nazi magazines and newspapers mushroomed, financed from Berlin with seemingly limitless funds. When one was banned by the federal parliament it simply appeared on the streets next day under a new name. Newspapers and journalists were inundated with material from the Nazi press agencies.

Goebbels preached the importance of the common heritage, the 'blood bond' of all Germans everywhere, both those living in the Third Reich and the *Auslandsdeutsch*, such as the German Swiss. One of the principal Nazi dreams was to see the creation of *Grossdeutschland*, 'Greater Germany', a super nation embracing all German-speaking peoples in Europe.

It was a doctrine which had a considerable number of supporters among the Swiss. Ironically, one of them was the professor of geography who became Radó's partner in Geopress, who drew and published a map showing the distribution of the Germanic race in Europe, which showed the Germans as populating not only Austria, parts of Czechoslovakia and Poland, but also most of Switzerland. There were angry scenes when it was displayed in a shop window in Berne, but the fact that it could be displayed at all was significant.

As a journalist, Pünter was aware of the pressures being applied by the Nazis, and of their methods. He was increasingly alarmed at the

55

dangers to the ancient Swiss democracy, and made complaints to the Bundespolizei, the federal police (the equivalent of the FBI or Scotland Yard's Special Branch) as the force responsible for dealing with subversive activities and crimes affecting the security of the state.

The Bupo, as they are known in Switzerland, were interested in Pünter. What he had to say confirmed much of what they already knew or suspected. Although they were aware of the influx of Nazi propaganda they had not realised its full extent, or the methods used to spread it. Pünter was able to give them the details, including names of journalists and editors who were in the pocket of Goebbels's ministry and of publishing firms and press agencies which were fronts for the Nazis. The Bupo was a small organisation working on a tight budget. A man like Otto Pünter, with an impeccable social democratic background, influential friends in politics and the trade unions, and useful contacts in Germany and Italy, who was willing to pass on valuable information, was well worth cultivating.

With the knowledge that the Bupo would protect him, Pünter was able to pursue his work with even greater vigour. In return for this protection he was able not only to pass on information about Nazi propaganda activities, but also to help in other ways. On at least one occasion he was able to save his country from a plot designed to embroil Switzerland, Yugoslavia and Republican Spain in one of Hitler's carefully-staged 'provocations' – a bombing raid on the Nazi party rally at Nuremburg, which would have made the later 'attack' on the Gleiwitz radio station, Hitler's excuse to invade Poland, seem small beer indeed.

With informants and contacts in various parts of Europe, Pünter had, by the mid-1930s, all the makings of a spy ring at his disposal. But it was not until the Spanish civil war that he decided to use his information for genuine secret Intelligence purposes rather than simply for publication to counter fascist propaganda.

It was inevitable that Pünter should become involved with the Spanish conflict, though, unlike Allan Foote, he did not go there to fight. True to his vocation as a communicator, he founded the Swiss-Spanish Society, which had the purpose of keeping the Swiss public informed of events in Spain through films, lectures, articles, pamphlets, and so on. He made two visits to Spain as a journalist with a group of like-minded friends to interview senior republicans, cabinet ministers and members of the International Brigades – in which some hundred and fifty Swiss were serving, despite the law which forbade any Swiss citizen to fight for a foreign power.

On the second of these visits, to Valencia and Barcelona, Pünter was introduced to a Russian Intelligence officer who was working for the Republican command under the pseudonym 'Carlo'. It was an important meeting for Pünter. It resulted in his putting the information obtained by himself and his collaborators in Italy and Germany at the disposal of the Spanish Republican government, and consequently to its Russian 'advisers' and through them to Moscow.

For Hitler and Mussolini, and for Stalin, too, the war in Spain was an ideal test bed, a military laboratory in which new theories of warfare, new weapons, even officers and men, could be tried out under real conditions. It was the finest training exercise imaginable, an opportunity to perfect techniques such as the *blitzkrieg*, aerial bombardment and tank warfare.

Of course, both Hitler and Mussolini denied any involvement with Franco. The League of Nations had decreed that the war was an internal matter which must be left to Spain herself to resolve without help or interference. If the Republicans, still the legitimate government of Spain, were to be able to protest effectively to the League and to other powers against the German and Italian intervention, they first had to be able to prove exactly what was being sent, and how. Pünter volunteered to go into Italy to visit the ports of embarkation for Italian and German troops and obtain first-hand evidence – even though he had a price on his head in Italy as a result of his involvement with the illegal republican movement there. Just as Radó was to do a year later, he watched, noted, and then reported. On his second trip he was joined by his wife Marta, a tiny, attractive girl from the Ticino, the Italian canton of Switzerland. From then on, she was his partner in all his secret activities, sharing the hard work.

Sadly, the information gathered by Pünter and other agents was of no avail. It was compiled into a dossier by the Spanish government and sent to the League of Nations and the governments of Britain, France and Russia – incontrovertible proof of the activities of Germany and Italy. But no action was ever taken. France and Britain were committed to the policy of non-intervention; Stalin was playing his own game with the Germans, more concerned for the safety of Russia itself; and the League, as usual, was utterly powerless.

By now Pünter was leading a well-organised ring of experienced agents spread throughout Europe, and was ripe for further work in the same field. The group had been forced to go underground when it began working for the Spanish, as the Swiss federal parliament had issued a decree in 1935 making it an offence punishable by imprisonment for anyone to set up on Swiss soil an Intelligence service with aims prejudicial either to Switzerland or to any foreign power. A later decree, issued on 25th August 1936, forbade any Swiss support to either side in Spain. The Swiss were reinforcing their strongest protection against attack – strict neutrality.

Even the Bupo could not protect Pünter against these laws, and he was forced to take precautions to safeguard himself and his growing ring of agents, beginning by giving everyone a code name. For himself, he chose the name 'Pakbo', which was composed of the initial letters of the principal meeting places of the group: Pontresino/Poschiavo, Arth-Goldau, Kreuzlingen, Berne/Basle and Orselina. As Pakbo, he continued to work against fascism by providing information to the Russians through Carlo, who had taken the new code name 'Kolia'. It was as Kolia that he handed over Pünter and his ring to the new resident director in Switzerland, Sándor Radó.

Kolia introduced Radó and Pünter over dinner in a Berne restaurant. At the end of the meal he said goodbye and walked alone to the station, where he caught a train direct to Paris. Neither Pünter nor Radó saw him again, though Radó received a postcard from him two weeks later sending greetings for May Day, posted in Moscow. From then on, Radó was in charge.

For the next year there was a steady flow of material from Pünter's ring, complementing that obtained by Radó himself. As tension grew in Europe, with the Munich conferences and Chamberlain's famous piece of paper leading to the occupation of the Sudetenland, Moscow grew more agitated and more demanding. In December 1938 Radó received this message from the Director in Moscow:

> Dear Dora, taking account of the situation which you know so well, I charge you to carry out your mission with the utmost energy, utilising the means at your disposal to the maximum. Rouse Pakbo. Demand from him more intensive work, to obtain interesting military information and to recruit valuable people . . . Pakbo is to concentrate his attention principally on Germany, Italy and Austria.

Radó and Pünter agreed that they should not only make use of their existing sources, but should also try to create new contacts. The flow of information built up rapidly, and for the next few months until the outbreak of war Radó sent to Moscow, via Paris, reports on Italian army and air force movements, naval construction, war industries and liaisons with Franco in Spain. Every warship or submarine that left Naples, Genoa or La Spezia was observed and reported. From Germany, too, came information on the armed forces and on political and military movements. In the summer of 1939, Pünter's agents reported on Germany's preparations for the occupation of the free port of Danzig. From France, too, Radó's and Pünter's agents and contacts sent information on political matters.

The network was still expanding when war was declared and Switzerland closed its frontiers. Radó was locked in Switzerland and with all postal and telephonic communications to France severed he had no means of contacting Centre. All he could do was wait.

In December a letter was placed in Radó's letterbox. It said a representative of Centre would call on him in the next few days. Shortly afterwards a woman arrived. She was about thirty-five years old, tall, slim and attractive, with dark hair, wearing a clinging woollen dress. Radó showed her into his study, where she gave the password and then said with a smile, 'I have been sent by the Director to make contact with you. My code name is Sonia.'

We have already met Sonia. She was Ruth Kuczynski, alias Werner, alias Schultz, alias Ursula-Maria Hamburger, Allan Foote's mentor.

CHAPTER FIVE

Marriages and Removals

Alone with Radó in his study, Sonia gave him the messages from Centre. The Director wanted to know how things were with Geopress, whether Radó had sufficient money, what the possibilities now were for obtaining intelligence, what help he would need to establish a transmitting station and how long it would take. Finally, could Radó maintain contact with Centre through couriers and agents in Italy? Sonia was to report Radó's answers to Centre in her next radio transmission, and she would then bring back the Director's instructions.

Radó told her that Geopress was still functioning. Although the agency had lost many of its clients and a large proportion of its income with the closing of the Swiss frontiers to the west, it still did good business in supplying maps to subscribers not only in Switzerland but also in Italy and even in Germany. He had collected a great deal of useful intelligence material and could obtain more, both through his agents and through Pünter's ring. However, until Sonia's arrival he had had no means of getting any of this material to Moscow. Contact by courier through Italy was both difficult and dangerous. He would rather have a transmitter of his own, but would need codes, ciphers, wavelengths, schedules and trained operators to work the set, since neither he nor Lène knew anything about radio.

All this would take time, and Radó proposed that he could meanwhile keep in contact with Moscow through Sonia and her transmitter. Sonia reported this to Moscow, the Director agreed, and from January 1940 the two rings began working together. The network was taking shape. To Foote and the British, this was an unexpected bonus, a surprise windfall. Foote was by now operating the radio set for Sonia most of the time and was thus in a splendid position to monitor and even control the reports of both rings. In March 1940, Sonia received a message from the Director saying that an important agent would be visiting Radó, bringing instructions for the setting up of his own transmitter, his own codes, schedules, and other details concerning liaison with Centre. He would also bring money for both rings. The agent's code name was Kent.

Kent's real name was Victor Sukulov. He was also known as the *Petit Chef*, and was second-in-command of a Soviet network based in Brussels, later to be known as the Red Orchestra. At the moment, this network was lying dormant, waiting for when it would be needed to work against Germany. It had several well-placed contacts in Berlin, who could provide high-grade intelligence material. It was an elaborate organisation, with lines stretching in many directions, but in spite of its subsequent fame it never matched the achievements or the ultimate size of the Swiss-based network.

Radó did not warm towards his visitor. Kent struck him as being far too much a man of the world, enjoying his comforts more than a good communist should. He boasted about the high life he lived in Belgium, with a cellar full of good wines, and the business he ran as a highly profitable cover. Nevertheless, he had brought a code book and Centre's instructions which would enable Radó to set up his own radio and communicate directly with Moscow. Kent spent many hours teaching him the techniques of coding and enciphering messages, and the rules governing secret radio transmissions.

Unfortunately, he had not brought any money. In fact, he asked the impoverished Radó to pay for his stay in Switzerland and his return fare to Brussels. When he departed, Radó had to get Sonia to ask Centre again for money, and eventually he had to travel with Lène through Italy to Belgrade – neither Yugoslavia nor Italy were yet in the war – to meet a courier from Moscow who gave him enough money to keep the network operational.

Radó's sources were still expanding, particularly those in Otto Pünter's Pakbo ring which, being independent, had not been affected by Moscow's orders to mark time. Material was still pouring in from many directions. The need for a radio set and for an operator to work it was becoming urgent. But how was Radó to find someone suitable in Switzerland? How was he to get the parts for a transmitter, since the laws against unauthorised radio transmissions in the confederation were strictly enforced.

The Communist Party in Geneva had been outlawed after a cantonal referendum in 1937, but the Swiss National Party was still in existence. (A federal ban on the Communist and Anarchist Parties was promulgated on 6th August 1940, and the dissolution of the Communist Party was ordered on 26th November in that year.) Under normal circumstances it was strictly against the rules of clandestinity to approach a national party in connection with work in its own country, but the circumstances in 1940 were not normal. Radó decided that he had no alternative but to ask Léon Nicole, the Swiss Communist Party leader, if he had any suggestions.

Nicole knew just the right man. His name was Edmond Hamel, and he ran a radio shop at Number 26, Rue de Carouge, Geneva, within easy walking distance of Radó's office. His wife's name was Olga – she had been given a Russian name as a mark of her parents' regard for the refugees from the Tsarist regime who lived in Switzerland before the 1917 revolution.

After checking out the Hamels' record with the party, Radó decided to put them to a simple test. He asked Sonia to visit the little shop in the workers' district of Geneva and buy some radio components. Sonia did so, and Hamel provided the parts without question. A few days later she appeared in the shop again, this time with a list of parts which she gave to the little proprietor. He said he would have to order some of them, and Sonia arranged to return after a week, declining to give either her name or address. When she went back, Hamel greeted her with a question – why did she want these parts? They were, he said, parts for a transmitter, and transmitters were banned. Sonia feigned helplessness. How clever of Hamel to have realised. She was trying to repair a set, but was not having much success. She had been told that the Hamels were good anti-fascists, and knew he would wish to help. Hamel nodded. He was hooked. He suggested that Sonia should bring him the set, and he would repair it. Or, better still, he would build a new one for her. He confirmed what she already knew, that he had not reported her to the police. He had talked it over with his wife, and they had already agreed that they would help.

Sonia left the shop well pleased, promising to return soon. But it was Radó who visited the Hamels next, with the proposition that they should not only build a set for him, but should also operate it, as paid agents. The Hamels agreed and Edmond began making a transmitter immediately. Radó told them their code names would be 'Edward' and 'Maude'.

As with Radó and Lène, Olga was the more dominant personality in the Hamel marriage. She was heavy-boned with thick black hair and big strong hands, a legacy of her peasant background. Edmond, on the other hand, was a small, quiet, mouse-like man, with dark hair and sharp eyes. He was, and still is, a neat, courteous man, taking pride in his work, content with his little shop, which has the words 'Radio Elemah' – his name in reverse – still unchanged above the window today. He learned about radio at the French merchant navy school in Paris, where he was trained as a ship's radio operator. The little shop, which he opened on his return to Geneva in 1933, has a workshop at the rear, which can be reached by a back door, and a flat above, also with a rear entrance as well as a staircase from the shop. It was well suited for secret work.

Although Hamel was already a skilled radio operator, trained to French merchant navy standards, he knew nothing of the specialised techniques of secret transmission, nor of codes and ciphers. His wife knew nothing of either, and would have to learn morse and all the other techniques. Radó asked Sonia to undertake the training of the Hamels. Sonia in turn gave the task to the two Englishmen, Foote and Brewer. Once more, fate had played into Foote's hands.

After the business with Kent and the shortage of funds, Sonia had moved yet again and had installed herself, her children and her transmitter in a chalet just outside Geneva. Foote and Brewer had moved too, so the daily visits to the Hamels after the shop had closed were no hardship. Hamel's existing knowledge and training made his instruction simple, but Olga surprised everyone by proving to have a natural aptitude, and soon excelled her husband as an operator. When they began making actual transmissions, however, they refused at first to believe that they were really in touch with Moscow, for the operator at Centre was so bad!

A radio shop was an ideal hiding place for a transmitter, and Sonia moved her set there. Now training and actual transmission to Moscow could be combined. While both proceeded, Hamel worked at making a second set to help cope with the steadily increasing amount of material to be transmitted.

Sonia worried for her children as the Germans swept through Western Europe and closed around the borders of Switzerland. She feared that if the Germans occupied the country, or even if they began to exert sufficient pressure on the Swiss, German citizens such as herself would be forcibly repatriated. She wanted, therefore, to leave while there was still a chance of passing through southern France and Spain into Portugal, and from there to England.

Foote, waiting to take over the ring, encouraged her and no doubt fed her fears with sympathetic advice. He suggested that she should marry Len Brewer and so obtain a British passport. If one is to believe Foote's heavily-edited book, it was to be a *mariage blanche* – one of thousands contracted for similar reasons at that time – but Brewer and Sonia fell genuinely in love, whereupon Sonia retired from the spy business altogether and escaped to England. There Brewer joined her, after he had completed the training of Olga Hamel, and they lived happily ever after.

However, in an interview with the American historian David J. Dallin on 31st October 1953, Foote said that Sonia was *transferred* to England by Centre and worked there with the Soviet apparat based in London. He went on to say that she operated for a time as a channel for Klaus Fuchs's atomic reports to Moscow before escaping to East Germany. We will return to that later.

Sonia herself says that Foote was actually the intended bridegroom, but that he cried off at the last moment, explaining that he was engaged already to an English girl and suggesting instead that she marry Brewer who, it turned out, had been in love with her in his quiet way for some time.

Once again, we can see the master fixer at work: Foote persuading Sonia that Len was the man for her; Foote convincing Len, who may not have needed much persuading, that Sonia was the woman for him. With one simple manoeuvre he gained control of Sonia's network and at the same time removed a tiresome and dedicated English comrade who had known him too long for Foote's peace of mind.

The marriage took place on 23rd February 1940 – an appropriate date, since it is Red Army Day – and Len moved into the chalet with Sonia, to the great disgust of the old German nanny, who, on being told that she was to return to Germany, went to the Swiss police and denounced Sonia and the others. It must have been a nasty moment, but fortunately the police were being plagued at that time by de-nunciations from all quarters and so were not inclined to take such accusations very seriously, and in any case the old woman's French was so bad that what she said came out garbled. Sonia, Foote and Brewer were able to convince the police that the old woman was more than a little crazy, and the moment passed. They quickly packed her off to friends and relatives in Germany who would look after her.

In December, Sonia and her two children set out for England via Spain and Lisbon. Brewer was the only remaining problem for Foote. He was anxious to be on his way, too, but could not travel through Spain, since he was a wanted man as a result of fighting for the Republicans in the civil war. Foote's connections came to the rescue again. Mysteriously, the British consul in Geneva was able to provide Brewer with a British passport in a false name. Perhaps it is not so mysterious when one realises that the consul, Victor Farrell, was an agent of the SIS, working to Vanden Heuvel and Dansey. Brewer returned to England, where he served first in the RAF and then in the Coldstream Guards – though he was still an officer in the Red Army.

With Sonia and Brewer gone, Foote could now concentrate on the real game.

The ring which Foote inherited from Sonia was not large. There was a contact with the Swiss Workers' Party, through Léon Nicole, his son Pierre, and Jules Humbert-Droz, leader of the right-wing faction of the party, with a woman codenamed 'May' as go-between and cut-out. Droz, formerly secretary of the Comintern, had many useful contacts with Germany through the workers who crossed the border between Switzerland and Germany every day. As well as a few unimportant potential sources in Switzerland itself, there was a line into Germany via a woman called Anna Müller, who lived in Basle.

Anna acted as Foote's contact with a character known as Max the Cobbler, who also operated out of Basle, and who was the organ-isation's supplier of passports. In the jargon of the secret agent a passport is known as a shoe, and a forger or supplier is therefore a shoemaker or cobbler. Max Habijanic was a police official in Basle, who had been working for Moscow, with Anna Müller as his liaison, since 1926. In his official capacity he had access to genuine Swiss passports, and he supplied these to agents of Centre for twenty-two years, until he was arrested in 1948. During the 1940s, his salary from Centre was 150 Swiss francs a month plus 100 francs per passport.

His method of working was the same as that of many other cobblers employed by Centre throughout the world. Centre would supply him with details about the person to whom the passport was to be issued – age, physical description, etc. – and he would then go through the Swiss police files until he found someone with roughly the same particulars. The passport would be issued in that person's name, so that in the event of a check it would seem genuine.

Anna, a woman in her sixties, was an important 'letter box' and call address for Soviet agents. She received newly arrived agents and directed them to their destinations. She looked after the transfer of money from France and Germany, in times when this was possible. As a cover, she ran a Moscow-financed private employment agency. Her monthly salary from Moscow – apart from any profit she might have made from the agency – was 450 Swiss francs ($110 US or about £28 at the rates of exchange then).

Anna Müller's most important area of liaison, however, was with a network of agents in Germany. These included a girl with the code name 'Mikki', who lived in Munich and was none other than Agnes Zimmermann, Foote's German fiancée.

Although Foote's own autonomous ring was not large or par-ticularly complex, it was very important to the organisation of the whole Soviet apparat. He controlled the supply of passports, the liaison point for newly arriving agents, an important financial source, and lines into both Germany and France. In addition, he had virtually taken command of all radio communications. He must have been well satisfied with his progress as he received from Sonia a new set of codes, new schedules and new radio call signs. At the same time, he received orders from Moscow to move from Geneva because he was considered to be too close to Radó and the others. His new base was to be in Lausanne, where he moved on 15th December 1940, with a new transmitter built for him by Edmond Hamel. Foote was now on his own. Only Radó stood between him and complete control of Russia's Swiss-based network.

Lausanne is a pleasant town on the north shore of Lake Leman, otherwise known as Lake Geneva. It has often been called 'the city of kings' because of the number of exiled monarchs who have lived there, and has always had a large expatriate community. In 1940 it was full of wealthy refugees – and spies of all nations. It was an eminently suitable place for Foote to live.

There was a curious air of unreality about life in the town at that time. Switzerland was surrounded, the enemy was at the gates – yet the country was not at war and life went on as though everything were more or less normal. The Swiss even took up skiing, replacing the foreigners who normally thronged the slopes. Since there was no petrol for private cars except for doctors or those on essential government service, anyone wishing to travel to Davos or to Geneva or Berne, as Foote often had to, was forced to use trains or buses. In consequence, most people did not bother to travel at all, and towns such as Lausanne turned in on themselves and became self-reflecting and introverted.

Accommodation in the town, as elsewhere, was difficult to obtain. There was an acute shortage caused by the huge and sudden influx of refugees after the fall of France and the Low Countries. The situation was not made easier by a decree issued by the police forbidding foreigners to rent apartments. These were reserved for the native Swiss, partly as a protection for them and partly because of the death of the tourist trade. Since most foreigners had plenty of money, it was felt that they should live in hotels and thus provide a living for Swiss hoteliers during the difficult years of war.

Allan Foote, however, was never a man to be beaten by such minor obstacles. To a man who had been able to rustle up a flock of sheep or a lorry load of sugar in the thick of the Spanish civil war, a Swiss police decree presented no problem. In no time, he had found himself a flat on the fifth floor of a block near the centre of town. When a plainclothes officer from the cantonal police headquarters on the corner of the same street called to check on him and to ask by what authority he had moved into a private flat, Foote turned on the charm and brought out the whisky bottle. Between large glasses of good Scotch he professed ignorance of the order, expressed his willingness to move, but pointed out that it was an expensive flat in an expensive block and that he was therefore contributing far more to the Swiss economy than he would be living *en pension* in a modest hotel. As the whisky in the bottle diminished he suggested that since he was already in residence, it would be simpler for everyone if he were granted official permission to stay there for a further six months. They could discuss the matter again at a later date. Through a haze of de luxe Scotch, the police officer accepted the argument and granted Foote the permission he sought. It was renewed every six months afterwards.

Number 2, Chemin de Longeraie is a six-storey block of apartments built in the early years of the century. It stands three-quarters of the way up a steep hill, from which there is a good view of the lake. The interior of the building has been remodelled recently, but in 1940 flat 45, on the fifth floor, was self-contained and at the end of a short corridor. The flat consisted of a living room, a bedroom with alcove in the French manner, kitchen and bathroom. The furnishings were old and worn and the rent was expensive at 200 francs a month, with six months payable in advance. But it was worth it. The flat was perfect for a man in Foote's peculiar profession.

From inside the flat he could hear the footsteps of anyone approaching along the corridor, so that he would have warning of arrivals. He drilled a hole in the front door in order to see out. Later, he asked a friend to stand outside and check what he could see of the interior of the flat when Foote lifted the cover of the spyhole. The answer was encouraging: 'Nothing'. In his living room he was far enough away from his neighbours to prevent them hearing his transmitter. When it was not in use, he hid it, with his code books, in a secret compartment which he built into the roof of a fitted cupboard.

Foote was always good with his hands, and the hiding place was a work of art. It was undetectable by the naked eye and could only be opened by inserting the blade of a very thin knife into what looked like a natural crack in a panel, to release a spring catch. He packed the space around the transmitter with paper and telephone directories, so that if anyone tapped on the wall it would not sound hollow. As a further refinement, he disguised the transmitter itself by fitting it into a portable typewriter case. He even made a wireless key which could be strapped to his thigh, so that if the need ever arose he could walk along a street carrying the 'typewriter' in one hand while tapping out a message with the other in his pocket. As far as we know, the need never did arise, but the device is a further illustration of Foote's ingenuity.

Yet one problem remained. It was impossible at that time to transmit powerful signals to Moscow without a fairly large outdoor aerial – but such aerials were banned in Switzerland along with private transmitters. Without an aerial, Moscow might as well have been the moon, so Foote again decided that boldness was the only answer.

Adopting, as he said, 'the air of an idiot and foreign child', he went to a local radio shop and explained that he wanted an aerial for his radio set, so that he could listen to English medium-wave broadcasts because his French was not good enough for him to follow local and continental stations. Surprisingly, the man believed his story – even though the mere explanation of the problem required a considerable command of the French language. But then people usually did believe Foote. In due course, the mechanic arrived at the flat with a variety of aerials designed to receive medium-wave signals with minimum interference, none of them remotely usable for the purpose Foote really had in mind. It took several glasses of Scotch whisky from Foote's seemingly inexhaustible supply to persuade the man that what was needed was a long, straight aerial, not one of the fancy contraptions which would stand out from street level like a sore thumb.

The aerial was duly erected, and Foote was ready to begin transmissions to Moscow. But when he tapped out his call sign for the first time the set refused to work, a further example of the difficulties under which the secret agent operates. He had been forced to smuggle the pieces from Geneva wrapped in his dirty laundry. When the set was assembled, the crystal refused to oscillate. It took a further and maddening two weeks, during which he could receive but not send, before he finally got through. Moscow continued sending its call sign, 'NDA – NDA – NDA', indicating that he should reply to their signals, but it was not until 12th March that, after tapping out yet again his call sign 'FRX – FRX – FRX', he received the reply 'NDA – NDA – OK – QRK5', meaning that Moscow was hearing him loud and clear.

In his role as an eccentric British exile, Foote began establishing himself in Lausanne with typical thoroughness. First, he secured his base, charming his landlady and winning the devotion of the *concierge* Mme Müller, and of his charwoman, Hélène. He always took time to chat to Mme Müller, who stopped him each morning with the question: 'Well, Mr Foote, what do you think of this morning's news?' She said he was a better source than any newspaper, 'but he didn't keep you talking for ages'. He obviously understood when a lady was busy. His relationship with his char took a more practical form. One of his acquaintances recalled after the war that his friends had always suspected Foote of having left-wing sympathies, because he gave his charwoman a rise without her asking for one, and still paid her when he was away. 'You have to eat, even if I'm not there,' he used to tell her. Living amid the hard-nosed bourgeoisie of Switzerland, it is no wonder he won her absolute loyalty.

These sound small victories, but they were in fact extremely valuable. Foote was constructing round his flat a *laager*, a protective wall, of devoted middle-aged ladies. They proved to be a remarkably effective defence, even against the German agents who were later to come looking for him.

Outside the flat he avoided the company of other foreign exiles, particularly the few British residents, whom he did not like in any case. In the local cafés and bars, he soon acquired a host of drinking companions, mostly Swiss, for whom he played the role of the eccentric British expatriate, *un peu snob*, with a modest private income and a prodigious thirst. He was something of a cook, too, and his rice puddings were said to have been exquisite.

Lausanne café society liked Foote. Not only was he a good listener and excellent company, but he could also take a joke. To the Swiss, all foreigners at that time were spies. When Foote was jokingly accused of being a secret agent he simply roared with laughter.

'Of course I am,' he agreed. 'Oh, my dears, it's impossible to hide anything from you!'

One of his drinking set recalls how he and a group of friends once went to 2 Chemin de Longeraie and rummaged through Foote's drawers and papers, saying they were seaching for his code books and secret documents. Foote was vastly amused and entered into the spirit of the game by helping them search with great thoroughness. Needless to say, they found nothing.

Only very rarely did the mask of amiability slip. His friends vividly remember a mysterious telephone call he once received in a café, when his curt, monosyllabic replies and the suddenly intense, thoughtful expression on his face were quite unlike the man they thought they knew. On another occasion, a group of friends tried to play a joke on him when they called at his flat for a drink and he excused himself, saying he was expecting a visitor. They pretended not to understand, and settled themselves in. When he asked them to leave they refused, saying that they were determined to see his mysterious friend, who was undoubtedly another spy. Suddenly, they found themselves facing a totally different Allan Foote. They left, quickly.

Stories such as these, however, are all from people being wise after the event. At the time, they accepted him for what he seemed to be, and were all genuinely surprised when he was eventually arrested. Even while he was lying in prison in 1943 and 1944, most people thought the police had made a dreadful mistake. They would have been more astonished had they known the amount of work he accomplished. The professionals who finally hunted him down were full of admiration. As the codebreaking specialist Marc Payot told us, 'Most spies are very lazy – but Foote worked like a Trojan.'

During the day, Foote kept up his cover as the friendly neighbourhood drinker and English eccentric, boozing in bars and cafés with his friends. But at the same time he was arranging secret meetings with his informants, couriers and members of his own ring. He explained his absences from the café scene by saying he was going to cinema matinées, though the times when he travelled further afield to visit Radó in Geneva, Anna Müller in Basle or Pünter in Berne must have called for something more elaborate.

In the evening, at about nine or ten o'clock, he would return to his flat, lock the door, take his code books and transmitter out of the secret compartment, and start work. In the early weeks the pace was not hard, and he could enjoy the clandestine task. But when the quantities of material increased, it became impossible just to encipher and send it in the time available for transmission. Enciphering and deciphering messages is a slow and tedious business, and Foote had to edit and shorten the messages first – providing himself with a further opportunity to tighten his grip on the network's communications.

Foote's regular time of transmission to Moscow was usually one o'clock in the morning. Since radio signals are not discriminatory, his messages could be picked up and checked by his British masters at the same time as by Centre in Moscow, with no one even suspecting. All they needed was his code or cipher. If reception was good and the night's messages short, he was usually finished in two or three hours. But if the messages were long and the atmospherics bad, he often found himself still sending at six in the morning. Several times he only

71

signed off at nine, and on one occasion at the peak of the network's activities he worked for three nights in a row without sleep while still collecting and enciphering material during the day. Long radio sessions are dangerous, increasing the risk of detection. But as the network moved into gear, Foote had no alternative.

CHAPTER SIX

The Last Link: Lucy

Early in 1941, while Foote was busy settling in to his new life in Lausanne, Lène Rado bumped into an old friend in a Geneva patisserie, a plump Polish Jewess whom she and Radó had known by her maiden name of Rachel Gaspary. She had been a shorthand typist in the propaganda and agitation department of German Communist Party headquarters at the same time as Lène had worked there. The two women greeted each other effusively, surprised that neither had known of the other's presence in Geneva, though they had both lived there for some time. But when they parted, they both 'forgot' to exchange addresses.

Lène hurried home to consult Radó, worried that the woman's presence in Geneva might pose a threat to their security, since she knew very well that the Radós had both been active workers for the communist cause all their lives.

But the meeting in the patisserie had not been entirely accidental. At the beginning of May Radó had a message from Centre. The Director told him that there was yet another Soviet ring operating in Geneva, and that he was to make contact with its head, whose code name was 'Sissy'. Her real name was Rachel Dübendorfer – the former Rachel Gaspary. Radó's instructions were to meet Sissy and take her ring into his network.

Radó was not pleased at this order. It seemed to him to break many of the rules of clandestinity. Sissy knew too much about him and about Lène – who was now officially working for the network herself under the code name 'Maria'. The network was becoming dangerously large, he thought, and therefore more vulnerable. Already, with his own, Pünter's and Foote's rings, he controlled over fifty agents, and although he insisted on a proper use of cut-outs and took every possible precaution, the sheer size of the network increased the chances of discovery. To take on Sissy's ring, too, would only add too these dangers.

However, when he found Sissy – by the simple method of looking her up in the telephone directory – he was agreeably surprised to find that she had known for some time that the Radós were in Geneva, but had avoided making any contact for fear of compromising them or herself. She knew the rules of the game.

But this was not the only surprise for the Radós. When they arrived at Sissy's flat they discovered that the man she was living with as her common-law husband was none other than Paul Böttcher, the former minister in the government of Saxony, who had given permission for the Radós to marry twenty years earlier. Böttcher had no papers and was living in Switzerland illegally, another reason for Sissy to adhere strictly to the rules of absolute secrecy. He used the passport of the man with whom Sissy had made a marriage of convenience in order to obtain Swiss citizenship, a man named Dübendorfer. Sissy had divorced Dübendorfer as soon as he had served his purpose, and he no longer had any connection with her.

Sissy's small ring had been operating for some time in the International Labour Office where she worked as a secretary. The ILO, a semi-autonomous organisation within the League of Nations, offered excellent facilities for espionage activities. Its officials were generally treated as diplomats. They enjoyed many of the privileges of the conventional diplomatic world and were issued with a special travel document along the same lines as a diplomatic passport, which enabled them to move freely between countries without customs checks when times were normal.

During the late 1930s there was a strong communist cell in the ILO, and at least six Soviet Intelligence agents were employed there, the most important for our purposes being Christian Schneider, code named 'Taylor'. This ILO ring had access to vital information about the German economic scene, but had been unable to pass anything to Centre since the fall of France. Sissy needed the communications system of Radó's network, which was why Centre had put her in touch.

The risks of absorbing Sissy's ring into the larger network were not as great as Radó had feared. On balance, he considered they were well worth taking – just how well, neither Sissy nor Radó could possibly have foreseen. It was through Sissy that the most important, the most astonishing link was to be made, a link with one single source which was to outweigh the total of all the other sources in the network, a link which would be unique in the entire, tangled history of international espionage.

During 1940, Centre had asked Radó for any information he could obtain on Germany's intentions towards Russia. Apart from one message received through Pünter saying that the Japanese attaché in Berlin had been told by Hitler himself that Germany and Italy would attack Russia after a rapid victory had been won in the west, all the indications were that Russia was safe for some time to come. The Germans appeared to have their hands full elsewhere.

Hitler, however, declared his true intentions behind the locked doors of a conference of his military directors at the Berghof, on 31st July 1940. 'If we crush Russia,' he told them, 'the last hope for England will sink with it. Germany will become mistress of Europe, including the Balkans. For this reason, Russia must be liquidated. The date set for the attack: spring, 1941.' Hitler's choice of date was careful. He told his closest followers, 'I shall not commit the same mistake as Napoleon; when I set out on the road to Moscow, I shall leave early enough to arrive before winter.'

From that moment, the German high command began making plans. Hitler set about securing his flank by establishing friendly relations with the pro-fascist regimes of the Balkans and thus gaining control over the south-eastern part of Europe before the attack on Russia. Units of the army, especially motorised and armoured divisions, were gradually withdrawn from the west, one by one, and sent on manoeuvres in Poland. In September 1940 Germany signed the Tripartite Pact with Italy and Japan. The pact was joined in November by Hungary and Romania, and later by Bulgaria. On 18th December 1940, unknown to Stalin, Hitler issued his Directive 21, the order for Operation Barbarossa, the invasion of Russia.

These preparations included a carefully worked out deception plan by which the Germans hoped to persuade the Russians that they meant them no harm, and that Hitler was actively considering inviting Russia to join the Tripartite Pack, along with Spain and Vichy

75

France, to form a continental bloc against the Anglo-Saxon powers. The plan, with typical German thoroughness, was committed to paper under the heading 'Guidelines for the Deception of the Enemy'.

There were fifteen numbered copies only, marked 'Matter for Chiefs', the Germans' highest category of secrecy and security, and they were distributed by hand. Their contents were never mentioned in radio transmissions, and the existence of such a plan remained secret. One of its principal aims was to convince Stalin that Germany would never attack the Soviet Union without first issuing an ultimatum. In this it seems to have been completely successful.

Stalin continued to believe that his bargaining power with Hitler was strong, and set out on a policy of appeasement and placation. He believed that the Germans would eventually be forced to come to terms with him, if only because of their need for supplies of food, fuel and raw materials which he could provide while the Allies tightened the blockade from the west. He was therefore determined to avoid war at almost any cost.

A great deal has been written and spoken about the responsibility which must be borne for the second world war by the appeasers such as Neville Chamberlain. But the blindness of the Russians, and the cynical way in which Stalin signed the Non-Aggression Pact in 1939, as well as further trade agreements in 1940 and even in January 1941 – after Hitler had given the order for Barbarossa – count equally as heavy. Indeed, in a speech made on 1st August 1940, Molotov, the Russian foreign minister, stressed that German victory over France in that year would not have been possible without Soviet help. During April 1941 Soviet deliveries of raw materials were being made at the full quota, with 200,000 tons of grain and 90,000 tons of petroleum being delivered in that month – at the same time as the British ambassador in Moscow, Sir Stafford Cripps, was trying to persuade the Russians that he had firm information that Barbarossa would begin in June. The last grain train, in fact, crossed from Russia into Germany only three hours before the invasion began.

During this time, the flow of information from Radó's many agents was growing steadily. There were reports through Sissy on the state of German industry, there were political and military reports brought to Radó by Pünter, and there were the first reports of troop movements and military matters from Christian Schneider, again through Sissy.

The nature of Schneider's reports was something of a puzzle to those who knew him, for he was a translator at the ILO concerned with political matters. The previous information he had given had always been concerned solely with politics. Suddenly, he had begun to provide detailed reports of a purely military nature. Sissy questioned the gloomy-faced little man when he met her, wearing as always his black Basque beret and sour expression. He told her that he had found a completely reliable source, who would continue to supply information to the Soviet network with the guarantee that it would be authentic and valuable, on the strict condition that no one but Schneider should know his identity.

Sissy accepted the material gratefully. She passed it on to Radó, who enciphered it and gave it to Foote or the Hamels for transmission, along with the other messages. Schneider's source, in fact, was a German refugee publisher living in Lucerne and working for Swiss Intelligence as an evaluator – Rudolf Rössler.

Rudolf Rössler was born on 22nd November 1897 at Kaufbeuren, near Munich, where his father was a minor official in the Bavarian Forestry Commission. The family were Protestant, God-fearing, and highly respectable – Rössler's sister became a grammar school teacher and his brother a public prosecutor.

Rössler was educated at the *Realgymnasium* in Augsburg, at the same time as another boy, a year younger than himself, Bertholt Brecht. It is intriguing to imagine the future dramatist and director of the Berliner Ensemble and the future publisher and reputed master spy as school friends. Their subsequent careers were very different, yet there are similarities in their characters. Some men are born dangerous not because they are violent – violence can be curbed, after all – but because they are morally inflexible. Both Rössler and Brecht fit into this category. Both, in their different ways, were visionaries, political romantics. Rössler's vision was of a superior German moral spirit that could perhaps be summoned into physical existence.

By the time of Rössler's schooldays, Augsburg had long since left behind the splendours of its ancient past and had become a quiet, provincial Bavarian backwater. No doubt the young Rössler and his friends reacted against the stuffy provincialism of their surroundings, so that when war was declared in 1914 they were eager to volunteer for the army if only to break free of Augsburg and breathe fresher air. But the experience of the years between 1914 and 1918 changed everything. Always intensely serious, Rössler emerged from the conflict with the rank of corporal and a profound horror of war. He was to remain a devout pacifist for the rest of his life.

At the same time, however, his military experience gave him an insight into the workings of the German military machine, which has always relied heavily upon its non-commissioned officers. This understanding was to prove extremely valuable to him in the years ahead.

After the war Rössler became a journalist with the *München-Augsburg Abendzeitung* and the *Allgemeinen Zeitung*. His career advanced steadily, and in 1925 he became editor of the magazine *Form und Sinn* (Form and Meaning). In 1928, he moved to seek fame and fortune in Berlin, plunging into the heady world of 'little magazines' devoted to literary and artistic matters which mushroomed during the uneasy twilight of the Weimar Republic, when the giant shapes of the future were stirring in the darkness, ogres struggling to be born.

Rössler found his place in the intellectual life of Berlin through the theatre, then a vital force in German political development. He became manager of an organisation called the *Bühnenvolksbund* (literally, the popular association of the theatre) which had been set up in a 'national and Christian spirit' as a counter-balance to the left-wing organisation called the *Volksbühnenbund* (the people's theatre association). The *Bühnenvolksbund* combined the roles of producer, agent, publisher and ticket agency, and at one time had five companies touring theatres all over Germany.

In this influential position, Rössler built up connections with clerical, liberal and conservative organisations. He numbered many of the leading literary and intellectual figures of the day among his friends – in particular, Thomas Mann, the author, and Stefan George, the poet. He also became a member of the prestigious *Herrenklub*, which has been described as the Berlin equivalent of London's White's in St James's – an interesting comparison, since White's was the club of Stewart Menzies, the SIS chief, and even came to be regarded as a principal recruiting ground and annexe to the SIS. The club in the Vosstrasse was frequented particularly by staff officers of the German army, so that Rössler's contacts were considerably extended and strengthened.

Although he showed a great interest in military matters, the theatre was still Rössler's main preoccupation at that time, not the theatre as entertainment, but the theatre as an intellectual and political force. He became a noted dramatic critic, but the criticisms he wrote were hardly conventional. He disdained to review plays and performances as such, devoting his articles to analyses of the political role of the theatre in the twentieth century. It was these articles which brought him into contact with a young man from Switzerland who was to become his greatest friend and disciple, and who was to lead him into the area for which he is now best remembered, espionage.

The young Swiss was Xaver Schnieper, twelve years Rössler's junior, the son of a government minister in the canton of Lucerne. In Berlin to study at the university, he had been impressed by Rössler's articles, one of which he discussed with his professor, who knew Rössler slightly and introduced them. Their first meeting was at Rössler's home in the Templehof district of Berlin in 1933, the same year that Hitler came to power and the Radós were fleeing the city.

There are some chemical compounds which are normally inert and only became active in combination with one particular substance. Some people, too, are like that – men or women who go on their undistinguished way, until they meet the one other person whose intellectual or emotional chemistry combines with and complements their own. Such was the case with Rössler and Schnieper. Alone, they were unremarkable; together, they were combustible.

Rössler was then thirty-six years old, a small, spare, bespectacled man with thinning hair and nervous manner, an inveterate smoker in spite of chronic asthma. His wife, Olga, was an attractive woman, some years younger than her husband, who also came from Augsburg. She took no part in her husband's political or espionage ventures, remaining a pretty, provincial *hausfrau*. They had no children.

Schnieper was dazzled when he first met Rössler. A small man with dark hair and the blazing eyes of a Robespierre, he still lives in Lucerne, where he works as a journalist. He talks with clarity and intensity, recalling his friendship with Rössler vividly. Were he religious, Schnieper would have made a formidable Jesuit. He is, in fact, a Marxist, though he is quick to point out that Rössler was never a communist ar,d had no association with the party. Schnieper describes Rössler as a progressive conservative (with a small 'c'), a man of conscience, a patriot and a Protestant, above all intensely German and as such appalled at what was happening to his beloved country.

A Jesuit priest who knew Rössler well, Father Otto Karrer, has written: 'His love of Germany made him a fanatical adversary of Hitler.' German author Wilhelm Ritter von Schramm, who was theatre critic for the *München Neuesten Nachrichten* and used to meet Rössler regularly at first nights, gives a slightly different picture of the man. In a Swiss television programme in May 1966, he described him as a German dreamer devoted solely to the arts, and said he could never understand how this man, whom he regarded as totally apolitical, ever found his way into Intelligence work.

It may be that a certain amount of injustice helped, largely suffered at the hands of Alfred Rosenberg, the man whom Goebbels christened 'the Reich philosopher'. For some time, Rosenberg had cast envious eyes on the *Bühnenvolksbund*, which by then had an annual turnover of more than thirteen million marks. When the Nazis came to power, Rosenberg ousted Rössler and took over control of his profitable business. Rössler was deprived at one stroke both of his income and of what he regarded as his life's work. The experience hardened his attitudes and turned him into a ferocious anti-fascist. He had at last discovered a cause he was prepared to die for.

Schnieper had by that time returned to Lucerne, where he had taken up a post as cantonal librarian. He persuaded Rössler to leave Germany and settle in Switzerland. In the summer of 1934 the Rösslers took a small villa on the outskirts of Lucerne.

While Radó in Paris was setting up his anti-fascist news agency, Inpress, Rössler in Lucerne was renting offices and setting up an anti-fascist publishing house, which he called Vita Nova (New Life), with funds from both Swiss and German sources. Rössler was managing director and editor of Vita Nova, with the aim of publishing works of philosophy and theology by authors whom he particularly admired, authors whose work was essentially anti-fascist. His list included F. W. Forster, Berdayev (always Rössler's favourite philosopher), Claudel (an unfortunate choice in view of his subsequent reputation as a Nazi collaborator), and many other poets and philosophers.

Vita Nova was never merely a publishing house to Rössler. He saw it as something much more important: an excalibur that would cut down the ideology of Hitlerism. Ironically, in its earlier years at least, it was not unprofitable. As the number of anti-Nazi publishers grew fewer and fewer under relentless pressure from Goebbels, so Vita Nova flourished, a combination of high-mindedness and commercial profitability which is peculiarly Swiss.

In 1936 Rössler undertook to publish a magazine called *Die Entscheidung* (The Decision) for a small group of young Swiss Catholics of liberal or leftist persuasion who also called their group by the same name. They included Schnieper and a young lawyer who was to play an important part in their future activities, Bernhard Mayr von Baldegg. Rössler wrote for the magazine himself under the pen name 'Arbiter', appealing to German expatriates everywhere to stop treating Naziism as an alien affliction forcibly imposed on an otherwise ordered and healthy German nation. They should, he wrote, recognise it as the most recent manifestation of a fundamental flaw in the German character, 'the belief that ideas are more important than people, and that the latter are there to be sacrificed to the former'.

There is little doubt that at this stage Rössler and his circle saw themselves as 'parfait gentil knights' defending Europe from a new scourge, albeit knights in shabby raincoats frequenting the Café du Gothard in Lucerne where Rössler often held court, drinking practically nothing save perhaps one glass of wine in an evening, but endlessly chain-smoking, indifferent to good food and even to his own comfort.

'He seemed to live entirely on coffee and cigarettes,' Mayr von Baldegg told us, adding, 'There was something very monastic about him.'

At about this time, in spite of the pressures of his publishing work, Rössler began writing political and military appreciations of events inside Germany, analyses which revealed an extraordinary perception. They also revealed a quality which was to give Rössler a very special talent in espionage – he had almost total recall of everything he read, and the ability to correlate everything he remembered.

Unlike ordinary people, whose memories function in more or less vague and disordered ways, Rössler absorbed information like a sponge. His mind held and stored anything which interested him, particularly military and political information which had come to him over the years from perfectly respectable sources: from conversations in the *Herrenklub*, from chats with old comrades, from newspapers, magazines, books, army publications. When some fact or reference triggered him off, a reported promotion, perhaps, or the transfer of a unit from one place to another, his extraordinary brain automatically registered the new information and adjusted his mental 'records' accordingly. It was as if he held files in his head, constantly and instantly available, on every unit in the German army.

'He had a mind like a card index,' Dr Hans Rudolf Kurz, director of the Swiss Federal parliament's information and documentation division and adviser to the President, told us.

'He was a human computer,' said Bernard Mayr von Baldegg.

'He was a freak,' declared Otto Pünter bluntly.

As war approached, Rössler was given the opportunity to make use of his remarkable abilities. One day early in August 1939 he called on Schnieper and told him, in a voice full of emotion, 'Yesterday two friends of mine from Germany were here, two men in important positions. They were sent by a group of friends who are in top posts, friends who think in the same way as I do, politically and ideologically, all of them people from the right, from conservative circles. They told me, "We will keep you informed about everything important that happens and we will give you details. You are the living embodiment of our conscience. Deal with our information as you see best for the future of Germany."'

It may be that the visit never happened. Many people believe that it was the fantasy of a political dreamer seeking self-justification for the betrayal of his country. Schnieper, however, believes it was true. What was more, Schnieper was soon in a position to help Rössler to do something useful with the information. When the Swiss army was mobilised he was called up for service with the Intelligence Corps, and attached to a strange outfit called the Bureau Ha.

The Bureau Ha was a private Intelligence organisation created and run by a dealer in photographic and optical equipment from Teufen in the canton of Appenzall, Hans Hausamann. Its name was simply his initial, 'Ha' being the German pronunciation for the letter H. Hausamann was also an army captain, as is the way in Switzerland where every able-bodied man is a soldier, and very concerned for the safety of his country. He was a gaunt man, six feet four inches tall, with the appearance of a depressed ostrich, a dedicated man who was appalled by the weakness of the army, a weakness brought about by the Depression and the consequent shortage of money.

The Depression hit Switzerland hard, with unemployment rising by 1100 per cent in seven years. Many Swiss argued that in such a situation it was wanton foolishness to spend money on keeping up an army which would never fight. After all, it was nearly a century since the civil war of 1847 in which precisely 125 men were killed – and those by other Swiss. The last foreign army to attack the country had been Napoleon's.

Hausamann was a wealthy man. He organised a campaign to fight the anti-army prejudice, on the grounds that a strong army was Switzerland's only guarantee of independence and neutrality. He led a group of army officers who called for a strengthening of the country's military resources rather than a reduction, in view of the steady build-up of Germany's armed strength across the border.

Although the campaign was partially successful, there were still areas of pitiful weakness, most notably in the field of Intelligence. From 1930 to 1935, the army's Intelligence department consisted of just two officers with an annual budget of 30,000 Swiss francs, the equivalent of £1,500 at the rate of exchange then. It was an army joke that if one man was ill and the other away on business the telephone remained unanswered and Swiss Military Intelligence was out of action! To help overcome this weakness, Hausamann set up his own organisation with his own money.

At first the Bureau Ha was no more impressive than the official Swiss Military Intelligence establishment. It was housed in three rooms in Hausamann's own home and employed a staff of three – his brother-in-law who acted as secretary, a female typist, and a retired lady telegraphist who had once worked for the French Post Office and who was to show an unexpected talent for the communications side of espionage.

Hausamann began by setting up a German network of contacts who could provide him with information. Since he was adjutant of his regiment in the Swiss army he was ideally placed to make friends in the German army, particularly as the two countries frequently exchanged officers at that time for training purposes. Hausamann was responsible for looking after German officers temporarily attached to his regiment. When they returned home he kept in touch, making sure he met them again socially on his frequent visits into Germany on business. Through them he got to know other people including civil servants, politicians, industrialists and businessmen.

Because he was a soldier and known to them, German officers trusted him and would talk freely in his presence. Hausamann watched and listened, accumulating valuable information as Hitler and his generals created their new military machine. He shuttled backwards and forwards between Switzerland and Germany, travelling on legitimate business yet all the time gathering material for his bureau. Soon there were others helping him, as his contacts grew. It was not a professional spy ring in the true sense because there was not enough money to finance full-time agents. But Hausamann had many friends.

The information they acquired was coded and radioed to the Bureau Ha. As Hausamann himself decoded all messages – and coded his own replies too – there was no danger of a security leak. In this he was helped by the retired lady telegraphist, who at no time knew what she was sending or receiving.

Gradually, Hausamann extended his lines into other European countries. The amount of material grew steadily, and all was turned over regularly to the army.

In 1936 he had the chance of proving the worth not only of his own organisation but also of Intelligence-gathering and espionage in general. The Swiss Nazi leader, Wilhelm Gustloff, was assassinated by a young medical student, the son of a Yugoslav Jewish rabbi, in his office in Davos. The Swiss Nazis had found themselves a martyr and the propaganda machinery began to work overtime. Hitler himself delivered an hysterical funeral oration. The Swiss government lived in terror that the Nazi dictator would use the assassination as an excuse for military action, or for reprisals against Swiss nationals living in Germany. Hausamann was able to put their minds at rest by obtaining a copy of Hitler's secret order 37/16 from the office of no less a dignitary than Rudolf Hess, the Führer's deputy. The order stated in unequivocal terms that there were to be no reprisals for the Gustloff affair. The Swiss relaxed. Hausamann had proved his value to his country.

In 1937, Hausamann established contact with Czech Intelligence, which had just come under the command of the brilliant General Moravek. The Czechs, even more than the Swiss, had every reason to fear the new Germany, and were delighted to have the chance of co-operating with the Bureau Ha and sharing vital information. Moravek already had an excellent understanding with the Swiss army, where his contact was one Roger Masson, who had made several visits to Prague. The Czech connection was to prove extremely valuable later.

By now the Bureau, having outgrown Hausamann's own house, had moved to the Villa Stutz, which stood in its own grounds on a promontory jutting out into the lake near Lucerne. It was here, at 8.00 a.m. on 1st September 1939, that Hausamann was informed by telephone that the Federal Council had ordered general mobilisation and that he was thus a full-time major in the army. Later in the day, Roger Masson, now head of Military Intelligence, called him and asked about his plans for the Bureau Ha. Hausamann replied that he would continue to work at the Villa Stutz, and formally placed his organisation at the disposal of the general staff.

Masson was delighted, as his own official organisation had been extensively reorganised and re-equipped. But he chose to keep the Bureau as a separate entity under the code name 'Pilatus', after the mountain near Lucerne. It was to be independent of the military Intelligence-gathering centre, Department NS1, commanded by Major Max Waibel, which was also stationed at Lucerne, with the code name 'Rigi', after the other mountain which overlooks the town.

As a liaison between the two organisations, Masson appointed an officer who in civilian life was a lawyer in Lucerne, Bernhard Mayr von Baldegg, Rössler's friend from *Die Entscheidung*, who was also instructed to act as liaison with another private Intelligence organisation, Otto Pünter's Pakbo ring. The Intelligence threads in Switzerland were already becoming intertwined.

Although he liaised effectively with the Pakbo ring, providing as well as collecting information, Mayr von Baldegg never met Pünter until several years after the war, when they were introduced by the television producer Werner Rings at a chance encounter in a restaurant. During the war, he was known to Pünter only by the code name 'Louise'. Women's names were obviously popular in the world of Swiss espionage. As we have already seen, there were already Dora, Maria, Sonia, Sissy, and Louise, and soon there would be another – Lucy.

When Xaver Schnieper was posted to the Bureau Ha, he was asked by Hausamann to recommend the names of suitable people who might be prepared to work for the Bureau. Naturally, Schnieper thought immediately of his great friend Rössler. He therefore showed his chief some of the assessments of political and military developments inside Germany which Rössler had written for *Die Entscheidung*. Hausamann was clearly impressed, and invited Rössler to work for him.

Following classic espionage procedures, Hausamann never met Rössler personally – he used Schnieper as a go between. It was excellent security, but very irritating for Rössler, who complained bitterly to Mayr von Baldegg that Hausamann treated him like a machine. The complaint was justified, but then there was something very machine-like about Rössler.

His precise role with the Bureau Ha was two-fold. First, he was a source of information through his own contacts in Germany, though these were never as many nor as highly-placed as has been suggested. Second, and more important at the start, he was used as an evaluator of Intelligence, for without proper evaluation much of the information obtained by agents in the field is useless. In peacetime it is difficult enough, but in war it becomes a monumental task of enormous complexity. It can be best compared to trying to complete a variety of different jigsaw puzzles all at the same time, without knowing what each picture is supposed to look like. A piece of information may seem significant by itself – but the evaluator has to decide which puzzle it fits into.

Of course, sometimes the information comes complete, such as the directive from Hess's office concerning the Gustloff affair. But more often it is a mere shard of Intelligence, such as a report of the movement of an infantry brigade from point A to point B. The evaluator must decide what significance that may have on overall strategy, if any. He must work out if it fits with another isolated piece of information already received, such as a report that a clothing factory in Westphalia has just received an urgent order for white ski suits. Does that mean Germany is about to launch a winter offensive somewhere? And if so, where? Russia? Norway? Finland? Sweden? Switzerland? If the infantry brigade happened to contain a high proportion of trained ski troops, the two reports could well be linked to give a positive indication of a future plan. But it is just as likely that they are completely unrelated and belong in different jigsaw puzzles.

The assessment of each item in this way requires encyclopaedic knowledge of military matters and of the way the German army operates. It calls for a man like Rudolf Rössler. In September 1939 Rössler suddenly found himself at the heart of Swiss Intelligence.

With the amount of work he was doing for the Bureau Ha, Rössler found it difficult to continue running Vita Nova virtually single-handed. He decided he needed help, and advertised in the newspapers for someone to read proofs and do part-time editorial work. The advertisement was answered by Christian Schneider, who happened to be Sissy's agent 'Taylor' and who was also a professional translator. Rössler gave him the job, and Schneider, who worked at home, began to travel regularly between Geneva and Lucerne to collect copy and proofs and to return those already corrected. Being interested in politics and the international situation, he frequently discussed the news with his employer, who impressed him with his knowledge and understanding of events.

Before long, Rössler confided in him that he was receiving Intelligence information from friends in Germany. Naturally, he was passing this information to the Bureau Ha along with his evaluations of the material Hausamann gave him, but since Switzerland was neutral obviously the information could not be used actively against Nazi Germany. To Rössler this seemed little short of criminal. Hitler must be stopped; Intelligence helpful to the anti-Nazi cause must go to those able to make the most effective use of it. (It was a view shared by Hausamann himself.) Schneider agreed, and told him that he was in a position to pass information on to Soviet Intelligence, if Rössler so wished. Rössler did, for it had become obvious to him that Russia, although now Germany's latest ally, was next on Hitler's list.

So along with the sheaves of proofs and manuscripts which he gave Schneider to correct each week, Rössler included copies of his evaluations of military events in Germany. Schneider in turn passed these to 'Sissy' (alias Rachel Dübendorfer) the head of the Soviet spy ring at the ILO in Geneva, who then gave them to Radó. The Hungarian enciphered them and passed them, with the rest of the Intelligence material which came in from other sources, to Foote or the Hamels for transmission to Moscow.

Unknown to Radó, Rössler had also made contact with the British mission in Berne, where Count Vanden Heuvel was now installed as station chief of the Secret Service, answerable directly to Colonel Dansey in London. Rössler had been disappointed by the response from the British. They did not seem to take his information seriously, no matter how hard he tried to persuade them of its authenticity. He was afraid that it finished up in the waste-paper bin, for he received little encouragement from them.

The British, as it turned out, *were* interested in Rössler's information. It gave them a means of cross-checking some of the information they were already receiving through other sources – which in turn enabled them to test the accuracy of Rössler's own, more limited, sources. It also gave them a potentially useful liaison man who had already established himself as a supplier of information, originally to the Swiss and now to the Russians – for Hausamann, without doubt, informed Vanden Heuvel of Rössler's other activities when he gave his approval. Directly or indirectly they now had four ways in to the Russian network: Foote, Sissy, part of the Pakbo ring, and now Rössler.

Knowing nothing of this, however, Rössler went on passing information to Schneider as he received it from his contacts in Berlin and from his work for the Swiss.

Meanwhile, in the spring of 1941, the messages began to take on more and more urgency. In April for the first time the date of Operation Barbarossa was given, first as 15th June, amended a few days later to 22nd June. In May came news that the German forces, now massed along the Russian frontier, were all in a state of alert, and at the beginning of June that their preparations were becoming still more intensive.

At this time, Foote was ordered by Centre to meet Radó at least twice a week, and to take over a large part of his transmissions. He was being promoted to deputy head of the network, which meant that he had to be in a position to take charge if anything happened to the Hungarian. Hence the need for them to keep in contact during the day-to-day running of the network. Moreover, since Radó was not a radio operator and could not transmit his own material, he had to rely on the Hamels, who also had a business to run. Foote, on the other hand, could encipher and send the messages himself in a single night. He was an incredibly fast operator with amazing powers of endurance and a huge capacity for work. He could transmit as much in a night as three other operators. As a result more and more of the material he sent came from Rössler.

Radó was worried about the origin of this material. He knew that it came via Sissy. She, in turn, told him it came from Schneider, who obtained it from an unknown source in Lucerne. The information was undoubtedly good. But the unknown source just might be a German plant, intended either to penetrate his network or to lull the Russians into a false sense of security by providing good information, so that at some really important time they could be deceived by the sudden introduction of false material. It would not be the first, nor the last time, this sort of deception was practised. The British were already working such a system using known German agents sent to Britain, controlling the information transmitted back to Germany, and the Germans were beginning to play the same game against the British from Holland.

Radó consulted Centre in Moscow, who were extremely sceptical. They told him to go on receiving information from Schneider's unnamed source, but to exercise the utmost caution. Centre normally made it a firm rule never to take information from unverified sources, but since the material in this case appeared to be of exceptional quality, they were prepared to wait and watch. To identify the source of this material, Radó settled on the simple code name 'Lucy', meaning Lucerne – which was all he knew of Rössler.

CHAPTER SEVEN

The Most Secret Source

On the morning of 17th June 1941, Radó received a telephone call from a very excited Sissy. She said she wanted to meet him immediately, as she had some vitally important and urgent news. That night, Radó sent off the following message:

17.6.1941 To Director
About 100 infantry divisions are now positioned on the German-Soviet frontier. One third are motorised. Of the remainder, at least ten divisions are armoured. In Romania, German troops are concentrated at Galatz. Elite divisions with a special mission have been mobilised. The 5th and 10th divisions stationed in the General Government [the Nazi description of occupied Poland] are taking part. Dora.

Germany's intentions seemed plain at last. But according to Foote, Radó still refused to believe that Germany had any firm intention of invading Russia. Like most devout communists at that time, Radó chose to follow Stalin's line: that German activity on the frontier was part of a war of nerves designed to extract greater concessions from Russia by way of trade and strategic supplies. Any other interpretation had to be regarded as British provocation.

Almost immediately afterwards, however, Lucy delivered his most detailed and important message. Not only did he give the exact date and time of the Russian attack as dawn on 22nd June 1941, but he also supplied exact details of the German order of battle, and of the primary objectives of the various army groups. The detail was incredible. If it was true, the Russian army was being offered the most precise Intelligence ever known.

Radó was in a quandary. Centre had given him firm warnings against placing reliance on reports from Lucy – whom it still regarded as an untrustworthy source. He had sent previous reports only with the utmost caution, and it seemed that Centre had chosen to disbelieve all of them. But this was different. This was utterly precise. It could not be misinterpreted in any way, for it stated not only that Germany intended to invade the Soviet Union, but also the precise time of the invasion, the forces taking part, their positions, their objectives, everything. It was almost too good to be true.

Radó says that he sent off this report without question. Other members of the network, on the other hand, say that he could not make up his mind what to do. Foote says that Radó telephoned him to make an urgent rendezvous. When they met, he said, Radó was 'obviously worried and upset . . . He himself inclined to Centre's belief and thought that the whole thing was an Abwehr [German Military Intelligence] plan.' However, after much discussion Foote managed to persuade Radó that it would be criminal not to send it, and Radó left the message with him. Foote sent it that night.

For the first time, Centre completely believed what Lucy said. Unfortunately, Stalin himself chose not to. When the invasion took place, at exactly the time and in exactly the manner given by Lucy, Stalin was so shattered that he suffered a form of nervous breakdown, and locked himself away from everyone for several days. Lucy's warning had been one of no less than seventy-six messages, all giving the clearest possible indication of Hitler's intentions. They came from many different sources, from embassies and sympathisers, and from trusted agents such as Richard Sorge in Japan, but Stalin refused to believe any of them. When the German armies roared into action across the river Bug at first light on 22nd June, however, and the Russians realised for the first time what was happening, one report stood out as being more accurate and more detailed than any other. That report had been transmitted by Allan Foote, under the heading 'From Lucy'.

While still recovering from the shock of the invasion, Radó bustled around the most important members of his network. During the day of Sunday, 22nd June, he visited Sissy and Böttcher at their flat, the Hamels above their closed shop, and Allan Foote in Lausanne. He also called Pünter to arrange a meeting for the next day.

All through the day, the radios of Europe were filled with the rantings of Hitler. At one o'clock next morning, Foote tuned in to his receiving wavelength, and picked up the following signal from Moscow, which was being repeated over and over again:

Fascist beasts have invaded the motherland of the working classes. You are called upon to carry out your tasks in Germany to the best of your ability.

Director.

Next night, Radó sent a message to Moscow, pledging the support of his network:

23.6.1941 To Director
Always faithful at our post and conscious of our position in the front line, we will fight with redoubled energy from this historic hour.

Dora.

During the next few days, instructions, demands and admonitions poured in on the network from Moscow, as the Soviet military machine prepared for war. Foote received for the first time a detailed system of priorities for messages: top priority messages, to be deciphered at once, were to be marked VYRDO; urgent messages were to have the prefix RDO; routine messages which could be dealt with at leisure were to be marked MSG. Foote was to deal with the bulk of VYRDO messages. All information from Lucy was to be classified VYRDO.

'Gone now were the days,' says Foote, 'when Centre regarded Lucy as an *agent provocateur*. They were clamouring incessantly for more and more information, and Lucy produced it.'

On the first day of Barbarossa, as the German forces swept across the frontier along its entire length from the Baltic to the Black Sea, the Russians were in a state of total confusion. Red Army divisions were not in their defensive positions and many units were at training camps. To those who were at the frontier, Moscow issued orders that they were not to cross into German territory, and Russian aircraft were not to penetrate further than ninety miles. Incredibly, Moscow kept open its radio link with the German foreign ministry, and asked the Japanese to mediate. Stalin was still refusing to believe that the war had actually begun. By noon, the Luftwaffe had destroyed 1200 Russian aircraft – 800 of them still on the ground – for the loss of ten of its own, destroying airfields and gaining total superiority in the air.

Throughout the rest of 1941, the war in Russia was a succession of triumphs for Hitler, and it began to look as though he would achieve his aim of taking Moscow before the winter closed in. By 21st September, the German army was besieging Leningrad and had occupied Kiev after encircling and capturing more than a million Russian troops. On 6th October, Hitler's armies began the grand offensive against Moscow, reaching the outskirts of the city in only ten days.

Britain reacted publicly on the first day of the new conflict. On the evening of 22nd June, Churchill broadcast to the world his famous message in which, after restating his own hatred of communism, he said, 'I see the Russian soldiers standing on the threshold of their native land, guarding the fields which their fathers have tilled since time immemorial. I see them guarding their homes where mothers and wives pray – ah, yes, for there are times when all pray – for the safety of their loved ones, the return of the breadwinner, of their champion, of their protector.'

The speech was one of Churchill's greatest. It had, without doubt, been prepared long before, for Churchill had known for several months of the plans of the 'bloodthirsty guttersnipe', the 'monster of wickedness' in Berlin. He lamented the fact that he had given Stalin warning, but could only hope that it had not gone unheeded. He then went on to say of Britain, 'We have but one aim and one single, irrevocable purpose. We are resolved to destroy Hitler and every vestige of the Nazi regime. From this nothing will turn us – nothing. We shall fight him by land, we shall fight him by sea, we shall fight him in the air, until with God's help we have rid the earth of his shadow and liberated its peoples from his yoke. Any man or state who fights on against Nazidom will have our aid. . . . We have offered the government of Soviet Russia any technical or economic assistance which is in our power, and which is likely to be of service to them.'

Churchill kept his word, and Britain did everything possible to help Russia, knowing that if Hitler succeeded in gaining an early victory there he would be free to turn the entire might of his forces against the

British Isles. Britain sent convoys through the dangerous waters of the Arctic, carrying essential materials and supplies which she desperately needed at home, sometimes to ports which only a short time before had been made available by Stalin to the German navy as bases from which it could attack British shipping. But relations between the two countries did not noticeably improve. Stalin regarded any sign of generosity as weakness, searched for hidden motives, and demanded greater efforts and greater sacrifices, much of the time coupling his demands with insults.

Churchill bore the insults, and continued to send help. Until Russia could produce enough war materials for its own forces, there was no alternative. Without aid from Britain and America – to whom Stalin presented on 8th July a list of requirements costing almost two billion dollars – Russia could not hope to hold the Germans, never mind defeat them. But Churchill had more than materials to offer Stalin. He also had Intelligence of a higher order than had ever been achieved in any major war. Perhaps the Russians could still fight without it – they did after all have their own highly developed spy networks throughout Europe – but they would certainly be able to fight better with it.

Knowing nothing of this, Radó and Lène listened to the Churchill broadcast in Sissy's flat, and prepared themselves for the supreme efforts they knew they would have to make. It was small consolation to them to reflect on the accuracy of the reports Sissy had given Radó, and which he had sent to Moscow after so much heart-searching.

The information which Churchill had at his disposal has been described as 'the greatest Intelligence triumph of all time'. It emanated, however, not from spies in the enemy camp, but from a group of wooden huts clustered around a slightly dilapidated Victorian country house near Bletchley, in Buckinghamshire. Those who obtained it were not flamboyant or glamorous secret agents in the James Bond mould, but 'boffins' and 'backroom boys', some of the world's finest scientific and mathematical brains plucked from Britain's universities. In their wooden huts they laboured to find the answers to a puzzle called 'Enigma', the highly secret automatic cipher machine employed by the Germans.

Cipher machines were not new. They were merely a form of calculating machine, and man has been devising ever more complicated calculating machines since the invention of the abacus. What made Enigma different was that although it was light, portable and very simple to operate – and could therefore be used by commanders in the field under battle conditions – the ciphers it produced were incredibly complex. It looked like a large portable typewriter. Messages typed on its keyboard were automatically enciphered by ever-changing electrical contacts on a series of revolving rotors. As each letter was typed, it appeared as a different letter in an illuminated display panel on top of the machine, and every time it occurred the replacement letter was different as the revolving motors activated different contacts. Additional variations could be achieved by changing the rotors around or replacing them with different ones, or varying still further the system of electrical connections. Once a message had been enciphered it could be sent quite safely by radio, and deciphered at the other end on any other Enigma machine as long as the operators were both using the same prearranged setting of the rotor contacts.

There were various models of Enigma machine, and as the war progressed they were improved and developed, principally by increasing the number of drums, which increased the complexity of the cipher. The permutations of letter patterns possible on a three-rotor machine are 3×10^{18}, i.e. 30 followed by eighteen noughts. For a four-rotor machine the figure becomes four thousand million million million, and for the ultimate ten-rotor radio-teletyping *Geheimschreiber*, codenamed 'Fish', the possible permutations were incomprehensibly astronomic.

With odds like these against the ciphers ever being cracked, the Germans were convinced that the security of their cipher machines was impregnable, and they felt completely confident in using them at all times and under all conditions. Even if an enemy were to capture an actual machine, it would be useless to him unless he knew the key being used to determine each cipher, and could set the connections in the exact pattern being used that day.

This was the problem faced by the scientists and mathematicians at Bletchley. If they could penetrate the Enigma, and read the messages being passed with such confidence by the German armies, navy, air force and high command, they would be able to provide British commanders with absolutely accurate, up-to-the-minute information

95

of their opponents' plans, movements and conditions. It was a prize beyond the wildest dreams of commanders throughout history, made possible now by the modern use of radio communication.

In fact, the Germans' confidence was misplaced. The brilliant cryptanalysts of the Polish Secret Service had been working on the problem of cracking Enigma ciphers ever since the Germans started using the machines in the late 1920s. By the end of 1937 they were successfully deciphering some seventy-five per cent of all intercepted Enigma traffic. Unfortunately, however, this success was short-lived. In the autumn of 1938, at the very time when Hitler's aggressive intentions towards Poland were accelerating fiercely, the Poles' secret eyes and ears were blocked again. The Germans introduced modifications to the Enigma machine, principally by adding a further two wheels.

The Poles worked desperately against the clock, but events overtook them. When Hitler invaded Poland they were forced to flee, taking as much of their equipment with them as possible and destroying the rest. They had already been collaborating with the British and to a slightly lesser extent with the French, both of whom were also working independently on the problem of Enigma. Now, it was obvious that collaboration must become total.

In breaking a complex cipher of any kind, time is the enemy. The sheer mechanical drudgery of trying to work out all the possible permutations of letters and symbols is enormously time-consuming, and in the end it is usually of little use to crack a cipher that was used for one day several months ago. The information obtained will be a matter of history. What is needed is a method of shortening the time taken to examine all the possibilities, and the ideal tool for the job is the electronic computer.

In 1939, however, the science of electronics was in its infancy and although one of the mathematicians at Bletchley, Alan Turing, had been considering building a computer since 1936, it was still something of a dream for the future. The first ever electronic computers appeared at Bletchley in 1942, and swiftly developed into a machine with no less than 1,500 valves, capable of reading 5,000 symbols per second, aptly named 'Colossus'. Colossus Mark II followed soon afterwards, with 2,500 valves and able to scan an incredible 25,000 symbols per second. Judged by any standards, it was an astonishing technical achievement, and it was just in time to cope with the increasingly complex developments and modifications to Enigma, and with the 'Fish' *Geheimschreiber*.

Before the creation of the computer, however, Bletchley had machines to help the cryptanalysts in their struggle. These were known as 'bombes', and were basically electro-mechanical data-processors developed by Turing and the other Bletchley boffins with extraordinary speed from a machine called the 'Bomba', which had been designed and built by the Poles before the war, using parts of six Enigmas in its circuits. It was the Bomba which enabled the Poles to break the old three-rotor Enigma cipher, and when they decided to co-operate fully with the British and French the design for it was one of the priceless gifts they gave to their allies. Now, the British had developed the device to a high degree of sophistication and re-christened it the bombe. It was also known as the Oriental Goddess. With it, Bletchley achieved the long-awaited breakthrough in April 1940.

The first messages to be deciphered were short Luftwaffe signals dealing with personnel postings, useless in themselves but highly significant as the forerunners of what was to come. From that point on, with the development of more and more sophisticated machines and an increasingly efficient organisation, the British were able to decipher growing numbers of messages passing between the various German commands. The information received was evaluated and if thought relevant was distributed under conditions of almost hysterical secrecy to only the most senior British – and later American – commanders. Selected signals and a digest of the remainder were sent every day to Churchill, wherever he might be. Copies of all signals were sent by teleprinter direct to Stewart Menzies at the SIS headquarters.

The entire operation was given the title 'Ultra', standing for ultra-secret, the greatest secret of the war. It remained secret, in fact, for nearly thirty years after the war had ended, and notwithstanding the several excellent books on the subject which have appeared in the last six years there are still parts of the fascinating story which have not been made public.

It was through Ultra that Britain knew with absolute certainty the details of Hitler's plans to invade Russia. When Cripps, Eden and

Cavendish-Bentinck tried to persuade the Russians to accept what they were telling them, they were not offering guesswork but certainty. This was the Intelligence information which Churchill personally ordered Menzies to pass to Stalin.

Churchill had, however, also ordered that under no circumstances was Stalin to be told the source of the information. The operation was not known as Ultra for nothing – the very name signified a new level of secrecy, higher than the existing British labels of 'secret' and 'most secret', or the American classification 'top secret'. Churchill and his Secret Service chiefs knew that they had an immensely valuable tool, but it could become worthless if the Germans ever suspected their Enigma code had been broken. They would then find some new method of sending messages to which Britain did not have the key, and the Intelligence Service would have lost its ears. Stalin might be Britain's ally, but he most certainly could not be trusted with a secret as vital as Ultra. And Stalin would not accept anything the British said at its face value, for he, in turn, did not trust Churchill. Why should he trust a British aristocrat who had advocated military intervention against bolshevism in 1919, and whose anti-Soviet views were well known?

A former senior officer of the SIS described to us the secrecy of Ultra as having become 'an absolute neurosis', and said there were no lengths to which the Service would not go in order to protect it. Nevertheless, a way had to be found for Ultra Intelligence to reach Stalin in such a form that he would accept it as genuine and act upon it. The information had to be authenticated in such a way that even a paranoid dictator would never suspect its provenance.

Menzies probably had several roads to Moscow open to him – such as the Polish Resistance for example – and it is possible that jewels of Ultra Intelligence of particular interest to the Soviets were smuggled into the Kremlin along them from time to time. But the Soviet network in Switzerland, already virtually controlled by the British, might have been tailor-made for the job. Not only was its second-in-command and principal radio operator a Dansey agent, but the network was actively seeking new sources of information. The British and the Free French had strong connections with the Pakbo ring, and thus could easily keep track of that part of the network, giving an additional security factor. But there was yet another joker in the pack, a joker whose existence was unknown to anyone outside a very small part of British Intelligence – the head of the Soviet spy ring at the ILO, Rachel Dübendorfer, had been 'turned'. Sissy was working for the British!

When we talked to Victor Cavendish-Bentinck, wartime head of Britain's Joint Intelligence Committee, the overseer and co-ordinator of all Intelligence activity, he indicated Allan Foote as one point of access and control. Foote was the obvious way in for Ultra material, particularly as he had his own transmitter/receiver – which could be used to contact Britain just as easily as Moscow – and his own personal cipher, which was unknown to Radó. There was no way that Radó or anyone else in the network could have checked what Foote was sending to Centre. In any case, Foote also had his own sources of Intelligence in Germany and Switzerland, and so could be expected to send additional material to Moscow. He always remained semi-autonomous in the network.

However, it would have been rash for the British to have relied solely on Foote. The very fact that he was an obvious choice for use by London made it dangerous both to the security of Ultra and to Foote's own cover as a genuine Soviet agent. In any case, such simplicity and directness were not Dansey's way of doing things. He always favoured complexity, choosing twisting back alleyways in preference to the broad highway. The author of the first book on Ultra, Group Captain F. W. Winterbotham – who also confirms that Britain controlled the Swiss network throughout the war – told us that this was typical of the way Dansey operated, and that he revelled in the pleasure of being able to 'get one up' on his rivals in the SIS.

There were other dangers. Suppose Foote were to be run over, or fall ill, or be killed or kidnapped by the Abwehr. In Lausanne, as we shall see, he was always at risk. Consequently, there had to be other agents in the network who could be used to feed material in, other agents who were prepared to work for British Intelligence. All they would have to do would be to pass on pieces of information from their British contact to their contact in the network – Radó, or Foote, or Schneider, or Pünter, or whoever. They would not need to be told the significance of the additional material, for that could endanger the Ultra secret. Even Foote himself need have no knowledge of Enigma or Ultra.

The flow of material had to be carefully orchestrated. If too much went directly through Foote, Centre might begin to ask questions. They therefore built up the one supplier of information who was never controlled by Centre, who was German, had already proved that he had some genuine contacts highly placed in the Third Reich, and who also had access to Swiss Intelligence material. Rudolf Rössler, otherwise known as Lucy, was the ideal man for the job. Feeding the information to Rössler was the real trick, for once it had passed through his hands it would be authenticated, 'laundered' clean like stolen money being passed through a legitimate business. For this the British used two principal routes, though there may well have been other means of access to the network, which by then had over a hundred agents supplying information from various sources, many of them serving more than one master.

The first way in was beautiful in its simplicity. It was the same as the route *from* Rössler into the network – i.e. via Sissy and Schneider. When we interviewed Edmond Hamel in his little radio shop in Geneva, he recalled that Radó had told him that Sissy had found a marvellous new source of information, which she refused to reveal to him. This is hardly surprising since it is not likely that she would have been foolish enough to admit contacts with British Intelligence. It was not until the route had been thoroughly tested and proved, and Centre convinced of the value of her mysterious source, that she told Radó about the little man in Lucerne. Radó himself says that even then she did not identify the man. Only after the extraordinary accuracy and detail of his Barbarossa reports had whetted the Director's appetite, was she able to make a unique deal – Rössler would be known only as Lucy, and would continue to send material to Radó on the strict understanding that neither his identity nor that of his source would ever be revealed to the Russians.

Such an arrangement had never before been sanctioned by Centre, with its constant fear of *agents provocateurs*. But Lucy was simply too good to lose. Nevertheless, Centre kept trying to discover Lucy's identity. During the summer of 1943, when Lucy's messages were at the very peak of value and effectiveness, Centre pressed Radó several times to discover and inform them of the identities not only of Lucy's sources but also of Lucy himself. Radó's reply is most revealing when one is aware of the facts. It read:

27.9.1943

Regarding your Numbers 157 and 158.

. . . I myself believe that one could obtain much more from the Lucy group. Nevertheless, as you know, I have no direct contact with this group and from Sissy and her husband I meet with a resistance which I do not understand every time I try to stir up the group . . . At each criticism Sissy is annoyed and says that Taylor and Lucy also regard them as annoying, and that if she passes on the criticisms they will both stop working. Following your advice, I have written a friendly letter to Lucy, but Sissy says that Taylor will not deliver it because Lucy is already doing everything he can.

It is possible that Sissy considers this letter as an attempt by myself to establish direct contact with the Lucy group, which she and her husband wish to prevent for reasons which I do not comprehend.

Sissy's motive for working for the British was simple: money. We were constantly told during our investigations in Geneva that Sissy was always short of money – which is hardly surprising in view of the fact that she had to support her daughter Tamara as well as her own lover, Paul Böttcher. Sissy herself had only a lowly-paid job at the ILO in Geneva, where, until he resigned to devote all his time to liaising with Rössler on behalf of Sissy and Centre, Christian Schneider worked in the same office.

In a Swiss television discussion about the network, transmitted in May 1966, long before the existence of Ultra had been revealed, Hans Hausamann was asked, 'Was it known to the Swiss Intelligence Service, or to you personally . . . that Rössler was using the line [i.e. the radio link] via Foote in Lausanne?'

Hausamann replied, 'I know exactly how the information was passed to Geneva . . . It went to the Palais des Nations, in which was the office of an authority [i.e. the ILO] which then transferred it to the Russian resident director Radó, who evaluated it and then handed it over to two radio operators for transmission to Moscow. I even had the courier [i.e. Schneider] followed on several occasions. He could be followed as far as the entrance to the Palais des Nations, but from there the trail was lost.'

It is hard to believe that a man as determined as Hausamann and with the facilities at his disposal was stopped at the entrance to the building. He knew that Rössler was passing Bureau Ha material to the Russians, for he had given his approval. He must have known to whom the material was being passed. He also knew that it was a two-way traffic – information was received as well as given, in the true Swiss tradition of giving a little to get a lot. He 'tolerated' (his word) Rössler's actions because they aided both the Russians and the British and he had fought against Hitlerism for many years. With his good relationship with the British, he must have known that Sissy was serving two masters, even though he could not have realised the extent or even the true nature of the service.

When Sissy was arrested in the spring of 1944, it was her defence that she had been working all along for the British. Her defence lawyer, a communist sympathiser, must have believed her story. Conveniently he left his briefcase containing all the documents relating to Sissy's evidence in a friend's office overnight. During the night, Pierre Nicole, son of the Swiss communist leader Léon Nicole, slipped into the office, opened the briefcase and photographed the papers. It was not long before Moscow learned that one of its trusted agents had 'gone double' – knowledge that was later to pose problems both for her and for Foote.

Feeding the information to Sissy posed no great problem for the British Secret Service. They had a large, well-ordered organisation in Switzerland, with agents spread throughout the country. In Geneva their man was Victor Farrell, who operated under the guise of British consul, who had his own radio set, and who provided the false passport for Len Brewer. His office was only a few yards from the Palais des Nations, and he could always find reasons for visiting the building regularly in his official capacity.

The second means of feeding Lucy was Karel Sedlacek, a Czech agent. Sedlacek's boss, General Frantisek Moravec, director of Czech Military Intelligence from 1937 until the communist takeover after the war, had established friendly relations with Swiss Intelligence as early as 1934, and had an agreement with Masson that the Czech Intelligence Service would share its technical equipment and intelligence expertise with the Swiss, in return for being allowed to set up an outpost in Zurich without interference. It was a fair arrangement, since both countries had a very real fear of German territorial ambitions and it was most unlikely that their interests would clash.

Once again, the Swiss barter system worked to everyone's advantage.

Moravec sent Karel Sedlacek to head the Zurich outpost under the cover name Thomas Selzinger, ostensibly working as correspondent for a Prague newspaper. His reports did appear in the paper, but they were ghosted for him by a genuine writer in Zurich, since he turned out to be a good agent but a hopeless journalist. In Zurich, Sedlacek made contact with another friend of Czech Intelligence, Hans Hausamann, who owned photographic shops there. Hausamann was glad to look after Sedlacek, who became a close friend of the family and a frequent visitor for Sunday dinners and picnics. He even lodged with Hausamann's mother – an arrangement which was convenient and safe. Hausamann's two sons called him Uncle Tom, which became his code name with the Bureau Ha and eventually with the whole Intelligence community in Switzerland. It was through the Bureau Ha that Sedlacek came into contact with Rudolf Rössler.

When the Germans occupied Czechoslovakia, the Czech government fled to London. Moravek went with them, taking over three small houses in Rosendale Road, West Dulwich, as his headquarters until they were bombed and he moved to an office in the Bayswater Road. His organisation worked hand in glove with the British. 'We had,' said Moravec in his memoirs, 'a close collaboration with them.' In fact, they shared everything with British Intelligence. And all the while, Sedlacek kept in touch from Zurich.

Before he died Hausamann told his biographer Alphons Matt that his finest and most reliable source of information for the Bureau Ha was not Rössler at all – it was 'Uncle Tom', Karel Sedlacek. As we know, most of this information came from London, for Sedlacek was in regular radio communication with the Czech transmitter-receiver centre at Woldingham. Consequently he was a convenient point of access for British Intelligence, since he was in no position to question the nature or original source of the material, but was ideally placed to pass it on. He could hand it to Rössler at first hand.

The source of the original material passed in this way was therefore completely disguised. Rössler would evaluate it for Hausamann and Swiss Intelligence – and then pass it on to the Russians. It is ironic that the shortest safest route from London to Moscow was via Hausamann's mother's lodger!

So the smokescreen was complete. Dansey's tortuous mind had created an elaborate maze which any intruder would find almost impossible to negotiate. Churchill's two requirements, had been fulfilled: Stalin was getting and accepting the vital information, and the secret of Ultra was safely protected.

Interlude

The Intelligence Mart

'Positive neutrality' is a peculiarly Swiss concept, reflecting either the national paranoia or natural caution regarding their stronger neigh- bours, depending on one's point of view. If you want to retain your neutrality, the Swiss argue, be ready to fight for it. But since they are a small country with a small population, they cannot afford a large standing army. Instead the Swiss have opted for an army of part- timers. Today, for example, every able-bodied male is required by law at the age of nineteen to undergo an initial period of 120 days' training, and during the sixteen years thereafter – that is, up to the age of thirty-six – men must attend ten 'refresher courses', each of three weeks' duration. At the end of these courses the civilian sold- iery – bank clerks, dentists, farmers, shopkeepers – return home, taking their rifles with them. They are prepared, theoretically, for anything. They can be mobilised within a few hours. All in the cause of neutrality.

However, a part-time army cannot operate effectively without professionals. At the centre of the Swiss military machine is a corps of highly trained officers and NCOs. And it was to win over his full-time professionals that, on 25th July 1940, the *Oberstkorpskommandant*, General Guisan, called together his senior officers in a meadow on the shore of Lake Lucerne known as the Rutli. This was a place of historic pilgrimage for the Swiss, a cross between Runnymede and Gettys- burg, where in 1291 the cantons of Schwyz, Uri and Underwalden agreed to form an 'everlasting league' for their defence against all who might attack them. Guisan rallied his officers on the very site where the Swiss Confederation was born and presented his plans for the defence of the country in the event of attack by Germany.

107

The General's action, while now regarded with pride by all Swiss citizens, met with a far more mixed reception at the time. There was a large pro-Nazi element in the country, and an even larger number of appeasers, or 'adjustors', as they were known. The Federal President, Pilet-Golaz, was among them, a man who had so convinced himself of Germany's ultimate victory in the war that he was terrified of doing anything to offend his powerful neighbour. But while the politicians railed and Germany and Italy protested, Guisan went quietly ahead with his plans, preparing a mountain *reduit*, a natural fortress in the Alps to which the army would retreat in case of invasion.

At the same time, his enlarged Military Intelligence department set about strengthening its ties with Allied Intelligence organisations. Switzerland, being small and relatively weak, had even more need than most countries of good, reliable Intelligence. Thanks largely to the organisation built up by Hausamann, it received a great deal of high-quality information from many sources. But if Guisan was successfully to defend his country against Germany and Italy, the only possible aggressors, he had to fight their supporters, the 'adjustors', within Switzerland itself. For that he desperately needed accurate Intelligence, the kind of Intelligence available only to the Allied high command. Only by knowing exactly the Axis intentions, not just towards Switzerland, but also towards the rest of Europe, could he convince the doubters in his own camp to stand fast.

The Swiss are firm believers in the adage that you get nothing for nothing. Everything has to be bought, one way or the other, and in the Intelligence world the currency is the same as the commodity – information. When Switzerland became an island in the middle of occupied Europe, it also became a focus for Intelligence activity by the warring powers, who continued to fight their own vicious war in the shadows. The various Intelligence organisations gathered beneath the Swiss roof and set up a marketplace for Intelligence, a clearing house in which information could be exchanged or traded for favours.

Who was in the market, and how did it work?

For the Swiss the information which they had for trading was gathered together conveniently in one town, Lucerne, where the Bureau Ha and Department NS1 were stationed, and there too was the man who linked them, Bernhard Mayr von Baldegg. Lucerne was also the home of Rudolf Rössler who was to become, almost unwittingly, the fulcrum of the whole complicated mechanism.

The French Deuxième Bureau had ceased to be an effective supplier or gatherer of information with the fall of France, but several of its agents had refused to stay with the official organisation under the rule of Pétain and the collaborators. Some had gone to London with de Gaulle, others had stayed in Europe and either gone underground or moved into Switzerland to operate officially on behalf of the Free French. Others had chosen the most risky course of all, by staying with the Pétain government but working for the Free French. One such was a diplomat in his fifties who worked for Pünter under the code name 'Nègre'. He had served as consul general in several East European countries, was a brilliant linguist and had first-class connections in many areas, especially in German heavy industry. He later became the Pakbo group's liaison man with the Free French Resistance organisation Bir Hakeim.

The most important of those who had moved to Switzerland were two men who worked for Pünter under the code names 'Long' and 'Salter'. In reality, Long was a French journalist named Georges Blun, a man with a most distinguished record, a Chevalier of the Legion of Honour, who had been Berlin correspondent for a number of French publications, and a professional agent for the Deuxième Bureau. He had excellent connections in Berlin and specialised in providing reports on the political, diplomatic and economic life of the Third Reich. His most importance source, which figured regularly in Radó's messages to Centre, was a highly placed and remarkably well-informed official with the German foreign ministry, Ernst Lemner, code named 'Agnes'.

Salter was another French diplomat, Léon Sousse, who also had a distinguished military career behind him. He had studied in Germany and had maintained a great many useful contacts there. He, too, had been a journalist in Berlin for some time. Salter was a very active and energetic member of the Intelligence community in Switzerland, working for the British and the Free French as well as for Pünter and through him the Swiss and the Russians. When Allen Dulles arrived in Berne as head of operations in Europe for the American OSS, Salter was quick to establish contact with him, too.

The Pakbo ring therefore had access to excellent French sources, which Pünter in return was supplying with information received from his other sources. Mayr von Baldegg was detailed, under his code name Louise, to trade with the French through Pünter. In this way, several connections could be achieved simultaneously.

The French, notably through Salter, were in touch and trading with the British Secret Service, so there was also a two-way flow in and out of Pünter's ring from the British. This information naturally went out from Pünter in two directions – to Moscow via Radó and to the Swiss via Louise. But the Swiss also had their own direct link with the British, using as a liaison man Corporal August Lindt, a young member of the famous chocolate-making family who has since had a most distinguished career as a diplomat. Lindt was attached to the Bureau Ha, and also worked for Colonel Oscar Frey, who was responsible for keeping the trade unions informed on political and military matters. Lindt worked as a courier between the Bureau Ha and the British, and consequently was a means of keeping the British supplied with Rössler's information – useful, though Lindt did not know it himself of course, both for receiving information obtained by Rössler from his German sources and for checking on Ultra information which had come from London.

The Bureau Ha also had a two-way association with Czech Intelligence, through their man in Switzerland, Hausamann's friend Karel Sedlacek (alias 'Uncle Tom'). He was able to supply information to Hausamann from Czech sources, notably from a senior German officer in the Abwehr, Paul Thümmel, who worked for the Czechs as 'Agent A54'. Sedlacek's bosses, of course, were now in London, where they in turn had close connections with the British Secret Service.

The British set-up in Switzerland was based in Berne, but with offshoots in other towns and cities. In Berne the SIS station chief was Count 'Fanny' Vanden Heuvel, with Andrew King as his assistant. Their office was completely separate from the legation itself, which in any case had to accommodate the SOE representative concerned with resistance and sabotage in occupied Europe, Jock McCaffery. Air Intelligence was represented by the famous one-legged first world war air ace, Freddy West, VC. Military Intelligence was represented by the military attaché, Colonel Henry Cartwright, and his assistant, Herbert M. Fryer, a close friend of Vanden Heuvel. Fryer seems to have been active in liaising with the Swiss, and was constantly hurrying to and from Lucerne. After his escape from Colditz, the military staff were joined by Major Pat Reid, who stayed in Berne for the rest of the war, helping to debrief other escaped prisoners and putting them on their way home.

Outside Berne the principal British agents were Eric Grant Cable in Zurich and Victor Farrell, Sissy's contact man, in Geneva. Farrell was particularly valuable. He dealt with escaping prisoners, organising routes through southern France and across the Pyrenees into Spain, then Portugal and so to Britain, besides liaising with the French and with other agents working in the ILO and similar institutions in Geneva, on behalf of the SIS. He also looked after the smuggling of arms and strategic materials such as industrial diamonds. Farrell had his own radio transmitter/receiver, through which he could contact both Berne and London.

Information came to the British organisation from many sources, in addition to those we have already described. Official Intelligence-gathering was mainly concerned with information affecting the war in the air, and West was interested in passing on anything which could help to indicate targets, guide bombers on to them, and assess the results of raids. There were two main types of informant – those who wished to give their information freely, and those who wanted to be paid. The free suppliers were left to West, but those who wanted money were dealt with strictly by Vanden Heuvel.

Some of the informers was distinctly bizarre. West recalls one man who arrived in Berne speaking with a heavy Italian accent and wearing a large, false beard. West thought there was something familiar about the man's eyes, and correctly unmasked him as an Italian government minister whom he had known before the war. Germans also called in at Berne en route between Berlin and Italy, as well as Allied airmen who had been shot down in France or Germany and who had managed to make their way into Switzerland. These men, since they were all trained fliers and observers, often had useful information spotted while travelling.

Such information was rightly West's province. But he found that he had to be very careful about reporting anything else, for fear of arousing the jealousy of Dansey who still regarded Switzerland and all things Swiss as his private domain. In fact, West and the other attachés were relieved to be free of the need to dabble in what they regarded as murky waters. To them, Air Intelligence was all-important, and they regarded almost anything else as small beer.

Later in the war, West was approached by the Swiss police who told

111

him there was an Englishman named Foote transmitting radio messages from Lausanne. Was Foote working for the British, they wanted to know, and what did the British want them to do about this? West knew nothing about Foote and asked Vanden Heuvel, who told him to have nothing to do with him but to 'handle anything concerning Foote with a very long pair of tongs'. Vanden Heuvel told West that Foote's activities were nothing to concern him at all. The Swiss police were informed that the Englishman was doing nothing against Switzerland, but was passing information for the Russians – who were of course Britain's allies – though he had no connection with the British legation.

One interesting point about British Intelligence-gathering operations was the means of communication used between Berne and London. Information was carefully enciphered, using the one-time pad method where each sheet on a printed pad carries a different cipher, printed at random and coinciding only with one other matching pad held by the recipient of the message, so that each cipher is used once only and is totally individual. The messages thus enciphered were taken to the Swiss post office, who sent them to the Foreign Office in London as cables in the normal way. Vast amounts of Intelligence were passed in this way from the 'official' men in the legation, though the SIS still used its own radio links, choosing to remain separate and secret.

In 1942 the Allied Intelligence community in Switzerland was joined by the representative of America's OSS, Allen Dulles, who arrived on the last train from France before the Germans closed the frontier and occupied the southern half of the country. He brought an entirely different approach to Intelligence-gathering, quite the reverse of the other organisations' discreet and secret operations. 'He was,' says Freddie West, 'like a man with a big bell, who rang it to attract attention, saying "I've got plenty of money and I'm willing to buy information."' Dulles liaised with the Bureau Ha, and with the French through his agent in Geneva, Max Shoop. He also had contact with agents in Germany and with a German consular official, Hans Gisevius, a former Gestapo man who had turned against Hitler and who had valuable connections with other like-minded Germans in high positions. Naturally Dulles also had contact with the British from his base at 22 Herrengasse, in the shadow of the Gothic cathedral in the old town of Berne.

112

These then were the main anti-Nazi Intelligence activities going on in Switzerland during the war, all heavily intertwined and interdependent. Practically every other Intelligence service in the world was also represented, including the Chinese – one of whose attachés worked for Pünter under the code name 'Polo' – and the Japanese. But they were on the fringe of the busy market. The only network which did not officially trade in secrets and for which information flowed in one direction only was the Russian. Radó was under strict orders not to share his information with anyone. Centre deliberately chose to ignore the fact that much of the material it received came from other organisations. That was a fact of life which Moscow did not wish to acknowledge.

Centre's attitude was clearly demonstrated on an occasion when Radó obtained a quantity of documents and plans which would have been of great value to the British as well as to the Russians. The plans, of course, could not be transmitted and the documents were far too long and detailed for the radio time available. Rather than see them go to waste, Radó suggested to Centre that he should pass them to the British, as allies. The reaction was immediate – the material must be destroyed. It was Russian, and must not be given to anyone else, ally or not, no matter how valuable it might be in the common cause against Hitler. Russia, incidentally, was the only major nation to have no diplomatic representation in Switzerland, and therefore no embassy, legation or mission from which to operate an official Intelligence service.

The information market did not stop at the Allied and neutral nations. The Swiss, being neutral, could still have contact with Germany in the Intelligence field, just as they still maintained diplomatic and trade relations with their powerful neighbour. Germany had need of Swiss products and of Swiss rail links to Italy, and was happy to deal with Switzerland, though Hitler was less happy that Switzerland should display so openly its firm determination to defend itself. The Swiss had insured against possible German invasion by placing explosive charges on all important road and rail bridges, passes and tunnels, so that they could be destroyed in an instant and thus denied to the aggressor.

Since Germany, and to a lesser extent Italy, were the only countries which posed a threat against Switzerland, the relationship between Swiss and German Intelligences was radically different from those with the Allied powers. German agents in Switzerland were concerned mainly with counter-espionage and trying to uncover and destroy the Allied networks. There were also, however, agents spying on the Swiss, obtaining information which would be useful to Germany in the event of an invasion or which would provide useful bargaining power in trade and diplomatic negotiations.

The Swiss authorities estimated that during the war there were some thousand German-trained spies operating in Switzerland. Most of these were Swiss supporters of the Nazis, giving saturation cover in frontier areas: on one section of the Swiss-German frontier between Basle and Lake Constance, some 150 kilometres long, for instance, 206 agents worked for German Intelligence. The Swiss counter-espionage service caught 865 such 'spies', of whom 523 were Swiss citizens. In the main, these were simply Nazi supporters who kept their eyes open and passed on anything which looked interesting. But there were more serious spies among them – thirty-three were condemned to death and seventeen were actually executed – in a country whose last canton abolished the death penalty for murder in 1927.

In spite of this activity, or perhaps partly because of it, the chief of Swiss Intelligence, Brigadier Roger Masson, had dealings with General Walter Schellenberg, the notorious thirty-two-year-old head of German SS Intelligence. Schellenberg visited Switzerland himself several times, and on one occasion even met General Guisan personally. Although there were factions pressing Hitler to invade Switzerland, and he himself threatened to teach the Swiss a lesson for being so cocky, Swiss Intelligence was still able to report that the general staff was opposed to such a move on the grounds that Switzerland was Germany's 'only eye out into the world' and that it performed valuable services as a point where information could be exchanged.

Thus the circle was complete. Directly or indirectly all the Intelligence services of the world were talking to each other and making deals with each other in the only country in the world where such a communal meeting place could have existed at that time – Switzerland. In fact, Schellenberg even contacted the British directly, through Eric Grant Cable in Zurich, in late summer 1942 in an attempt to set up a deal on behalf of the anti-Hitler faction. Later in the war he also made contact with Dulles, with the same intention. In time of war, the only way enemy nations can talk directly to each other without using neutral go-betweens who may complicate matters, is through their Secret Services. Sadly, the same often applies to allies, too.

Part Two

CHAPTER EIGHT

Lorenz and Laura

With so much going on in the secret world of Intelligence in Switzerland, it would have been surprising if the Germans had not suspected the existence of the Russian network. The German radio detection unit at Cranz in East Prussia first picked up strong signals beamed to Russia in July 1941, though they were unable then to break the cipher in which the messages were being transmitted, or to locate the transmitters with any real accuracy.

At the same time, the Germans had picked up signals from other transmitters in Belgium, France and Berlin. They created a special unit to work solely against Soviet Intelligence operations, in a rare example of co-operation between the various German Intelligence services. For once, Canaris's Abwehr, Müller's SD, Schellenberg's SS Foreign Secret Service and the Military Wireless Counter-Intelligence Department worked together, under the direction of the head of the RSHA, Reinhard Heydrich. The new unit was given the name *Sonderkommando Rote Kapelle* – the Red Orchestra Special Commando.

The Kommando moved swiftly and efficiently in the occupied countries and in the Reich itself. By the end of 1941 it had smashed the Red Orchestra network in Brussels and Berlin. Most of the agents had been captured, as had their contacts in the various German ministries and commands. 'Kent', the man who had brought code books and instructions to Radó in Geneva only twelve months before, managed to escape from Brussels, however, and fled to unoccupied southern France, where he found a hiding place in Marseilles.

With the Red Orchestra smashed, the Kommando took over many of its transmitters and started a *Funkspiel* (literally 'radio game') trying to deceive the Russians and to extract useful information from them by sending false information over their own transmitters. Schellenberg, who later became chief of the combined German Intelligence services, claimed that at its peak the *Funkspiel* operation employed no less than sixty-four transmitters. Many of these belonged to individual agents dropped by parachute, and were of little importance, but the overall effect must have been considerable. With so many attempts to confuse them, Centre must have valued even more highly the steady and generally reliable flow of information from Switzerland.

Knowing there was a network operating independently of the Red Orchestra in Switzerland, the Kommando tried its best to locate it and put it out of action. It also tried, naturally enough without success, to find its sources in the German high command and ministries. It seemed incredible to the Kommando investigators that even after they had undertaken the most intensive searches and had weeded out those who had been feeding the Red Orchestra, the Swiss network was not only continuing to receive Intelligence of the highest grade, but was actually increasing the amount.

From captured agents and intercepted radio messages, the Kommando began piecing together scraps of information about the Swiss organisation. But there was little they could do about it until they had much firmer evidence. Smashing spy rings in occupied countries was all very well; trying to break up a network in neutral Switzerland was dangerous indeed. In any case, it was more important to discover the network's sources. An agent can always be replaced – his informers cannot.

The German Intelligence services were asked by the Kommando to put their agents in Switzerland on the alert to hunt for the network. As we have already stated, there was a large number of Nazi agents in the confederation. In addition to native Swiss, there were also many Germans. The SD in Germany ran a school for secret agents, under the command of SS *Sturmbahnführer* Klaus Hugel, which turned out 300 agents per course, and an increasing number of these were being sent into Switzerland, some with specific aims, others with instructions simply to keep their eyes open. Now, they were given something specific to keep their eyes open for.

Naturally, the various German consulates were all working for their country's Intelligence services in addition to their normal duties, as were the British. In Berne the consul-general, Hans Meisner, was responsible for running the Abwehr's 'Bureau F', which was also given the job of seeking out the network. Two men were put to work on the problem full-time, Captain Hans Pescatore and Corporal Willy Piert. They found they had a very difficult job, since they got no help from the Swiss authorities and had to rely largely on other Abwehr, SD and Gestapo sources, mainly in other countries. However, they persevered, and gradually began to draw nearer to their target.

In Geneva the consulate provided a base for an Abwehr 'V-man', Hermann Henseler, who was given the task of tracking down the transmitter based in Geneva. Henseler had formerly worked as a German agent at the ILO – the Russians were not the only ones to use that organisation for espionage purposes – so even at the beginning of the hunt, he was dangerously close to the Radós, Sissy and Taylor.

The first real sign of danger, however, did not come directly from Henseler or the Bureau F. The Kommando had managed to 'turn' some of the captured agents, whom it put to work to help penetrate the Soviet networks. Among them were two old-established members of Russian Intelligence, photographic experts who had been active abroad since 1926, named George and Joanna Wilmer, alias Charles and Elsa Martin, code names 'Lorenz' and 'Laura'.

Lorenz and Laura, after a spell in Japan, had been stationed in Germany immediately before the war, and had lost touch with Centre after the Nazi-Soviet pact. Meanwhile they had been discovered by the Germans. They arrived in Switzerland with German help, were established in a villa above Lausanne, and then made contact with Moscow through the rather indirect route of an agent whom they knew from their Japanese days, code named 'Louis', who operated from San Francisco. Centre took the bait, glad to hear that two such trusted and experienced agents had reached the safety of Switzerland, and instructed Foote to contact them.

Foote, ever cautious, visited the address given to him by Centre and gained admission by saying that he had heard the villa was up for sale. He found the two agents living in considerable luxury, in itself something of a surprise since they had been out of touch with Centre for two years, and had received no pay in that time. Lorenz was the most smartly dressed spy he had ever met, and Laura had several good fur coats. Foote immediately wondered who had been paying them, for even if they had kept in touch with Moscow it was doubtful if they could have supported such a standard of living. Centre not only regarded luxury as bourgeois and decadent *per se*, it also never managed to make very much money available to any spy. Moscow was noted neither for the promptness nor for the regularity of its payments, and its agents all too often had to fend for themselves, as Foote knew only too well.

Nevertheless, Foote gave them the right passwords, and finally managed to persuade them that he was genuine. For some reason they were at first very reluctant to trust him. Maybe they could not believe that everything had worked out so easily, and suspected him of being some sort of plant. However, they explained that they had two very highly-placed sources of information in Germany, codenamed 'Barras' and 'Lambert', and wished to pass the material thus obtained to Centre through the network. Centre agreed that they should work through Foote, and instructed him to visit them twice a week, despite his suspicions.

As Foote dealt with Lorenz and Laura, he grew more and more uneasy about them. The information they produced was of poor quality, simply reports of routine troop movements in France, the sort of thing the Germans could easily afford to part with. Then they kept trying to discover his true name and his address. This was strictly against all the rules of espionage and clandestinity, for what an agent does not know he cannot be made to tell if he is ever captured. He discovered that they were going through the pockets of his overcoat, which they made him leave in the hall of their house when he visited them, even heating the house to tropical intensity to make sure he would have to take it off. Foote, however, was highly professional and would never have dreamed of leaving papers of any sort in his coat. He had had two detachable pockets made which hung down inside the front of his trousers – trousers in those days were more generously cut than they are today – where he carried his passport, his *permis de séjour*, messages and other papers, and a small .32 automatic pistol.

Foote reported his suspicions to Centre, who declared he was suffering from nerves – 'out-station suspicions' was the way they described it. But when Foote detected Laura secretly trying to photograph him, he had no more doubts. He knew for certain that the two agents had been 'turned' and were working for the Germans, a fact which was more than usually dangerous for him, in his position as a double agent.

Perhaps sensing that Foote was on to them, Lorenz finally tried a more direct approach. At a dinner party at the villa he suggested that Foote should retire, hand over his codes and contacts and let him, Lorenz, run the network – for he believed that Foote was the resident director. He argued that he was a more experienced Soviet agent and that Centre would raise no objections to his taking command. In return, he would pay Foote $500 a month and $500 expenses, over and above what he received from Centre. Foote naturally refused, perhaps amused by the bizarre irony of the Germans trying to take over a Russian network which had already been taken over by the British. Nevertheless, bizarre or not, the Germans were too close for comfort. The threat to his safety was real enough, but he could not lie low or move out. He still had much important work to do.

CHAPTER NINE

Full Stretch

As soon as the network had been placed on a war footing, Centre gave Radó and Foote orders to develop and expand with all possible speed, searching for new contacts, new collaborators and new sources of information. At the same time, they were to concentrate their attention on German troop movements, particularly the transfer of units from France and other Western European countries to the eastern front.

Pünter's French agents were particularly valuable in this area, and his contacts in the diplomatic world were also bearing fruit. For example, on 7th August 1941 Radó was able to send the following message:

> The Japanese ambassador in Berne has declared that there can be no possible question of a Japanese attack against the Soviet Union, for as long as Germany has failed to win any decisive victories on her fronts.
>
> Dora

This confirmed information already sent by Richard Sorge from Japan – the information on which his fame as an agent has been based. It enabled the Russians to transfer troops from the Far East to help in the defence of Moscow. It was the first small turning point in the war. The weary German armies, finding themselves in the suburbs of Moscow after their great advance across Russia, and believing victory was within their grasp, were suddenly confronted by fresh troops. And this time the troops were not battle-weary Europeans, but fresh, well-fed Mongolians used to fighting in the extreme cold. The German attack was halted.

Throughout the German advance, the network had been busy sending information from Lucy and other sources about German plans and strengths. But on the night of 19th October, halfway through a message, Centre suddenly went off the air. Try as they might, neither of the transmitters could raise Moscow. The silence continued, night after night, and Foote says Radó was in despair and even talked of going over to the British! For six weeks, at the height of the battle of Moscow, the network had no voice. Then suddenly, the radio began again. Centre started transmissions at the normal scheduled time, at precisely the point halfway through the message where it had stopped. There was no explanation.

What had happened shows just how near Moscow had been to capture. On 16th October 1941, after the Russians had lost at least 650,000 men to the Germans, with no less than forty-five divisions destroyed, the population of Moscow had panicked and fled. Stalin and his headquarters staff – including Centre – stayed in Moscow, but most other government departments and the diplomatic corps were ordered to leave the capital and move to the city of Kuybyshev in the interior of Russia. In Moscow itself chaos reigned, with looting in the deserted streets – the British embassy, for example, was stripped of anything worth stealing – and by 19th October a state of siege was declared. That night, without warning even the operator who was in the process of transmitting to Foote, Centre was ordered to move out. As Foote says, 'The unhappy operator had been practically wrenched from his set and put in a lorry for the long trek eastwards.'

Without the troops from the east and Intelligence about German plans supplied by the network, it is possible that Moscow would have fallen. But the Russians had other factors on their side. The Germans had been pushed almost beyond endurance by the immense distances they had covered, and their supply lines were stretched to breaking point. The Russian weather entered the game, with torrential rains that turned the ground to mud and made the German tanks all but useless, followed by the onset of winter. Hitler's gamble had failed. In spite of his earlier statements he had not started his attack early enough. On 8th December he issued his Directive 39, abandoning the assault on Moscow and blaming 'the surprisingly early severe winter weather'. On that same day (Japanese time) America was brought into the war when Japan attacked Pearl Harbor.

The network had been transmitting furiously since contact had been re-established with Centre, passing on all the Intelligence that had been piling up during the six-week silence. Some of it was out-of-date, of course, but much of it was still valuable: detailed information about the strength of German forces, their losses and their needs; the state of reserves and replacement equipment; the numbers and descriptions of units transferred from France to the eastern front; German objectives and plans; and even reactions in the German high command to events in Russia. The network's messages began to reflect the growing disillusionment and dissatisfaction with Hitler.

During the early months of 1942 Radó was also able to send to Moscow, by courtesy of London and Lucy, detailed information of Hitler's orders for spring and summer offensives. In this the Ultra cryptanalysts at Bletchley had an unexpected bonus when Hitler sacked his commander-in-chief and assumed direct personal control of the war in the east. Hitler could not resist meddling in every smallest detail, and it seemed that every decision taken by any commander in the field, no matter how small, had to be referred to the Führer himself. Naturally, almost all communication between the front and Führer headquarters was made via Enigma machines. As fast as the radio messages shuttled backwards and forwards between Hitler and his commanders the British listening posts picked them up and relayed them to Bletchley. Within hours the relevant parts were on their way to Switzerland, and thence to Russia. Often the gap was less than twenty-four hours from the time the original message left Hitler's lair.

The generals wanted to attack Moscow, the nerve centre of the Soviet Union. But Hitler would have none of this. His main plan was to forget Moscow for the time being and concentrate instead on the south-west of the Soviet Union, thrusting through the Ukrainian 'Black Country' at Kursk, Voronezh and Kharkov to occupy both the Caucasus with its rich oilfields and the mountain passes into Turkey and Iran through which Anglo-American supplies were carried to Russia, at the same time cutting off the vital river traffic along the Don and the Volga.

As part of this plan, Hitler had given orders for the taking of the industrial city of Stalingrad. Originally known as Tzaritsyn, the city had been held for the Reds during the civil war in 1918 by Voroshilov, Budenny and Stalin. All three claimed credit for the victory, but when

Stalin assumed absolute power he rewrote the history books to give himself all the honour, renamed the city after himself and turned its defence into a Soviet military legend. Naturally, Hitler saw the chance of destroying it as too good to miss.

The network reported all this, and the Red Army began making what preparations it could. But the problems which had halted Germany – weather conditions, overstretched lines of communication and the exhaustion of troops after a long and gruelling advance – now came into play against the Russians. The Germans, while retreating through the winter snows, had been busily re-equipping and reinforcing, and when the spring cleared the snows from the ground their mobility and generally superior equipment came into their own once more.

To clear the way for the main offensive the Germans attacked in the Crimea and inflicted a heavy defeat on the Red Army. Having been told by Lucy that the main attack in the Ukraine was due to be launched on 18th May, Stalin ordered Timoshenko to attack the Germans in the Kharkov area and to destroy the forces being assembled there. For once, however, Lucy's information seems to have been incomplete. Stalin miscalculated, and the result was a defeat that cost the Red Army dear. They lost 214,000 men as prisoners, 1,200 tanks and 2,000 guns. Soviet official sources have never given the number of Russians killed and wounded, but when Foote was confronted with the 'faulty' message by the Director in Moscow at the end of the war, he was told it was 100,000.

What is particularly interesting is that Centre should blame Lucy for the defeat, which shows just how much they had come to rely on the information he supplied. No mention was made of the part played by bad assessment of the information, or of Stalin's orders that there was to be no retreat of any sort, or of the elaborate German deception plans, which he largely swallowed, pigheadedly, holding back too much vital Russian strength in the north. Operation Kremlin, as it was code named, was specifically intended to mislead the Russians into believing that the Germans' main offensive was to be against Moscow and that a considerable portion of their strength was positioned for such a move. Added to this, the Germans knew all about Timoshenko's forthcoming attack at Kharkov.

In April, a new commander had taken over *Fremde Heere Ost*, the German Intelligence staff on the eastern front – the legendary

Reinhard Gehlen. He had quickly demonstrated his skill in dealing with prisoners and had managed to 'turn' one of the more important, a senior political commissar named Minishki. In a secret operation, code named 'Flamingo', Gehlen had arranged for Minishki to 'escape' from captivity with a great deal of genuine, valuable information, as a result of which he was duly installed in the heart of the Kremlin among Stalin's senior staff. From there, he began reporting high-grade Intelligence back to Gehlen, who assessed it and advised the army commanders accordingly.

At the same time, Gehlen began to score successes with one of his other specialities, his own form of *Funkspiel*, creating confusion by the use of radio messages from phantom formations in the German armies, or from genuine formations and units but indicating totally false positions, objectives and strengths. So although, thanks largely to London, Lucy and the Swiss network, the Russians were well ahead in the Intelligence war, they by no means had everything their own way.

By this time the Russian network had over a hundred agents supplying information. Operation Lucy was gathering momentum. Vital, detailed material – often in reports covering several pages of typescript as the British cipher-breakers at Bletchley became more expert at deciphering Germany's Enigma wireless traffic – was being transmitted to Moscow. The small 'headquarters' staff of the network responsible for enciphering and transmitting – Radó and Lène, the Hamels and Foote – were stretched almost beyond endurance. However, Lucy's messages were now reaching the network so quickly that any delay in enciphering and sending seemed almost criminal, so Radó began looking for ways of improving the situation and of getting more help.

First, he turned to Otto Pünter, asking if he would help with enciphering. Pünter agreed readily, but soon found that the amount of material involved was so enormous that it was interfering with his other activities and preventing him from carrying on his profession as a working journalist. He was an ingenious man with a quick mind, and soon thought up ways of improving the situation. He had already built his own apparatus for making microdots during the days when messages could be sent in this way through the post or by hand. Now he turned his inventive abilities to developing a machine which would speed up the process of encipherment.

He had been given a German edition of Sven Hedin's book *From Pole to Pole* for use as his key. He laid out the relevant passages converted into numerals on a board of electrical contacts. This was then connected to a typewriter which he had adapted for the purpose. When the clear message was typed, the equivalent enciphered symbols would light up on a display unit at eye level. While Pünter typed the original messages, his wife sat on the other side of the table with another typewriter and copied down the enciphered message. It worked beautifully, and saved a great deal of time. Without realising it, Pünter had invented a simple form of Enigma machine, the original source of much of Lucy's information.

Even with Pünter and his wife, Radó and Lène, Edmond and Olga Hamel, and Allan Foote all working flat out, they still could not cope. With the quality of material being handled, the operators had to spend more and more precious time travelling about the country to meet couriers and cut-outs in prearranged places, which were changed daily. Foote recalled that he had to break all the rules of clandestinity and continue enciphering in all sorts of places. He sat in buses and trains on his way to the various meeting places, in busy cafés, restaurants and railway stations, frantically enciphering messages on scraps of paper for transmission when he got back to his flat that night.

Through Léon Nicole's workers' party, Radó met a young woman who had already shown herself to be an enthusiastic anti-fascist. Her name was Margrit Bolli, an attractive, dark-haired girl of twenty-two. She lived with her family on the outskirts of Basle, and leapt at the chance of working with the network. With the permission of Centre, Radó recruited her and put her to work initially as a courier, a job which she did eagerly and efficiently. He gave her the code name 'Rosie', and asked Foote to teach her the rules of clandestinity as well as how to encipher messages and operate a radio set. Rosie was an attractive girl and Foote accepted the task willingly, the more so since it increased his control of the network's communications. He could not keep travelling to her home in Basle, however, so it was agreed that she should visit him in Lausanne. She told her father that she was visiting her grandparents who lived in the town. Meanwhile Foote persuaded his neighbours that she was his girl-friend – a romantic

129

notion which no doubt had great appeal for the middle-aged ladies who guarded him so zealously. Rosie proved to be a good pupil, and by late spring Hamel installed a radio set at her parents' home, where she transmitted messages – simple ones at first, but rapidly becoming more complicated as she gained assurance. Soon she moved to Geneva, where Radó found her a flat in a modern block at Number 8, Rue Henri Mussard.

It has been said that Radó moved her there because she had become his mistress, but this is a very doubtful supposition. In the first place, Radó always seemed to be a devoted husband and father – and he also had his mother-in-law on hand to keep an eye on him, which would surely have discouraged any 'extra-mural' relationship. And on a simple, practical level it is most doubtful whether he could ever have found time! Those who knew him then agree unanimously that Radó was always in a hurry, with no time for anything other than essential business. He was not only running a huge, complex spy network, dealing with hordes of agents and enciphering much of the information himself, he was also continuing to run his Geopress agency, which was still flourishing.

According to Inspector Charles Knecht, then chief of police in Geneva, 'He might have found time to make love to her once – after all, she was a young, pretty girl. But regularly? Never!' In any case, Rosie soon found another lover.

Rosie was installed in her flat with the cover story that she was a student from the German-speaking part of Switzerland who had come to Geneva to improve her French. It was thus quite natural that Radó and Lène should call on her regularly, as the neighbours would take Radó for her teacher. Indeed it would have seemed odd if she had never had any visitors. Hamel fixed her radio set in its new quarters, and she began transmitting regularly from there in Radó's cipher.

The network now had three transmitters and four operators working at full stretch, and still continued recruiting new sources. Apart from the danger of discovery with such a large organisation, the main problem was the old, recurring headache of money. It had been difficult enough for anyone to cross into another country such as Yugoslavia before Italy came into the war. After that it was impossible.

Identity photograph of Allan Foote in 1939, from police records. (*Police Cantonale, Lausanne*)

Foote at the time of his arrest. (*Archives Drago Arsenijevic*)

The end of a double agent. (*Der Spiegel*)

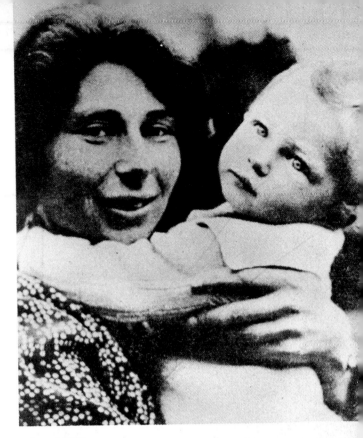

Sonia (Ruth Kuczynski) with her child, Micha. (*Anthony Read*)

Len Brewer, alias Burton, alias Phillips. (*Anthony Read*)

Fred Copeman today. (*Anthony Read*)

Sándor Radó. (*Ringier Dokumentationszentrum*)

Edmond Hamel today outside his shop. (*Anthony Read*) *Inset*: Edmond Hamel during the war. (*Police Cantonale, Lausanne*)

Otto and Isabel Pünter. (*Anthony Read*) *Inset*: Margrit Bolli. (*Police Cantonale, Lausanne*)

No. 2 Chemin de Longeraie, Lausanne. Foote's apartment, showing the radio antenna. (*Archives Drago Arsenijevic*)

Inspector Charles Knecht. (*Ringier Dokumentationszentrum*)

Rudolf Rössler and Xaver Schnieper at the time of their trial in 1953. (*Photopress*)

The cupboard in Foote's apartment where he hid his transmitter.
(*Archives Drago Arsenijevic*)

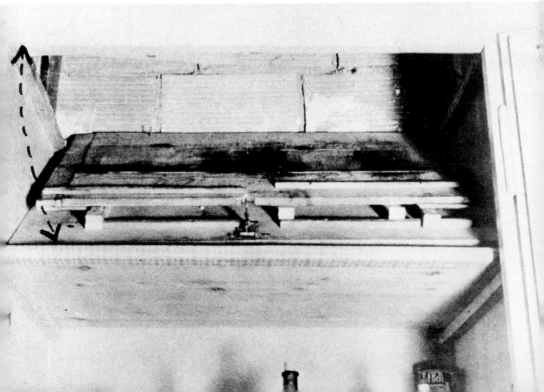

The hiding place of the Hamels' transmitter in their villa, Route de Florissant. (*Archives Drago Arsenijevic*)

Olga Hamel photographed by her husband while transmitting to Moscow. (*Archives Drago Arsenijevic*)

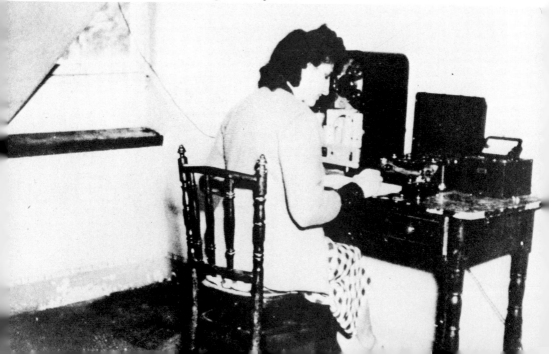

Full Stretch

Radó seems to have been more adept at spending money than raising it. He had become accustomed to living a comfortable bourgeois life in Geneva, and his personal expenses appear to have been high. Certainly a great deal of money passed through his hands – Foote stated after the war that he had given him about $100,000 between April 1941 and August 1943, though Radó was unable to account for a large part of this.

It was left to Foote to organise the finances. Although Moscow had unlimited credit at its disposal in the United States, Centre seems to have been very lackadaisical and unimaginative in trying to find ways of transferring funds to Switzerland. Their first suggestion was that Foote should make regular journeys to Vichy to meet a courier there, a wildly incredible scheme since it would have called for the Englishman to travel openly in Occupied France! They then declared that it would be impossible for them to have the money paid into a bank in France or elsewhere and then transferred in the normal way to Foote's account in Switzerland, since this would necessitate the courier who paid in the money knowing Foote's real name.

With typical ingenuity Foote took matters into his own hands and went into the black market currency business with the help of some of his shadier friends. It would be interesting to know whether the 'shady' British friends had any connection with the elegant, charming papal count in Berne and the bird-like colonel in London! Swiss firms who did business in the United States had to forward money from Switzerland to New York, where it would be changed into dollars at the official rate of 4.30 francs to the dollar. Some of them were persuaded to allow Foote to do the exchanging at black market rates of about double the amount. Centre paid the money into the firms' accounts in New York in dollars, and the firms in Switzerland then handed over the required amount of Swiss francs to Foote. It was expensive, but it worked.

At first, Foote also used American firms, but when the US authorities tightened up their currency regulations he had little difficulty in finding individual Americans who were quite happy to make a profit from this 'eccentric millionaire' in Lausanne.

When a particularly large sum of money was required on one occasion, Foote decided on boldness. He went to see the most important lawyer in Lausanne to seek official help in getting the money transferred from New York. Interestingly, the lawyer records that in order to make the whole transaction seem respectable, Foote took along with him a genuine *British* Intelligence agent.

It is one of the many ironies of this story that Roger Corbaz, the lawyer Foote chose – presumably by accident – turned up later as president of the military tribunal which tried him in his absence at the end of the war and found him guilty of espionage. Corbaz suspected that there was something odd about Foote's request, in spite of, or perhaps because of, the presence of the British agent. He told him he would only arrange the transfer if Foote could bring him proof that the money legally belonged to him and that the whole affair was above board. Foote never went back, but found another way of getting the money.

Moscow was never particularly generous to its agents, and payments were normally geared not to the work done or to its value, but simply to the needs of the agent concerned in obtaining information and maintaining his cover. According to notes made by Radó which were found by the Swiss police later, his own salary started at 1,270 Swiss francs a month and was raised in September 1942 to 1,775 francs a month. In the period between June 1941 and September 1943 he received a total of 40,850 francs by way of salary. Presumably Lène was included in Radó's salary, because there is no mention of her receiving any separate payments. According to Foote, his salary was at first 650 francs a month, rising to 870 and then to 1,300. Radó's records show Foote as receiving a total of 21,730 francs during twenty-four months.

Payments to other leading members of the network showed some discrepancies between the amounts agreed or stipulated by Centre and the amounts actually paid them by Radó. The Hamels began by trying to refuse payment, until they were persuaded by Foote that they must accept something or they would be regarded as suspect by Centre. Hamel says that Foote also told him he would be stupid not to take the money that was available, since he was working extremely hard on Moscow's behalf. In any event, Centre agreed to pay the Hamels 1,000 francs a month between them. Radó paid them only 150 francs a month, plus expenses, making a total of 12,100 francs for twenty-seven months. Margrit Bolli, Rosie, was supposed to earn 500 francs a month, rising to 800, but never got above 400, receiving a total for twenty-one months of 8,350 francs.

Although there may have been perfectly valid reasons for them, discrepancies such as these were to play a very large part in Radó's downfall. Centre has always been suspicious about its agents' handling of money, fearing that they may either develop the taste for expensive living and thus lose their revolutionary zeal or that they will abscond with the money and 'go private'. Foote, although giving the appearance of being something of a pirate, a man who could fix anything or anyone, was meticulous in his handling of money. His books always balanced. He could account for every penny he received. In his position he could not afford any carelessness. For the moment, it suited his masters in London for him to go on working for the Russians in an apparently straightforward way, contributing to the eventual defeat of the common enemy. But Russia had not always been an ally of Britain, and the time would come when he would have to revert to his original role as a penetration agent with the mission of working against Russia. So he watched Radó, noted the Hungarian's mistakes and recorded them for future use.

'I knew, of course, about the operations of Radó,' he told the American historian David Dallin in 1953, 'but I did not inform Centre. Later in Moscow I was severely reprimanded for having withheld the truth from my superiors.' Such loyalty to Radó was most touching – but Foote had always made sure that any dubious suggestion or request, such as possible co-operation with the British, had always been made by Radó and never by himself, even when it had been his idea.

Foote was already engaged in a deadly chess game for the highest possible stakes. But Radó was not entirely off guard. He had little confidence in Foote's loyalty to the Soviet cause, which is hardly surprising – the Englishman was far from being a political animal. In fact, he knew so little about communism that when Radó called on him with a bottle of champagne on 7th November 1942 to celebrate the twenty-fifth anniversary of the Russian Revolution – Radó was always happy to find an excuse for celebration, but this was something extra special to all communists – Foote looked at him blankly and asked what was so special about the day. It was like a Christian not knowing the significance of 25th December.

According to a former member of the network, Radó and a few of the others always suspected that Foote had been a British agent, through his time in Spain as well as in Switzerland, but they had no way of proving it. Consequently, the game was by no means one-sided. The two men, watching each other warily and weighing each move, were both experienced and skilful players.

For the moment, however, the network had desperate need of Foote's talents. He was still worth three other radio operators, was trusted by Moscow, and was the only one able to obtain money. And money remained a key factor in the network's operations, though most of the suppliers of information in the field were quite happy to work for nothing, because they believed in what they were fighting for. Pünter states that no one in the Pakbo ring received payment from the network. Travelling expenses amounted overall to only 800–1,000 francs a month, plus an additional 1,000 francs a month for the line to Agnes in the German Foreign Office, which entailed long courier journeys.

Schneider, who had given up his permanent job at the ILO in order to spend all his time dealing with the flow of information to and from Rössler, was given a monthly salary of 890 francs. Rössler himself accepted payment for his information, which, depending on quantity, sometimes came to as much as 5,000 francs a month. Rössler poured all this into his publishing house, Vita Nova, which was now ailing. Sadly, both Rössler and Schneider often went unpaid, and had to make do with promises from Centre, most of which were not honoured. ·

Where money was concerned, Moscow always had double standards. Its agents were not allowed to put a foot wrong and were required to keep their finances absolutely in order, but Centre itself could renege whenever it felt like it. Its most blatant example came later when Foote was in prison and Radó asked Pünter if he could help. Pünter went to great trouble to obtain some 65,000 francs in loans, mainly from Swiss businessmen who were either friendly to Russia or who hoped their actions might help them to obtain large orders from Russia after the war. Through their efforts, Radó was able to raise an additional sum, believed to be as much as 300,000 francs, for which he gave signed receipts under a false name. All the lenders were assured they would be repaid after the war. But the promises made by Moscow proved worthless: not a centime was ever handed over by Russia. Nor was a single order received by any of the businessmen.

For Otto Pünter, the memory of the affair still rankles. When the war ended, he and the creditors contacted the Russian embassy in

Paris, without success. It became obvious that the Russians were not going to pay, and some of the creditors accepted the matter and wrote off their losses. Others, however, held Pünter himself responsible. In 1946, when diplomatic relations were at last re-established between Russia and Switzerland, Pünter visited the new envoy, Anatoli Kulachenkov, who knew all about the matter but stated that he would not acknowledge it or do anything about payment. Pünter was left to repay the more insistent creditors himself, in monthly instalments.

All that, however, was later in the war. In 1942 the network was operating successfully at full stretch, though it was already facing renewed threats from the Germans.

In early summer, one of Radó's friends was approached by a man claiming to be a journalist who had good contacts and who wished to get in touch with Centre. He gave his name as Yves Rameau, and said that Centre would know him under the code name 'Aspirant'. At that time he did not manage to get to Radó, but the friend did pass on his message, with a description of the man. Radó discovered that Rameau was in fact born in Germany and that he had actually known him by his original name, Ewald Zweig. He had left Germany at about the same time as Radó, fleeing from the Nazis since he was Jewish, and had since become a naturalised Frenchman, taking the name of Yves Rameau. He had worked for the French Intelligence service, the Deuxième Bureau, had stayed on after the capitulation of France and had then offered his services to Germany. He had been sent to Switzerland by the Kommando, with orders to infiltrate the network. He had been unsuccessful, and Radó swiftly informed Centre, but it was another distinct sign of danger. They would all need to be much more on guard.

At about the same time Centre informed both Radó and Foote that a new Swiss passport was urgently needed for an agent in Italy called Paolo. Radó had control of the lines into Italy, and was to arrange for couriers to collect the old passport and bring it to him, so that it could be passed on to Foote, who controlled the line to Max the Cobbler in Basle. The first part of the operation went smoothly. An Italian courier took the passport to a tailor's shop in Como, on the Swiss frontier, where it was collected by a network courier, taken back to

Geneva, and given to Radó's friend and doctor, Emilio Bianchi.

Radó then paid a visit to the doctor's surgery, collected the passport and sent it via Rosie to Foote. Foote then took the train to Basle, where he gave the passport to Anna Müller, who in turn passed it to Max the Cobbler. Four days later, the passport was returned along the same route, officially renewed. When the network courier reached the tailor's shop in Como, however, he found it was being watched by Italian security men. He slipped away, reported to Radó, and in due course they managed to get the passport into Italy by another route, through Tirano. They need not have bothered. The whole thing had been set up by the Italian security service, who had arrested Paolo in June, a month before the affair began. The Italian 'courier' had been a member of the security service, and the agents of the ring had all been rounded up.

It was particularly disturbing that the Italians now had firm evidence that the network existed in some strength in Switzerland, that it was in direct contact with Moscow, and that it had agents working within the police force at Basle. The Italians, of course, worked closely with the German Abwehr, SD and Gestapo.

The next blow, however, came from a different direction – Hamel was arrested by the Swiss police for possessing an illegal radio transmitter. The arrest almost had disastrous effects, for while the police were actually searching the Hamels' apartment above his shop Radó arrived with the batch of messages for transmission that night. Fortunately, he spotted the danger signal put up by Hamel – an electric clock in the shop window showed twelve o'clock when all was clear, but if the clock's hands showed any other time, then it was dangerous to enter. The same clock, incidentally, is still in Hamel's shop window today, but it now works normally. Radó spotted the signal and walked on. Later, he contacted Olga Hamel from a public telephone box and was told what had happened.

The police had not been searching for a transmitter, but for subversive literature, as Hamel's brother had been arrested for distributing communist propaganda. They failed to find the actual transmitter, even though they arrived when the Hamels were preparing to send. Edmond was at the set when they heard the sound of the police arriving outside the front of the shop. While he had gone to let them in, stalling them as long as possible at the door, Olga had taken the set out through the back door and buried it in the back garden, throwing the evening's messages and cipher sheets on to the kitchen fire as she passed.

What the police actually discovered, hidden under the floorboards, was another set which Hamel was in the process of building as a reserve apparatus. It was not finished, however, lacking the transmitting key. Hamel had disguised it in the casing of a medical oscillator, which works on similar principles to short wave radio transmitters – indeed, British scientists at that time were using such equipment, borrowed from hospitals, to jam German radio direction beams used to guide bombers to their targets. Hamel produced a medical certificate stating that he was suffering from neuralgia and sinus trouble and said that he had needed the equipment to treat his ailments. Since such equipment could not be bought commercially at that time, he had been forced to manufacture it himself. He had not obtained a licence, and for that reason had hidden it under the floorboards because he knew that he was technically breaking the law.

Having no reason to doubt this honest tradesman, and since they had not in any case been searching for radio transmitters, the Geneva police believed Hamel. The case was not treated with any urgency. It was six months before he was called to court, where he was found guilty of possessing an illegal medical short-wave oscillator and given a suspended sentence of ten days imprisonment.

According to the strict rules of espionage, Hemel should have been dropped immediately the police raided his premises, even though nothing incriminating had been found. But during the hectic days of 1942 the pressure on the network was so great that they could not manage without the transmitter and its two operators. The Hamels must continue their work, but Radó decided that a new address had to be found. He therefore rented a luxurious villa standing in its own grounds just outside the town on the Route de Florissant. The Hamels moved their radio equipment into the attic, and from then on spent their nights there, taking it in turn to transmit furiously as the volume of messages increased.

Even while Radó was rehousing the Hamels' transmitter, another, greater danger was looming. It started from the apparently harmless event of Margrit Bolli (Rosie) falling in love with her hairdresser, Hans Peters, to whom she had been introduced by another customer, Lène Radó. The affair might have remained harmless – though any emotional involvement is potentially dangerous for a secret agent, particularly one as young as Rosie, who was then only twenty-two. But Peters was a German.

He told Rosie that he was a convinced communist, and had fled Germany to escape from the Nazis. No doubt he had gauged her political feelings and thought this was the best way of establishing a friendly relationship. In fact, he was a Nazi supporter, a member of the *Deutsche Arbeitsfront* and of the Nazi sports club in Geneva. Foote, with intentional irony, described him as a handsome, blond Aryan youth. In reality he was born on 26th March 1905, and so was eighteen days older than Foote himself, and his photograph shows a rather sallow-faced man in glasses. Presumably the thirty-seven-year-old appealed to the young girl from Basle. Before settling in Switzerland he had worked as a hairdresser on ocean liners, where, no doubt he found plenty of opportunities to practise the arts of seduction.

The love affair could still have been harmless, but for one other factor, which changed everything. Peters's closest friend was Hermann Henseler, the Abwehr V-man, who had been assigned to search for agents of the network. It has been said that Peters was a German agent specially sent to infiltrate the network and discover its secrets. In fact, he did not become an Abwehr agent until November 1942, when he became suspicious of Rosie and reported his fears to Henseler, who enlisted his support and saw to it that he was paid for his efforts on behalf of the Fatherland.

At that time, Peters had nothing positive to go on, and was prepared to bide his time. It would be some months before he had discovered sufficient to make action worthwhile. Anyway he was in no hurry. He was enjoying his work.

In the autumn of 1942 there were more immediate dangers threatening the network. The Kommando had moved its headquarters to Paris, first sharing offices with the SD in the former French Sûreté building in the Rue des Saussaies, and then setting up its own offices in a block on the Boulevarde de Courcelles. From there it began scoring notable successes in capturing Soviet agents in France and Belgium, many of whom had links in one way or another with the Swiss network. A large proportion of them were persuaded by the Gestapo, using its own well-practised methods, first to talk and then to collaborate.

In September they caught a Swiss national living and working in Brussels under the code name Niggi, who knew Sissy and Anna Müller. Two months later, on 12th November 1942, they picked up several other agents in France, including Victor Sukulov ('Kent') who had been hiding in Marseilles. Kent, of course, knew a great deal about Radó, for he had taken him a new code book and instructions for radio transmission.

At first, Kent staunchly refused to say anything other than 'I am a Russian officer. I don't deny having worked against Germany, I had to carry out my orders. You can shoot me.' Nothing the Kommando interrogators could do would budge him: he remained silent. But they knew from messages found in Brussels that he had been connected with the groups in Belgium and Berlin, so they flew him to the German capital where the trial of other members of those groups was being prepared. He was put into the Gestapo prison, where his identity as Kent was confirmed by other agents who had not been as strong as himself. Yet still he refused to talk.

However, during an interrogation session a few days after reaching Berlin, the guards suddenly brought into the room Margarete Barcza, a beautiful young Czech widow with whom he had been living for some time. According to eye-witness reports, Kent behaved like a lunatic, embracing her wildly in front of everyone. The Gestapo had found his weak spot. He offered to tell them all if they would set her free.

'What do you know about Robinson, Jim, Radó, Lucy, Sissy?' he is reported as crying. 'I will tell you everything – but you must set her free!' And then he fell to his knees and wept like a child.

Soon afterwards, the Kommando took Kent and Barcza back to Marseilles, where Kent was put to work as a 'turned' agent, operating the radio contact with Centre. He worked well, and performed many useful services to his new masters, who kept their part of the bargain. They did not harm him, his mistress or their child. He told the Kommando all he knew about the Swiss network, which meant that from the end of 1942 they not only had Radó's name but also details of his cipher.

CHAPTER TEN

Success – and Failure

Throughout the summer of 1942, the German advance had continued, grinding its way onwards towards the Volga. At every point they met with fierce, often fanatical resistance from the local populations as well as from the Red Army and the militias. There are reports that in places local women charged the approaching German troops in hopeless desperation, linking arms so that none would falter. In other cases local commissars blew up themselves, their defence volunteers, women and children, together with their attackers. But it was all in vain. By September Stalingrad was under siege, its defenders trapped with their backs to the Volga in a pocket which measured only ten miles by four at its widest. The German advance gradually squeezed the pocket even smaller. Victory seemed within their grasp.

The Russians have consistently claimed that Stalingrad marked the turning point of the war on the eastern front. Other historians see it only as the moment when the Russians stopped losing; the actual turning point they regard as the battle of the Kursk Salient. But there is no doubt that Stalingrad assumed an almost mystical significance to the Russians. As the pocket grew smaller and smaller, they continued to resist. Surrender or evacuation were unthinkable.

Through October, the Soviet high command in Moscow worked frantically at plans for a counter-offensive. In this they were helped considerably by the Intelligence received via Switzerland of the enemy's positions, strength, reserves and intentions. The network became almost a direct extension of the high command structure, in a unique relationship with Moscow which can never have occurred elsewhere in the history of espionage.

Historically, the role of the spy in wartime has been to penetrate an enemy's defences in some way, perhaps with a specific target in mind, and to feed back to his own headquarters whatever he was fortunate enough to discover. His directors at headquarters accept what he is able to send, and try to fit the information into their overall pattern. Whether the information is or is not relevant remains a matter of chance.

With Lucy, however, the situation was anything but normal. The volume of radio messages flowing from Moscow to Switzerland became almost as great as that in the other direction, as the Soviet high command, through Centre, used the network like a reference library. Whatever they wanted to know about the Germans, they simply asked Lucy. And Lucy, his amazing human computer memory bank stocked with first-class, up-to-the-minute information from Ultra in London, provided the answers.

Was Guderian really on the eastern front? Were the 2nd and 3rd Armies under his control? Was the 4th Panzer Army attached to List's army group, or had another Panzer army been posted to him? Who was commanding the 18th Army – Lindemann or Schmidt? Had the 9th Army Corps been posted to Army Group North, and what were the divisions which constituted it? How was Model's group made up? Who was attached to it? Which sector of the front was he responsible for, and where was his headquarters situated? How was Kluge's group organised? What had been allotted to it? Was the headquarters of the 3rd Panzer Army at Vyazma? Who was attached to this army, and who was in command? Where were the German defences to the south-east of Stalingrad, and along the Don? Where had lines of defence been established on the line from Stalingrad to Kletskaya and Stalingrad to Kalach? What form did these defences take? Where exactly were the 11th and 18th Armoured Divisions and the 15th Motorised Division which were previously engaged on the Briansk-Volkhov front? What was the composition of Weichs' army group? Who was on his staff? These were only a few of the questions put to Lucy by Centre. Many others required much greater detail. And, of course, along with the other sources in the network Lucy continued to provide fresh information at the same time as answering Moscow's questions.

On 1st November, the first snow of the winter fell on Stalingrad, yet still the defenders held the German armies at bay. The Volga was swollen to such an extent that it took four hours for ferries to cross it, instead of the normal forty minutes, and floating ice made every journey dangerous. Where the river narrowed, the bridges had all been destroyed, and the only way the trapped forces in the city could be supplied was by small boats during the night. The principal pocket of Soviet resistance was now reduced to an area measuring no more than 700 metres by 400 metres, from which even the wounded could not be evacuated. The defenders were in a desperate state, but while the pockets remained undefeated, large German forces were kept from moving on elsewhere. What was more, through the Intelligence received from Switzerland coupled with that gained on the spot, the Russians knew just how many German forces were gathered around Stalingrad, where they were positioned, and how vulnerable they were to counter-attack. Stalin began planning Operation Uranus, a great two-pronged attack which would cut off the entire German 6th Army and turn the besiegers into the besieged.

As the plan progressed, commanders in the field were kept informed by representatives of the high command who flew back and forth from Moscow. Everything was done by personal word of mouth. Nothing was written down or sent by radio. The value of the Intelligence received from his own agents had taught Stalin the dangers involved. And so the secret preparations proceeded, and the questions and answers flew backwards and forwards between Moscow and Switzerland.

On 2nd November came news that the Germans had suffered their first important defeat outside Russia at El Alamein, where Montgomery had also benefited from Ultra Intelligence sent from Bletchley – though in his case he knew its source. Compared with the size of the forces ranged around Stalingrad, however, Alamein was a small skirmish. Montgomery had defeated an Axis army consisting of four German and eight Italian divisions. In the south-west of the Soviet Union at that time, the Red Army had a strength of sixty-six rifle divisions, seventeen rifle brigades, five tank corps, fifteen tank brigades, three cavalry corps and one mechanised corps. German forces were of much the same size. In all, the Axis forces had some 258 divisions and sixteen brigades ranged along the Russian front. Nevertheless, the news that Rommel was in full flight in the North African desert was a splendid morale booster for all Allied troops. Then, on

142

8th November came the news of the successful Anglo-American landings in Morocco and Algeria.

In a message at the end of October, Centre told Radó: 'Keep in mind, dear Dora, that the work of your organisation is at present more important than ever. You must do everything to continue the work.' A few days later Radó received a message congratulating him and his team for their 'excellent work'. The Director told him that Maude and Edward (Olga and Edmond Hamel) had been awarded decorations for their tireless efforts, and that a decoration had been sought for Sissy. He was also told that his own decoration was waiting for him (he discovered later that it was the coveted Order of Lenin) and that the Director was certain many more would follow. Centre sent good wishes to all in the network on the twenty-fifth anniversary of the Soviet Union.

It was then that Radó bought a bottle of champagne and travelled to Lausanne to tell Foote of his good fortune, and to celebrate. Whether the Englishman had received a Soviet decoration at that time we do not know – in any case he would have been informed direct by Moscow, on his own radio set. Perhaps Radó wanted to know, too. In all, Foote was decorated by the Russians no less than four times during the war, and attained the rank of major in the Red Army.

On 19th November, the Russians launched Operation Uranus with two great armoured thrusts in a classic pincer movement from north and south of Stalingrad. The Germans had been expecting some form of counter-attack, but this time had no firm idea where it would come from, or when it would begin. Stalin's precautions against any leak had been exceptionally thorough. The Germans, on the other hand, had few secrets from the Russians. Within four days, the Red Army was poised to close the jaws of its pincers at Kalach.

Kalach was an undistinguished Russian town on the River Don. It had been bombed, shelled, fought over, taken and retaken – until just about all that remained standing was the huge temporary bridge across the swollen river which the Germans had built to replace the bridges the Russians had blown up in the summer. The bridge at Kalach was vital to the Reich; it was the last lifeline to the German 6th Army which, under the command of Field Marshal von Paulus, was caught in the bear-trap that was Stalingrad. Across the bridge flowed the food, ammunition and spares that would keep the 6th Army alive and fighting.

On the afternoon of 22nd November a platoon of German engineers was on duty on the bridge. Demolition charges were already in place so that it could be destroyed immediately the order was received, and so denied to the advancing Russians. At about 4.30 p.m. the engineers heard the clatter of tanks approaching in the darkness from the north-west. The lieutenant in charge of the engineers wondered for a moment if they could be Russian? Surely not, he thought. Not from that direction. It was much more likely that they would be German reinforcements.

As the armoured vehicles approached and slowed down, he saw that the first three vehicles were Horch personnel carriers with 22nd Division markings. He ordered his men to lift the barrier. The Panzer personnel carriers rolled on to the bridge, then stopped. The doors opened and sixty Russian soldiers armed with sub-machine-guns leapt out. Within moments, they had mown down most of the engineering platoon.

The Russians removed the demolition charges and secured the bridge, then their commander, Leiutenant-Colonel Filippov, ordered twenty-five tanks to push across the bridge and drive south-east in the direction of Sovietski, which lay on the railway line running westwards from Stalingrad. That evening they made contact with the 14th Independent Tank Brigade, the advance guard of Major-General Trufanov's 51st Army which was driving up from the south-east. The trap had finally sprung. The German 6th Army, nearly a quarter of a million men, was surrounded.

The end of the battle of Stalingrad seemed in sight. But there were to be many more days of bloody fighting before the Germans surrendered, and the Russians could move on westwards at the beginning of the long advance that would take them into the heart of Germany. For the moment, there were urgent questions for the Red Army Intelligence network in Switzerland.

It was true that the Russians had encircled a large German army. But exactly how large was it? The question was critical. If there were too many Germans in the trap, or if the enemy had many more reserves to throw into the forthcoming battle, then it could be the Russians and not the Germans who had a tiger by the tail. It was imperative that the Soviet high command should know the true facts of the situation. The questions began to flow again. Lucy reported that there were three times more Germans inside the trap than Moscow had thought. On Christmas Day 1942 the Director at Centre in Moscow sent the following message to Geneva in Radó's cipher:

> Werther is to state clearly how many replacement divisions in all are being formed from recruits by 1st January. Reply urgent.

The message was intercepted by German radio detectors and given to the Kommando, who had just succeeded in breaking Radó's cipher with the help of the information given to them by Kent. Eagerly, they deciphered the message and read it. It was the first time the Germans had heard the code name 'Werther'. They were to hear it many more times during the next two years.

Who was Werther? It was a question that was to haunt German Counter-Intelligence agencies during the war, and even after more than thirty years is still capable of inflaming passions. A number of writers have made much of the Werther mystery. It has encouraged the kind of lunatic logic that haunts the Shakespeare-Bacon controversy. Was Werther a code name that disguised the identities of a group of ten or twelve senior Werhmacht officers who were anti-fascist or pro-communist, and who worked at Hitler's headquarters? Or was it the code name for one man? Since it has been the cause of so much dangerous speculation, let us pause for a moment to dispel the various delusions.

After the war there were many Germans for whom the invincibility of the Wehrmacht was an article of faith. How could the greatest military machine in history, they asked, have been defeated by *Untermenschen*, the sub-humans of Hitlerian mythology, the Slavs and Mongols? There could only be one explanation – treason. The Wehrmacht must have been betrayed from within. A number of right-wing newspapers and magazines began a witch hunt that was intended to smoke out the traitor or traitors. But though the campaign caused considerable anguish and blighted several blameless careers, no one ever discovered the identity or identities of the mysterious Werther.

The failure to identify Rössler's conspirators is hardly surprising, for in truth there never was a Werther or a group of Werthers. The name was not a personal code name at all, but simply a file heading applied by Radó to denote the subject of information supplied by Rössler. When Rössler passed his messages via Sissy or Schneider, he put the department it referred to at the top of each, thus: 'From the OKW' (*Oberkommando der Wehrmacht*, the army high command), 'From the OKL' (*Oberkommando der Luftwaffe*, the air force high command), 'From the *Auswärtiges Amt*' (the Foreign Office), and so on. When Radó enciphered the messages, he put a new heading on each one to guide the Director while further disguising the source. Material referring to the Wehrmacht was given the heading 'From Werther'; that from the Luftwaffe, 'From Olga'; and that from the Foreign Office, 'From Anna'. Like most of the code names devised by Radó, they were very simple. Other names which signified subjects rather than people were Teddy, Ferdinand, Stefan and Fanny.

Although these names were applied principally to material supplied by Rössler, Rössler himself had no knowledge of them, any more than he knew at the time that he was called Lucy. Only Radó, the members of the network who helped encipher his messages, and the Director in Moscow, knew what the names signified. When Radó chose them to confuse the enemy, he could hardly have imagined how successful he would be!

Of course, there were a number of Germans in all branches of the forces who were anti-Hitler and who gave information to the Allies. The famous Viking Line is one example, which did indeed feed the Swiss NS1 among others, but which had no connection with Lucy. There has even been speculation that Admiral Canaris himself, chief of the German Abwehr, passed information to the British. Nevertheless common sense alone denies the possibility of any single spy or group of spies, however highly placed in the OKW, where at most only thirty people, probably less, could have had access to the sort of information regularly received by Rössler. No spy or spies could have worked there undetected through all the most difficult days of the war, surviving all purges and postings, and finding time to encipher and transmit vast quantities of information. Such a premise simply does not hold water.

Thirty years and more after the war ended, with revelations and investigations following each other constantly, there remains only one possible source for the most important material Rössler gave to Radó – the Ultra secret organisation based in Hut 3 at the Government Code and Cypher School, Bletchley Park, Buckinghamshire, England.

After the triumph of Stalingrad the Russians believed that they were now invincible. The accusations levelled at Lucy after the disaster of the last battle of Kharkov had been wiped out by the string of Intelligence successes scored during the long battle for the city on the Volga. The Swiss network's stock was again riding high. The Soviet high command felt they could rely on it to provide infallible information to help plan their next move, a grand offensive to retake Kharkov.

Kharkov is built on a plateau in the midst of the black earth region of the Ukraine, whose capital it was until 1934. It is close to the river Donetz, at the centre of what Hitler called 'the Russian Ruhr', the industrial heartland of the Soviet Union, rich in coal and iron, crammed with vital heavy industry. It is also one of the major rail junctions in the USSR. By any standard it was a prize worth winning and holding. Already there had been two major battles fought for it, both of which had been won by the Germans.

The Russians initially had two plans for retaking Kharkov. Stalin examined them, and saw the possibility of combining them into a gigantic move to achieve a double encirclement of German forces. The Soviet 6th Army would make for the Dnieper and cut off all Axis forces caught in the triangle formed by the Donetz, the Dnieper and the Sea of Azov. Meanwhile, Lieutenant-General Popov's armoured group would drive towards the sea, splitting German Army Group South in two.

The overall plan had much to commend it. It was bold and it was imaginative – but it was risky. As the Germans' front contracted, thus becoming easier to service, the supply lines of the Red Army were again being stretched to breaking point. This problem might have been overcome if the Russians had been able to maintain tactical air superiority, but the very speed of the Russian advance was to take them to the limits of the operational capability of their own air force.

Given these dangers, good and reliable Intelligence became even more important. But in this area fate again intervened against the Russians. The third battle of Kharkov was one of the rare occasions when Hitler surrendered overall strategic control of a major battle to one of his generals, in this case Field Marshal von Manstein. We do not share the view of so many German military historians who would blame every Wehrmacht defeat on Hitler, and claim that Germany would have won the war if he had only left things to his generals. Much of the time, the Führer's famous intuition was remarkable, particularly in the politico-military field. In this case, however, his handing over control had extremely beneficial results for the German army.

One of the side-effects was a drastic reduction in wireless traffic between von Manstein and Hitler at the Wolf's Lair, since it was not necessary to clear every detail with the Führer. The reduced flow of messages dried up altogether on 17th February, when Hitler arrived in person at Zaporozhe, von Manstein's command post.

With less material to intercept, Bletchley had little to offer the Swiss network in up-to-date, accurate Intelligence. The Stavka (the Russian General Staff) was consequently forced to fight the third battle of Kharkov half blinded, without its usually reliable prime source of Intelligence. Nevertheless, the operation began well.

Since the end of January, the Russians had been hammering away at the German line between Belgorod and Voroshilovgrad, to the east of Kharkov, which was held by a mixed collection of Romanian, Hungarian and Italian troops, stiffened by Germans. In February the line collapsed, leaving a 200-mile gap through which the Soviet armies poured towards Kharkov, seemingly unstoppable.

Kharkov was defended by General of the Waffen SS Paul Hausser and the SS Panzer Corps, a completely fresh outfit newly arrived from France, which included two crack divisions, *Das Reich* and *Leibstandarte Adolf Hitler*. As the Russian T34 tanks reached the outskirts of the city and the Russian armies threatened to encircle it, Hitler ordered that it should be defended to the last man. Hausser, however, had no intention of sacrificing his crack troops simply for the sake of obeying an order from the Führer. First, he appealed to his superior, General Lanz, whose reply, signal number 24, sent at 17.25 hours on 14th February, could not have been more to the point: 'Panzer Corps will hold to the last man its present position on the east front of Kharkov in accordance with the Führer's orders.'

Hausser waited until 13.00 hours on the following day, then ordered the withdrawal. Two and a half hours later he received the final, unequivocal order: 'Kharkov will be defended under all circumstances.'

Hausser ignored the order, and saved two Panzer divisions and the *Grossdeutschland* Panzer Grenadier Division, to fight another day.

With such confusion in the German camp, it is hardly surprising that the Intelligence reports received by Centre were equally confused and misleading. Since there was little Ultra material available to the Swiss network, it had to rely on other sources, which were not as sound. Rössler had only the material he was evaluating for the Bureau Ha to draw on, and it was this which he passed to Radó via Schneider and Sissy. Among the Hausamann papers today we find secret reports which appear to be Hausamann's assessments of Rössler's evaluations of information received from other Bureau Ha sources. The first declares that from 11th February the German troops in the Donetz area were in retreat. In report number 284 of 16th February we read: 'All German counter-attacks have failed . . . The Germans are being overtaken by a new disaster. Losses to be expected on the German side will greatly exceed their losses at Stalingrad.' Report number 291 of 17th February states: 'The object of German resistance . . . is now confined to covering the German withdrawal from the Donetz bend.'

With Intelligence reports based on such information, Stalin was convinced that the Germans were in retreat everywhere. He immediately ordered further offensives. It seemed that the great encirclement plan was succeeding. The Soviet 6th Army was now driving hard for the Dnieper and Popov's armoured group was only a hundred miles from the Sea of Azov.

Suddenly, on 19th February, von Manstein counter-attacked. Popov's brigades found themselves running short of supplies and meeting heavy opposition in the shape of the 11th and 7th Panzer Divisions and the SS *Viking* Panzer Grenadier Division. One of the crack divisions which General Hausser had saved from Kharkov was attacking the Soviet 6th Army on its flank. The Red Army had over-extended its supply lines and was virtually without tactical air support.

In spite of the actual situation on the ground, however, Lucy's reports were still sounding notes of optimism. Report number 307, dated 21st February, read: 'The consequence of the fall of Kharkov and the collapse of the improvised German Donetz front are assessed as disasters at German high command. More than forty German divisions are in danger of being cut off.' Stalin believed Lucy, as did

149

most of the Soviet high command. When Popov begged General Vatutin to permit the withdrawal of his shattered armoured group, Vatutin refused.

'Attack the enemy,' he ordered. 'The enemy is retreating across the Dnieper!'

Even as late as 23rd February, Vatutin, under constant pressure from Stalin, sent Popov the following signal: 'I wish to remind you emphatically that you are to use all means available to you to annihilate the enemy. I am holding you personally responsible.' It was not until late the following day that Vatutin was forced to face the unpalatable truth – the Russians were facing a major disaster.

On 8th March, Hausser's SS Panzer Corps reached the outskirts of Kharkov. It took them a further six days of hard fighting to complete the encirclement, but by 15th March Kharkov was besieged. Only then did the Russians realise the full extent of the disaster. In just over four weeks they had lost no less than fifty-two divisions.

The refusal of the Soviet high command to take account of the reports coming from the front line is hard to understand. True, Stalin was a fearsome war lord and reporting failure to him can never have been a comfortable business. But he was kept continually informed of every development and personally updated his war maps. The only explanation is that he chose to believe the reports from Centre rather than from the front.

Centre was the highest Soviet clearing-house for Intelligence. It reported directly to Stalin himself. In the past, Centre's information, particularly from its Swiss network, had been almost impeccable. Its only previous lapse had been more than outweighed by its subsequent record. Therefore, if Lucy in Switzerland reported that the German forces were fleeing, then fleeing they must be. What neither Centre nor any of the Swiss network had any means of knowing was when the information from Lucy was *not* based on Ultra Intelligence. Without access to the Enigma radio intercepts from Ultra, the Swiss network was reduced to routine Intelligence from agents in Germany, Switzerland, Italy and France. On the occasion of the third battle of Kharkov, that was simply not good enough.

Stalin blamed Centre for the disaster, and Centre in turn held the Swiss network to blame. The irony, of course, is that the network was suffering because of its previous successes. The only way it could redress the balance was by achieving an even greater success.

CHAPTER ELEVEN

The Turning Point

The opportunity to achieve the success the network so badly needed was not long in showing itself. Immediately after their victory at Kharkov, the Germans began preparing for their next great assault, which was to be against the Russian-held line to the north, around the city of Kursk.

The battle of the Kursk Salient in 1943 is now regarded by most historians to be the most important battle of the second world war. It was also the greatest tank battle in history, with some 6,300 tanks and over two million men engaged in an area no more than fifty miles in length and fifteen miles in depth. It was the nearest thing to a Verdun in the second world war, an extraordinary, complex battle of attrition, a battle from which the German Panzer forces were never to recover. Never again would they be able to gather together such a mass of *matériel*, never again would they be able to regain the initiative. Before the Battle of Kursk, German victory was still possible; afterwards, defeat was inevitable.

Kursk lies between Orel and Kharkov on the north-south line. After von Manstein's victory, Kharkov was again in German hands, as was Orel. But between them, the Russians still held Kursk and a front which bulged out like a giant hernia – the Kursk Salient. Hitler and the German high command planned to cut off the bulge and straighten their line, thus trapping hundreds of thousands of the enemy. Von Manstein was to strike north from Kharkov at the same time as Kluge drove southwards from Orel. It was in every respect a classic textbook manoeuvre straight out of Clauswitz. It was, however, a massive operation calling for considerable preparation. And there were problems, too – not least caused by the beginning of the thaw, which turned frozen Russian earth into a sea of liquid mud. There were also arguments among the German generals on various aspects of the operation.

Long preparation periods were ideal for Ultra – and for the Swiss network – particularly where there were disagreements between the various commands. The longer the preparations and the more intense the arguments, the larger the number of signals to be intercepted, deciphered, and used. The network followed the development carefully, until on 8th April Radó was able to send this message to the Director in Moscow:

> The differences between the German high command and the army command have been settled by the decision to postpone to the beginning of May . . . the attack against Kursk.

On 11th April a plan for a short, sharp, convergent attack was submitted to Hitler. But the Führer dithered, wanting to wait until there were more of the new Tiger tanks available, or even for the very latest in German armoured design, the Panther tank, which would soon be ready for its first action.

Moscow knew about the new tanks, and as early as 28th March had asked Radó for further information about both the Tigers and the Panthers demanding 'tactical and technical data: thickness of armour, armament, speed'. The network had been able to supply the details, with the result that Russian tank crews were given instructions on dealing with them. The instructions could not have given them much encouragement, however, for the Tigers completely outgunned the Russian T34s and their frontal armour was proof against the Russians' 76.2mm shell. The principal advice given was to get in close as fast as possible, since Tigers were said to be more vulnerable from the flanks. How the Russian tanks were to get close was left to individual commanders.

The planned German offensive had now been named 'Operation Citadel', and was already assuming a kind of lunatic momentum of its own within Hitler's headquarters. On 15th April, in his Operation Order number 6, marked 'Most secret, 13 copies only', Hitler declared Citadel to be an operation of the greatest importance. 'The attack,' he wrote, 'must succeed, and it must do so rapidly and convincingly. It must secure for us the initiative for this spring and summer . . . The victory of Kursk must be a blazing torch to the world.'

'It is vital to ensure the element of surprise. To the very last moment the enemy must remain uncertain about the timing of the offensive,' Hitler declared. A deception was planned, to take the form of a supposed drive towards the Caucasian oilfields, code-named 'Operation Panther'. Hitler continued, 'Preparations for Operation Panther are to go ahead in the zone of Army Group South. They are to be emphasised in every possible way (conspicuous reconnaissance, appearance of tanks, deployment of bridging equipment, radio, agents, creation of rumours, employment of Luftwaffe, etc.).'

In spite of all the Germans' efforts at secrecy and deception, the network kept Moscow informed of every move. As Hitler was celebrating his fifty-fourth birthday on 20th April, Radó was able to report to the Director that Citadel had been temporarily postponed. Nine days later, he informed Moscow that the new date for the German attack had been fixed as 12th June. Moscow knew well that Hitler could change his mind again, and on 7th May the Director demanded to know the current German plans and intentions. He instructed Radó to report urgently. Two days later he received from the network a lengthy signal of more than 120 cipher groups, giving a detailed assessment of the high command's intentions. Preparations were advancing rapidly. There were delays in the delivery of the new tanks, but Albert Speer, in charge of armament production, promised Hitler that 324 Panthers would be available by 31st May. The stage was set.

While preparations were continuing at full speed for Operation Citadel, the Kommando were aware that the Russians were still getting details of German plans, and redoubled their efforts to break the network. The importance of destroying this source of information was becoming more vital for the Germans every day.

With the help of Kent, they continued decrypting those messages which they had managed to pick up in Radó's cipher, but they were still unable to make any impression on the ciphers used by Foote or Sissy, and therefore could not be sure how much the enemy actually knew. In view of the importance of Citadel, the Kommando decided on extreme measures: if they could not crack the ciphers, they must take out the agents themselves.

In spite of the efforts of Lorenz and Laura, they did not know who Foote was at that time, or where to find him, except that he transmitted from somewhere in Lausanne. Kent, however, knew that he was responsible for finding money for the network and figured that this might be a means of getting to him. Centre believed Kent was still working for them, and when he informed them that the French ring he was supposed to be running was desperately short of funds, they responded as expected by telling him to send a courier into Switzerland to collect money from Foote.

The Director informed Foote of the plan, and gave him four different days and two places of rendezvous for meeting Kent's courier, allowing time for overcoming any problems in crossing the frontier. On the fourth day and at the final meeting place, inside the main entrance to the Botanical Gardens at Geneva – coincidentally only a few yards from Radó's front door – a man eventually contacted him. They exchanged passwords and Foote handed over a parcel of money. The courier in return gave him a large book wrapped in bright orange paper and told him he would find three messages hidden between two of the uncut pages. These were urgent and must be enciphered and transmitted to Moscow that night.

Foote had been told nothing of this by Centre, and was immediately suspicious. His suspicions increased when the courier suggested a further meeting after the messages had been transmitted, when he would give Foote some more valuable information. As a rendezvous the courier proposed a place close to the German-controlled French frontier near Geneva. Foote replied that he could not attend any meeting for at least a week, and left. Guessing that the bright orange paper was intended to serve as a beacon for anyone following, since there would have been no problem in buying less conspicuous wrapping paper, he tucked the book inside his coat and took evasive action, not going home to his flat until he was certain he had lost any possible followers.

Although Centre had not listened to his fears about Lorenz and Laura – and indeed had reprimanded him for suspecting them – this time they, too, were uneasy when Foote reported the matter, and the Director forbade him to meet the courier again. He told him to send the messages found in the book, but to disguise them in such a manner that they could not be recognised and used to help break his cipher. Two weeks later, the Director told Foote that the courier had indeed been a German plant, and that he himself had narrowly escaped being kidnapped by the Kommando. He was ordered to work with particular caution and to reduce his contacts with other members of the network to the absolute minimum, since he had been seen by an enemy agent who would be able to identify him.

Foote was only too happy to comply with this order, and used it as an opportunity to break contact completely with Lorenz and Laura. He learned in Moscow after the war that captured German documents had revealed that his suspicions were well founded. The German plan was that if the first kidnap attempt failed he was to be taken during his next visit to their villa. It is perhaps just as well for them that the occasion never arose. Considering Foote's record in Spain, they would have found it more than a little dangerous to try to overpower him.

With the failure of their plan to capture Foote, the Germans began to increase their pressures on the network in other ways. In March, Schellenberg made two visits to Switzerland to talk to Col. Roger Masson. The first of these, on 3rd March, was in the Hotel Bären, at Biglen, near Berne, when General Guisan himself was present. The conversation centred mainly on Switzerland's attitude towards any potential aggressor, and whether the Swiss would fight. Hitler needed to know this, since he was again considering the occupation of Switzerland in order to have the Alps as a defensive barrier against the Allied thrust through Italy, for there were already clear signs that the Italians might pull out of the war.

The second meeting remained secret until after the war, when Schellenberg talked about it to the British Security Service investigators who questioned him at their centre at Ham, near Richmond, Surrey. It took place on 12th March at the Hotel Baur au Lac, Zurich – ironically the very hotel which Alexander Korda and Claude Dansey had always used when they visited Switzerland before the war in the days of the Z Organisation. This time the meeting was private between the two Intelligence chiefs alone. And this time the principal item on the agenda was the Russian network. Schellenberg received no direct satisfaction from Masson, who declined to take any action against the network, on the grounds that it was not operating against Switzerland or Swiss interests. But the young SS General never played simple games.

155

During the same visit to Zurich Schellenberg also made contact with British Intelligence, passing messages to Churchill to test Britain's reaction to possible peace moves. While talking to Masson he kept returning to another theme, his concern for Hitler's safety. Next day, while Schellenberg was still safely in Switzerland, a bomb was placed in the aircraft taking Hitler back to his headquarters from a visit to the eastern front. Unfortunately, it failed to go off, and the Führer escaped once again. Schellenberg, in the clear, hurried back to Germany.

A few days later, on 18th March, Swiss Intelligence received news through Lucy that Hitler had ordered active preparations to be put in hand for the military occupation of Switzerland. Masson used his liaison with the SS General to ask indignantly if the report was accurate. Triumphant, Schellenberg sent back a message saying that there had been an invasion plan, but that he had been able to persuade the high command that it was not necessary; he knew the Swiss would not allow the Allies to cross their country. He had achieved his purpose – the original report had been a plant, issued under a careful control to a selected number of men in high positions, but in a manner which made it seem normal and genuine. The fact that it had reached Lucerne so swiftly indicated to Schellenberg that there were traitors in the high command. It seemed to him that Werther must exist. Immediately, there followed a savage, ruthless purge of all the officers who could have been involved. Security was further tightened. Schellenberg must have felt very pleased with himself, convinced that he had eliminated the network's most valuable source.

In Switzerland there was fury at Masson's action. Hausamann in particular accused him of wantonly, foolishly, destroying the finest source of Intelligence ever known. But to everyone's astonishment, the information continued to flow – indeed, the best was still to come. Had Masson really been so utterly foolish, so completely trusting in his dealings with Schellenberg as everyone supposed? Or did he in fact outsmart Schellenberg by leading him to believe a lie? How much did Masson actually know or suspect about the real source of the wonderful Intelligence flow through Lucy? Two things are certain: Masson was a patriot, in spite of the vilification poured on him by some sections of the Swiss press, and he was no fool. The rest must remain his secret, taken with him to the grave in 1967.

Having failed to locate the source, the Kommando redoubled its efforts to trap the agents of the network. In April they found and arrested more Soviet agents in France, including one, code named 'Maurice', who was a liaison man for Sissy. He had visited her in her flat in Geneva, and knew a great deal about her ring.

On 23rd April, the radio section of the Kommando scored another success, picking up a message for Sissy which actually gave details of a new code for her use. On 25th April, the Germans deciphered the message, with great excitement. It read:

23.4.1943 To Sissy
We are giving you the title of your new code book. Buy it, and we will give you the instructions for its use. Albert must know nothing of this new book. Title: *Storm Over the House*, Editions H. Jebers. Page 471. Director.

A few days later, the Swiss press announced the appearance of German vehicle-mounted radio goniometry (direction-finding) units on the French shore of Lake Leman. Officially, they were searching for secret radio sets operated by the French Resistance in the mountains. In fact, they were directed against the three transmitters in Geneva and Lausanne, which they had given the name 'Red Three'.

It could not have taken them long to locate the Hamels' set, for the villa on the Route de Florissant stood alone in its own grounds less than a kilometre from the frontier. Rosie's and Foote's sets were more difficult to locate precisely, because they were both working from flats in the centre of towns.

The radio set is both the spy's most useful tool and his Achilles heel, for radio transmissions can be picked up and traced by the enemy without the agent or his director realising. Today, high-speed morse – the microdot of the radio world – and other devices developed since the war make transmissions so short that detection is very much more difficult. Even in 1943, Schellenberg's technical experts in Germany had already invented a high-speed automatic transmitter using magnetic tape, which could transmit two typed pages of material in three-fifths of a second. The equipment was only the size of a cigar box, and could be easily disguised. But for the Soviet operators in Switzerland, there was no such wonder equipment. They had to rely on more basic methods of security, using good ciphers and changing

157

call signs and wavelengths at frequent intervals. Rosie's transmission schedule, for instance, was as follows:

DAY	CALL SIGN	START TIME
Monday	DVS	00.40
Tuesday	FSY	12.00
Wednesday	INK	00.20
Thursday	FBT	00.40
Friday	DPW	00.20
Saturday	IKW	12.00
Sunday	FWI	00.20

Her wavelengths changed according to the following table:

TIME	12.00	00.30	01.00	01.30	02.00
WAVELENGTH	37m	37.5	39	40	42

TIME	02.30	03.00	03.30	04.00	04.30
WAVELENGTH	43	45	46	47.5	49

TIME	05.00	05.30
WAVELENGTH	50	51

Such precautions were partially successful, for the German detectors both in Cranz and in France had only managed to intercept some ten per cent of all the messages transmitted by the network. Since over half of these had been sent by Foote, in his own unbroken cipher, it followed that at most only five per cent of the grand total could have been deciphered. However, in the espionage business, even five per cent is too much for an enemy to know.

Fortunately, most messages from Lucy, as well as many of those concerned with the recruitment, training and use of new agents, had been sent by Foote – a fact which had strengthened the British grip on the network at the same time as keeping it secure from the Germans.

Radó could not be sure how much the Germans knew, or how close they were to unmasking him. But he was worried by the various danger signs and communicated his fears to Centre. The Director ordered him to keep working, and to find and train new operators. He was also told to move the Hamels to a new base, but this was impossible. When he suggested that enough time had passed for it to be safe to install a reserve transmitter in the Hamels' old apartment above the shop in the Rue de Carouge, however, he received a very sharp reminder of the rules of clandestinity.

The next blow fell much nearer home, in Geneva itself. In May, one of Sissy's own sources of information, a secretary with the German purchasing mission in Geneva who worked for the network under the code name 'Bill', was discovered by the Germans. Fortunately, she did not know Sissy's real identity, but the situation was dangerous. She had been discovered through messages picked up and deciphered by the Germans.

The Kommando was getting close. Their agent Yves Rameau reappeared, trying to infiltrate the network, as also did two other 'Russian' agents, Belov and Nemanov. Belov managed to unmask another of Sissy's ring, an agent known as Marius who worked as a liaison man between Sissy and one of her Vichy French sources. Belov succeeded in gaining the man's confidence to the extent that he was able to pass himself off to him as the chief of the network and to give him orders which he happily carried out. Fortunately the network's system of cut-outs functioned, like watertight compartments in a ship, so that it could continue working.

One message which the Kommando intercepted, at about the same time as that concerning the new code book, must have caused them even greater excitement, and perhaps some bewilderment. In it, Centre asked for precise details of Lucy's sources in Berlin, which of course, they still did not know. The Kommando must have been bitterly disappointed when there was no reply, nor even any indication of Lucy's own identity.

The Germans were not the only ones disappointed, for Centre instructed Sissy to stand down and stop working for a period, as a safety precaution after the capture of Maurice, Marius and Bill. Centre tried to persuade her to allow someone else to liaise with Lucy, but were again told that this was out of the question. She refused point blank. At the time, such insistence sounded like temperamental obstinacy, the actions of a prima donna. Sissy told Radó and the Director that the conditions were laid down by Lucy himself, an assertion which they had no means of checking. It is far more likely that it was British Intelligence who made the rules.

So Sissy stayed at her post and continued working, and the network was able to go on passing to Moscow some of the most important messages of the whole war, as the Russian and German armies prepared for the great battle of Kursk.

At the height of the build-up, on 26th June 1943, Sissy received a strange telephone call from a man whose voice she did not know. He asked to speak to M. Dübendorfer. When Sissy said he was not there but that she was his wife, the man apologised for disturbing her and hung up. Sissy was puzzled and perturbed. Her marriage to Dübendorfer had been purely one of convenience and she had had no contact with him for a long time. Why should anyone expect to find him in her apartment?

Two days later, the same man phoned again and asked Sissy to tell M. Dübendorfer that someone wanted to meet him and would like to arrange a rendezvous in Lausanne or Zurich. The caller declined to give his name, but said that he was speaking on behalf of a man who lived in Lausanne and that the matter concerned people who had recently arrived in Switzerland from France. The man he was speaking for was an Englishman, a Mr Allan Foote, whom she might know as Jim.

Sissy had never met Foote, though she knew of his existence. She did, however, know that he was an important agent within the network, and was worried that some stranger should be using his name. She asked the man to go to her apartment to discuss whatever it was he had to tell them, but he refused, saying that it was not possible because he had to leave Switzerland. Someone else would call her husband that night from Lausanne.

For some reason, Sissy asked her cousin, Water Fluckiger, who worked for her ring under the code name 'Brand', to be at her apartment that evening and to answer the phone pretending to be Dübendorfer. Presumably Paul Böttcher was there, too, but perhaps his voice was too distinctive, particularly when speaking French. In any case, Fluckiger took the call. The man suggested a rendezvous. But Fluckiger refused and demanded to know what he wanted. Secret rendezvous provide perfect opportunities for kidnapping, and by now everyone in the network was on the alert.

At this, the caller quoted the names of several agents who worked through the French consulate. Fluckiger, who used that connection himself, told the man he did not know what he was talking about and did not wish to listen to such senseless talk. In reply, the man said that in that case the Dübendorfers would be receiving a phone call from someone whom they would certainly know – Mr Allan Foote.

This was the second time Foote's name had been mentioned. Until the first time Sissy had only known Foote by his code name, Jim, and she was now very worried. She looked up his telephone number in the Lausanne directory – like her, he had his name listed – and Fluckiger called him and started to talk about men who had recently arrived from France. Foote told him he didn't know what he was talking about. Fluckiger apologised, then rang off, after giving Foote Sissy's telephone number and asking him to call if he heard anything. But he did not tell him who she was.

It did not take such an experienced agent as Foote long to find out that the telephone number belonged to someone called Dübendorfer. He immediately informed Centre and Radó that he suspected she was a German agent trying to infiltrate the network. Of course, Radó was able to put his mind at rest about Sissy. Nevertheless the affair was mysterious. Later they found out that on the day of the first call two people, an aristocratic-looking Frenchman and an elegant woman (possibly Lorenz and Laura?) had questioned the porter, the milkman and the cleaner at Sissy's apartment block, asking for Dübendorfer's address in Zurich and telling them to say nothing to Sissy.

The Director at Centre was very disturbed by this news, coming as it did on top of the various other danger signals. He again ordered Sissy to hand over the liaison with Lucy to someone else. Surely, he reasoned, Lucy would agree to dealing with another contact now, when he knew of the dangers. But Sissy was adamant, Lucy would not work with anyone except herself, whatever the risks involved.

The Director also tried to persuade Foote to stop working for a while, and to leave Lausanne. After the affair with the orange parcel and the kidnapping plot, the Director had ordered Foote to change his apartment and move to another town, but Foote had informed him that such a thing was impossible for a foreigner in wartime Switzerland. Now he was being told to take a holiday and to allow his sources, too, to work directly to someone else in the network. Like Sissy, and for exactly the same reasons Foote could do no such thing. In any case, he had too much in hand to leave his post at that moment.

161

Not only was he the only one who could get money for the running of the network – and there were many delicate and complicated negotiations and deals in progress – but he was needed to help cope with the biggest and most important battle of the entire war, which was just about to begin. He told Radó and the Director therefore that he was having a little difficulty over his *permis de séjour*, which needed renewing, and that he could not leave Lausanne until this had been done.

During this time, the Russians continued to prepare their defences in the Kursk Salient. They poured in men and equipment – nearly forty per cent of their total field armies and nearly all their available armour. They prepared for defence in depth. They laid mines at a density hitherto unheard of – 2,200 anti-tank and 2,500 anti-personnel per mile of front. By the beginning of July they had over 20,000 pieces of artillery in place, including over 6,000 76mm anti-tank guns, plus 920 Katyusha multiple rocket-throwers.

A message from Radó, dated 31st May, informed Moscow that the build-up had not gone unnoticed:

From Werther. 7th May.
The Germans have noted large concentration of Soviet troops at Kursk, Viazma, Velikiye-Louki. The high command think that the Russians could be planning a preventive assault on several sections of the front at once – similar to the tactic employed by Timoshenko last May when he tried to hold up the German advance on Kharkov. Dora.

Both the Russian and the German high commands were becoming increasingly nervous. When could the offensive begin? June seemed to be the favourite date.

From Werther. 23rd May.
On 20th May all preparations of von Manstein's and Kluge's army groups were completed; all motorised and armoured units stationed on the second line are in a state of alert, ready to leave for the front. These troops will be at their starting point on 1st June. Dora.

Was that the date for the start of Operation Citadel? Moscow

162

demanded further clarification. On 30th May, Moscow sent a signal to Radó in Geneva:

Order Lucy and Werther to establish:
1. At precisely what point of the southern section of the eastern front is the German offensive to open?
2. With what forces and in which direction is the thrust to be made?
3. Apart from the southern sector, where and when is a German offensive planned on the eastern front?

Moscow was kept informed of every change in German plans, every new development. Of course, they had other networks in other countries, which sent in information. They employed the normal Intelligence-gathering techniques of any army; they questioned prisoners; they made use of aerial reconnaissance, and every partisan behind enemy lines was a potential Soviet spy. But their use of such methods was never very effective, and it is doubtful if they ever obtained from any source, except the Swiss network, information of such importance and in such detail.

On 23rd June, Dora was able to tell Moscow that the German high command was beginning to consider an offensive against Kursk a very risky proposition:

Since 1st June, the Soviets have concentrated . . . such a quantity of troops that the Germans no longer talk of superiority. Hitler on the other hand wishes to attack.

By now, ironically, there was too much at stake for Hitler to withdraw. The very fact that the Russians had put so much of their strength into the Kursk Salient made it an irresistible objective. At one throw of the dice, with one extraordinary stroke, Hitler saw the chance to smash the Soviet forces, thus reversing the disaster of Stalingrad. If the Russians were defeated at Kursk, it was hardly likely that they would have the heart or the equipment to mount another offensive that year. He could then release troops to Italy, which the Allies were about to invade. His battle-hardened veterans would sweep aside any Allied invasion. It all depended on Kursk. Like Stalingrad, the place had begun to assume an almost mystical significance.

When should Hitler attack? If he waited another three weeks, he would have two extra battalions at his disposal. They would go to strengthen Model's divisions in the north. The 11th Panzer, the SS *Grossdeutschland* Division and the three divisions of Hausser's SS Panzer Corps were already equipped with Panthers. Hitler waited. On 1st July he called his generals to the Wolf's Lair, his headquarters in East Prussia. Operation Citadel, he informed them, was to open in four days' time. The orders were to go out immediately.

The following day, 2nd July, while at his headquarters near the village of Zorinskiye Dvory, the commander of 1st Tank Army, Lieutenant-General M. Y. Katukov, had an important visitor. It was Nikita Sergeyevich Khrushchev, who was then political commissar attached to the Stalingrad front. He was accompanied by General Vatutin. The two men brought vital secret information from the Soviet Supreme Command, which they were delivering personally to commanders in the field. It was nothing less than full details of the anticipated German attack, including the date. Moscow decided to hedge its bets, however: Krushchev told Katukov to be ready for an attack at any time between 3rd and 5th July.

On the German side fifty divisions, a total of 900,000 men, with a further twenty divisions in reserve, plus 2,700 tanks, many of them Tigers and Panthers, awaited the signal to move. About 10,000 pieces of artillery were in place, and the Luftwaffe had assembled some 1,860 planes, three-quarters of the total German air strength on the eastern front. Of these aircraft 1,200 were drawn up on sixteen airfields in the Kharkov area.

The Russians deployed in excess of one million men and 3,600 tanks, but at no time did they gain air superiority.

The German plan had not altered since von Manstein had first proposed the amputation of the salient. It was still a classic pincer movement – with Colonel-General Model's 9th Army and Colonel-General Hoth's 4th Army supplying the two prongs of the pincers.

Nothing happened on 3rd July. The Soviet armies waited. Before dawn on the 4th it began to rain, a thundery shower which made the atmosphere heavy and overcast. The earth and the troops steamed, like horses at the end of a race. The rain stopped before three, just as the first waves of Stukas struck the Soviet positions facing the SS *Grossdeutschland* Division.

General Rokossovsky, who was in command of the Soviet central front facing the German 9th Army, was able to anticipate the German attack. At 1.10 a.m. on the 5th he ordered his artillery to open fire. The Germans were caught at their assembly positions. Nevertheless, at 3.30 a.m. they attacked.

The battle of Kursk sometimes appears to be like a huge and complex mechanism which, once started, no one could stop. Events have their logic and their own momentum. In the end, no matter how clever the spies, no matter how accurate their information, it is only the soldier in the field who can change the logic, affect the momentum. Although the Swiss network kept in almost constant touch with Moscow, although every fresh piece of Intelligence was radioed to Centre, the fate of the battle was now out of their hands. They had done all they could, and they had done it magnificently. Now it was up to others to make the best use of their efforts.

On 13th July, after eight days of some of the most savage fighting of the war, Hitler called a conference. What was the position at Kursk? Kluge's report was gloomy. The 9th Army had not made the expected breakthrough. It had lost 20,000 men and was now having to withdraw mobile troops to stem the Russian advance to Orel, which threatened his rear. Von Manstein was for going on – his 4th Army had enjoyed considerable success. He believed that, in the south of the salient at any rate, victory was still possible.

Hitler allowed von Manstein to continue the offensive until the 17th but then was forced to transfer two Panzer divisions from his command in order to protect Orel. Von Manstein had no alternative but to withdraw. It was a costly withdrawal – costly in terms of weapons and *matériel* and men. By the beginning of August he was back in his original position of 4th July but now he was being harried by the Soviets.

The Battle of the Kursk Salient was over. The war in the east had been turned. Lucy and the Swiss network had more than justified themselves.

CHAPTER TWELVE

Under Doctor's Orders

With the turn of the tide in Russia, Lucy and the Swiss network had served their purpose as far as Britain was concerned. The Russians had smashed the German armies at Kursk and their eventual victory was assured. The massive strength of the Axis divisions on the eastern front could not now be used against the west. The threat against Britain had been averted.

Churchill no longer felt the need to risk the security of Ultra by continuing to feed information to Stalin via Switzerland. Indeed he could foresee with some alarm the distinct possibility of the Russians advancing too quickly into western Europe, with all that implied. It was time to break connections.

The battle of Kursk was the last time Ultra material was fed to Russia on any regular basis. A rather plaintive signal from Radó to Centre at that time clearly shows the changed situation:

> Concerning our last questions on the eastern front, Lucy communicates only that events are moving so fast that it is impossible to give precise indications of troops in different sectors of the front.

Such a response was a far cry from the days, such a short time before, when Lucy was able to provide so much detailed information that sending it became a major problem.

London was not even interested in using the network to pass lower-grade, non-Ultra material, for by this time General Menzies had his own personal representative in Moscow liaising officially with Russian Military Intelligence. He had sent one of his most trusted permanent staff, Cecil Barclay, a member of the banking family, to

Moscow in June. He was responsible for passing non-Ultra material to the Russians through the established Intelligence Liaison Centre, where all the Allied missions operated. This material was described by Group Captain Winterbotham as 'low-grade cipher stuff' – though to Winterbotham anything other than Ultra was low grade, and Lord Dacre (Professor Hugh Trevor-Roper), then an SIS official responsible for feeding most of it to Barclay, feels it was more important than such a phrase implies.

Barclay did not pass anything concerning Kursk, all of which came through Switzerland. He was under instruction to tell the Russians if they asked – which they did – that Britain had not been successful in breaking the Enigma code, with which the Russians themselves were still struggling unsuccessfully. Although Barclay was supposed to be operating a two way exchange of information, most of the material passed in one direction only – from Britain to Russia. The Russians did occasionally pass some material, notably some Luftwaffe code books which they had captured, and Barclay sent such information home using his own one-time pads.

One day Barclay was taken to a large house on the outskirts of Moscow, where he met the Director, Lieutenant (later Colonel) General F. F. Kuznetzov, whom he describes as 'a short square man, very unyielding, with a handgrip like iron'. Kuznetzov had an air of great authority, as befitted a man who had direct access to Stalin, and the building buzzed about him with women officers and uniformed soldiers scurrying to and fro. It is possible that this house was the headquarters of Centre itself. If so, Barclay was extremely privileged, for its location and even its nature remain a closely guarded mystery to this day.

Kuznetzov liked Barclay, and the Englishman soon developed a good personal relationship with him and with his staff. Commenting on this to Menzies during a leave trip to London, Barclay suggested that as the Russians were apparently prepared to accept Intelligence information from him, perhaps he could pass other, more important material to them – if the SIS had anything of that sort. Barclay was not supposed to know about Ultra, though he had in fact learned about Enigma by accident before the war, and so had to approach the subject circumspectly. To his surprise, Menzies pointedly ignored the suggestion, and Barclay returned to passing his 'low-grade cipher stuff' in Moscow. Back in London, coincidentally, Dansey was knighted, becoming Sir Claude Dansey, KCMG. A reward, perhaps, for a job well done.

The Russian victory at Kursk had had one immediate effect – a reduction in the flow of information to the network. But the agents soon became aware of other signs of deterioration. With Britain's protection withdrawn they became vulnerable to the dangers which had steadily been building up against them. The reality of those dangers was brought home first to Foote.

After Kursk, he was free to take his delayed holiday in the Ticino. But first, there was another matter to be cleared up. In June, he had received a disturbing letter from his German fiancée, Agnes Zimmermann. They had been keeping in touch through an old friend of Agnes's mother, who worked in the German legation in Berne. Agnes sent her letters in the diplomatic bag to her mother's friend, who would then pass them to Foote inside Switzerland. In this way, Agnes overcame the ban on letter-writing imposed on her because of her job in the military censorship department. This particular letter, however, was not about love. It was very much to do with business.

As a Soviet agent, Agnes was a contact for Russian spies dropped into Germany by parachute. One of these spies, a girl whose code name was 'Inge', had lost the special suitcase containing her clothes, equipment and radio set during the drop. She had also been separated from her partner, who was picked up by the Gestapo. She had, however, gone to her first contact, Anna Müller's brother, Hans, in Freiburg, and had told him what had happened. He had sent a message to Anna, which she had passed to Foote for transmission to Centre, so that a new kit could be provided. Inge had then travelled on as instructed to Munich, where she met Agnes, who was to find her a cover job.

In April, Foote had sent instructions for Inge to go back to Freiburg to collect a new radio set from Hans. The girl had set off, promising that she would soon return. When she had not reappeared by June, Agnes became worried and wrote to Foote. With Centre's permission, Foote telephoned Anna to ask if she knew what had happened. There was no reply. After several further attempts at telephoning, he decided to go to Basle himself, to find out what had happened to

Anna. She might have been taken ill – after all she was sixty-three years old and living alone, although she always seemed in perfect health.

In Basle there was no sign of Anna. Her apartment was silent, and although it was then July and very warm the windows were all tight shut. There was no danger signal showing, but nothing else either. Foote thought she might be in hospital – but had no means of knowing which one. He dared not start questioning the neighbours, and the old woman had no friends or relatives in the town. He recalled that earlier in the year Anna had gone to Freiburg to look after her brother when his wife had been taken seriously ill. Perhaps something similar had happened again. Perhaps Anna would return home in due course. All he could do was to go back to Lausanne, inform Centre, and wait for a while before trying again.

Now there was another worry. He had heard nothing more from Agnes. Had something happened to her, too? At the end of August he received a letter from her at last – but it did nothing to allay his fears. To begin with, it came through the post, and not by the usual route. It was typewritten, did not have Agnes's usual signature, and had his full name and address on the envelope, something which Agnes never did. He was extremely suspicious of the letter, which said that there was no news of Inge, who had said she was going to North Germany, where her parents lived. Although she had left money for Agnes to buy various toilet things for her, she had not returned.

Foote telephoned the friend of Agnes's mother in Berne, who told him that she had received a letter via the courier in the usual way at the end of July, from Frau Zimmermann, in which she said everything was all right. This reassured Foote for a while, but his peace of mind was rudely shattered by the next message from Centre:

14.8. 1943
No news of Inge. It is important to find out what Mikki [Agnes Zimmermann] knows of her. You must reassure Anna, but if you go to see her be very careful: we have been informed that her brother, Hans, has been arrested by the Gestapo. Director.

Anna had disappeared. She never returned to her apartment in Basle. Agnes, too, had vanished from her home. Shortly afterwards,

Foote received a telephone call from an elderly woman who told him that she was a doctor, and had been in Munich where she had met Agnes, who had asked her to post the typewritten letter to him. Speaking in a strange, incoherent manner, she said she had been caught in a bad air raid, which had shattered her nerves. Foote informed Centre, who told him to search for Anna and for the strange woman doctor, but to proceed with the greatest care, in case she was working for the Gestapo. He found neither of them.

The Gestapo had indeed arrested Agnes and had also lured Anna into Germany by sending her a bogus message in her brother's name saying that his wife had been taken seriously ill again and could she come at once. She was arrested, taken to the Gestapo prison in Berlin and interrogated, but in spite of her age and her apparent frailty she told her captors nothing about the network. Agnes, too, said nothing, even under torture.

Hans and his wife, with the other members of their ring, were sentenced to death and executed. Anna was saved by diplomatic pressure from the Swiss authorities, who were told of her plight by a prison doctor. But she spent the remainder of the war in irons in the condemned cell until she was liberated by Allied forces on 8th May 1945, too weak to walk. It needed several months of hospital treatment before she was well enough to go back to Basle. With a certain bitterness, Foote records that Centre paid her nothing by way of compensation, turning her loose without a penny, and not even giving her back pay for the time she had been imprisoned. Like the Christian church, Soviet communism believes in rewards in heaven, it seems, though its heaven is centred in Moscow.

For the others, Inge disappeared without trace, and certainly never left prison alive. There is no record of her execution, and it is probable that she died under torture. And Agnes? She went mad in the torture chamber and never regained her sanity. Foote never saw her again.

It was with a heavy heart that Foote took his holiday in the Ticino, Switzerland's Italian canton south of the Alps, at the beginning of September. While he was resting there, and receiving a fresh briefing from British Intelligence about his revised role now that the war in eastern Europe had turned in Russia's favour, the news came that the Allied armies had landed in southern Italy on 3rd September. King Victor Emmanuel had signed an armistice.

Italy had changed sides, and the Swiss suddenly became concerned about the safety of their southern frontier. The Germans were now in complete control in the north of Italy, and it seemed possible that they would try to do something to make sure the alpine passes stayed open to them as supply routes. The Swiss radio Intelligence service was ordered to listen out for any radio traffic which might warn of possible German moves. They set up a special unit which they called the Lake Group, formed from part of 7th Radio Company, under the command of Lieutenant Maurice Treyer.

Treyer, who normally worked as a radio control officer at Geneva airport, had actually heard some of the network's transmissions nearly a year before, having accidentally picked them up while playing with his receiver during an idle night.

At that time they meant nothing to him, and although he reported the matter, the police took no action. They had no means of knowing what the cipher signified, nor where the transmissions were coming from or going to. They could easily have been from the French Resistance across the nearby border, or from British SOE agents who were known to be working both alone and with the Maquis in that part of France.

Now, however, Treyer was deliberately listening for anything suspicious – albeit from the Germans and their agents – and was using goniometry direction-finding equipment. Within a few days his unit picked up Hamel's transmitter. That was during the night of 11–12th September. They christened the transmitter Station LA and recorded the messages, which were in a cipher consisting of six-figure groups of numerals. The next night, they picked up another station also transmitting from Geneva in the same cipher, and christened that LB. That, of course, was Rosie.

It was then that Treyer made a fateful decision. He had been listening for Germany military traffic, and these two stations were obviously not that. While Rosie's set was difficult to pinpoint exactly, it was a fairly simple matter to locate the Hamels in their isolated villa. This he did by arranging to have the power supply to each house in the road cut off in turn, until a sudden break in transmission confirmed in which one the set was operating. Judging by their radio procedures, he guessed that they were Russian – or at any rate a local communist group – talking to party headquarters in Moscow. This was illegal, of course, but even so of no particular concern to army Counter-Intel-

171

ligence. Internal politics were a matter for the police, and so Treyer passed the matter on to the Bupo instead of to the army SPAB under General Jaquillard. Inspector Charles Knecht, head of the Bupo in the Canton of Geneva, took charge of the police inquiries.

On 27th September Treyer picked up Foote's radio transmissions from Lausanne. A second police officer, Inspector Pasche of the Canton of Vaud was brought in, since this third transmitter, christened LC, was in his territory. Had the matter been referred to Military Intelligence, it is probable that Masson would have ordered no further action. But in Switzerland there is a rivalry between the police and Counter-Intelligence authorities – as in Britain between the Security Service (MI5) and Special Branch on one hand, and the SIS (MI6) on the other. Once the police had started the investigation, nothing would stop them seeing it through to its conclusion.

At about the same time, they received a complaint from the German consul in Geneva that he had clear evidence of a Russian spy ring operating in Switzerland. He insisted that the police enforce the law and stop it. The Kommando were losing hope of uncovering the network's sources, and were now prepared to settle for breaking it up. Hans Peters, working under the apt code name of 'Romeo', had made good use of his time with Rosie. He had been able to give Henseler a great deal of useful information on her activities, including the name of Radó's cipher book *Es Begann im September*, Rosie's transmission schedule, and no doubt the identities of Radó, Lène and Foote at the very least.

This was not the first complaint the Swiss police had received. Radó had been denounced three times in 1943, but each time they had declined to take action, saying there was no proof of his activities. In any case he was too well known as a respectable and distinguished geographer to be arrested. Foote, too, had been denounced to the Lausanne police by an anonymous letter in which was enclosed one of the photographs taken of him by Laura. But they had shrugged it off as simply being one of dozens of unfounded accusations which they received at that time. It seemed far more likely to them that Foote was a British agent, and therefore the concern of the military authorities who would undoubtedly wish to protect rather than prosecute him.

Lorenz and Laura had reappeared briefly while Foote had been away in the Ticino. Somehow they had managed to track him down to his eyrie in the Chemin de Longeraie, probably with the help of

172

information obtained by the Germans through Peters, since Rosie worked as courier between Radó and Foote in addition to her role as a radio operator. However, although they succeeded in finding the building, they failed to get past Foote's redoubtable first line of defence – Madame Müller, the *concierge*, and Hélène, his char.

The two agents approached both ladies with a rather ingenious story. Foote, they said, had promised to marry Laura's sister, but having got her pregnant was suddenly losing his enthusiasm for the match! They explained that that was why they wanted to know about Foote's friends. Was there any particular woman in his life who might have replaced Laura's pregnant sister in his affections? Or had he any male friends who might have been leading him astray? It was a story designed to arouse the sympathy of Mme Müller and Hélène. Unfortunately for Lorenz and Laura the two ladies would not hear anything against their favourite tenant.

'I told them,' declared Mme Müller, 'that a tenant's love life was his own business. They also wanted to know if I had seen a woman who limped.' (Was this Sissy, or someone else, perhaps? Hermine Rabinovitch, another agent in the ILO, was crippled and used crutches, but she had left for Canada some time before.) 'It's true, I saw her. But was that any of their business?'

In spite of this rebuff the two Abwehr agents hung around outside the building for a few days, but without success.

'They didn't even offer Hélène and me money,' added Mme Müller indignantly. For someone who feels she deserves at least the chance to say no, there is nothing more galling than not being offered a bribe.

With that, Lorenz and Laura fade from our story. It would be satisfying to report that they came to a bad end, but alas, they did not. There is remarkably little justice in the clandestine world of spies. George Wilmer (Lorenz) was tried and convicted shortly after the war for procuring and using false papers. He was given a three-month prison sentence, but was only expelled from Switzerland, with his wife eleven years later, in February 1956 – which suggests that one of the various masters for whom he had worked may well have been Swiss Intelligence.

When Foote returned from his 'holiday' and started work again, therefore, it was the Swiss police and not the Germans who were searching for him, and within a few weeks Lieutenant Treyer's detector vans were circling the building like hungry sharks. For the

173

moment, however, they were prepared to let him carry on while they concentrated on the easier meat to be had in Geneva. There, the targets were at least Swiss citizens, and so offered less complications.

It had taken Treyer about two weeks to pin down Rosie's set to the apartment building at Number 8 Rue Henri Mussard in Geneva. Next he had to locate the exact apartment. One morning at the beginning of October, Lène came back from delivering a sheaf of messages to Rosie and told Radó the young woman wanted to see him urgently. Radó met her in a café in the suburbs of Geneva next day. She told him she was sure her flat was being watched. Strange men loitered outside the block, vehicles drove slowly past at night and a man had called saying he was from the electricity company and had come to check that her installation was in good order – though she had made no request for a service call. She had no doubt that he was a security man.

Radó was alarmed. The more Rosie told him, the more obvious it became that the Bupo had indeed discovered her flat and were keeping it under surveillance. He told her to stop transmitting immediately, and to destroy all papers and documents. He would send Hamel round to collect the radio set, which had been disguised to look like a portable gramophone, and take it to his shop for storage. As a local radio mechanic Hamel would be able to do this without arousing suspicion, and in any case the watching police would not know what flat he was calling on in the large block. Rosie herself must leave Geneva as soon as possible. Radó told her to go by train to stay with her parents in Basle.

But Rosie had not told Radó everything. She had not told him about Hans Peters, her Romeo. When she informed Peters that she was leaving he persuaded her to stay in Geneva and move in with him, rather than go to Basle. His orders from Henseler were to keep her in Geneva at all costs, and like a good Nazi he always obeyed orders – especially orders which involved keeping an attractive young woman in his bed. So Rosie left her flat, hurriedly. So hurriedly, in fact, that she did not destroy the papers and cipher books kept there.

The Hamels had not noticed anyone watching them, either at the shop or at the villa, and although there was danger in the air Radó and the Director agreed that they must keep transmitting. Foote, too, would have to work at full stretch, for there were still vast quantities

of material to be enciphered and sent, although the character of many
of the messages was changing. They were becoming more political as
British Intelligence began using Lucy to try to influence Moscow
rather than simply to keep the Red Army informed of military Intelligence. Nevertheless, Foote's workload was considerably increased
particularly as he had to travel to Geneva to collect his messages now
that Rosie was unavailable as a messenger.

Since the summer the network had been planning to train and equip
new operators, to help spread the load and to form a reserve in case of
arrests. With the help of Pierre Nicole and Otto Pünter, two young
people, a girl and a young man, had been selected and it had been
intended that Foote should train them. But life had been far too hectic
of late – with both the frantic efforts to keep pace with the flow of
messages during the great battles and the various domestic alarums
and excursions. The training therefore had been postponed. Now, it
was too late.

On the night of 13th October, Edmond Hamel went to bed in the villa
at 192 Route de Florissant while his wife took the first shift at the
transmitter in the attic. As he slept and she tapped furiously on the
morse key, policemen crept silently into position outside. Led by
Inspector Knecht and supported by Treyer and his technicians and a
bearded young cryptographer on attachment to the operation, Marc
Payot, no fewer than seventy armed policemen surrounded the
house. Standing behind them were police dogs and their handlers,
and a mobile searchlight borrowed from the army. Knecht had no way
of knowing exactly what he would find in the house, but he was taking
no chances – besides, it was a rare opportunity to put on a show for
the military.

At 12.30 a.m. a police expert picked the lock on the front door, and
Knecht and his men went inside. Swiftly they climbed to the attic,
burst in on Olga as she was transmitting, and gave the signal for the
lights to be switched on outside. As police swarmed through the
building a sleepy Edmond Hamel appeared, dressed incongruously in
an embroidered nightshirt. The operation was all over in a matter of
minutes. The Hamels were arrested and spirited away, and a search of
the building began. Olga was taken so swiftly that she did not even
have time to transmit a warning signal to Centre, never mind destroy
the messages and ciphers with which she was working.

On the table alongside the transmitter key were twenty-three pages of enciphered messages to be sent that night. There were also several other messages and enciphering notes, and hidden in a cleverly-constructed cache behind the skirting board with an electrically operated door, was a wealth of other material. The beautifully-constructed hiding place had the mark of Foote's craftsmanship, and would have been almost impossible to find. But the police had arrived while Olga Hamel was working, and the trapdoor was open.

The documents found by the police included Radó's accounts for the running of the network, two enciphered alphabets and notes on radio transmissions with details of times, wavelengths and call signs. It was a rich haul. By keeping such detailed notes, especially his financial accounts giving lists of all payments to agents, Radó had broken the most fundamental rule of espionage. It was something he would have to pay dearly for when he returned to Moscow.

As soon as they started to examine the various documents, the police realised what they were dealing with. But it was too late now to draw back and hand over to the army. Knecht had a great deal more planned for that night.

The first move was to send men to Hamel's shop in the Rue de Carouge, to search for anything incriminating. The second move was to raid Rosie's flat. Rosie, of course, was not there, but a copy of Radó's cipher book *Es Begann im September*, was lying on her work table, beside a typewriter in which were still the sheets of paper on which she had been copying the pages. Rosie tried to pass this off later as a typing exercise, but the fact that there were six carbon copies in the machine told the police otherwise. This was Rosie's part in the enciphering and deciphering operation. She typed out the key passage from the book, the Hamels wrote the messages between the lines and Radó and Lène completed the operation with the final part of the cipher. In this way, none of the operators held the entire cipher code, which was known only to Radó. It seemed a fairly secure system, though a good cryptanalyst would be able to break the cipher given time and the book on which it was based. Marc Payot was given both the book and the next stage. Within a few days he had broken the cipher.

From Rosie's empty flat the police went immediately to Peters's flat, which they had already marked out during their observation period. Rosie and Peters were in bed together when they were arrested. Peters was released after a few days, since he had no connection with the network apart from his affair with Rosie. He had done his job well and on Hitler's next birthday, 20th April 1944, was decorated by the head of the OKW in the name of the Führer, with the *Kriegsverdienst Kreuz* second class, with swords, a rare honour for an Intelligence agent. After the war, when the Germans moved out of the consulate in Geneva, a souvenir of his efforts was found there – a copy of *Es Begann im September*.

It had been a good night's work for Knecht and his men. The two Geneva transmitters had been silenced and a number of vital documents found. According to one report, the arrests did not end there – in their enthusiasm and determination to be thorough the police arrested another suspect that night, a man who turned out to be Colonel Meyer of Swiss Military Intelligence who had served as a liaison man with the British and French. Professor David J. Dallin also records this, saying, 'General Guisan, indignant about the "mess" made by "these fools" demanded the immediate release of the prisoners, and Colonel Meyer was, in fact, released within three days. But that was all the General could achieve.'

Radó did not learn of the arrests until the next afternoon. At four o'clock he went to the Hamels' shop to take a batch of messages for transmission that night, including some to be delivered by Hamel to Foote. To his surprise, the shop was closed and shuttered. There was no sign of the Hamels. He went to a telephone kiosk and tried phoning them, but with no success. Returning home, he bought a copy of the evening edition of the *Tribune de Genève*. Sandwiched between a brief report of a drunken brawl in the Rue de Mont Blanc and a crash between two cyclists in the Place de Molard were three short paragraphs:

Discovery of a Secret Communist Radio
For three days the Sûreté have been searching the canton for a radio which is transmitting tendentious information.
The search began on Thursday morning around 4 a.m. when this communist organisation was discovered near Meinier.
Several arrests have been made.

There was no doubt in his mind that those arrested could only be his own radio operators. However, to make sure he called a contact with the police. The man confirmed his fears and added that it was not only the Hamels who had been arrested, but also Rosie, whom Radó had thought to be safely away in Basle.

Radó knew that Hamel had a rendezvous in two days' time with Foote in Lausanne, when he was to deliver a large batch of information. If Hamel talked, the police would know about this, and might make the rendezvous in his place. Foote must be warned. Radó went to his telephone.

'Edward is gravely ill,' he told him, using the language of espionage. 'We have called the doctor who has taken him to hospital. No visiting is allowed at the moment.' Foote, who had already seen the piece in the *Tribune de Genève* and understood Radó's meaning perfectly, made sympathetic noises for the benefit of any listener, and asked the Hungarian to keep him informed. He was now the network's only means of contacting Centre. It put him in a very powerful position.

CHAPTER THIRTEEN

'Stone Walls do not a Prison Make . . .'

It is absolutely necessary that you stay in touch with Albert. You must both be very careful. Tell Albert that we approve the measures he has taken. The organisation will stop all work for the moment. We shall await your calls each day according to the programme.

That message was Centre's immediate response to Foote's news that the two Geneva transmitters had been seized. Radó went to ground in Berne for a while, having told Sissy and Pünter what had happened, then he returned to his flat to arrange his affairs.

The head of the justice and police department for the Canton of Geneva at that time was a leading politician of the extreme left. It was therefore not too difficult for Radó to establish contact with Hamel in prison, and to find out what was going on. Hamel's warder was also a communist sympathiser, and carried written messages for him. Through this channel, Radó was able to confirm that the Swiss police knew about him, since they had shown his photograph to the Hamels and to Rosie, saying that this was the head of the ring and asking if they knew him. They also had Foote's picture, and at one stage told Rosie that he was the head of the entire network. The Hamels remained firm, and said nothing, but Rosie broke down, identified Radó's picture and confessed.

Radó arranged lawyers for all three prisoners, and secured Moscow's approval of his choices. Unfortunately, lawyers in Switzerland were expensive, even those who were prepared to make allowance for the anti-Nazi nature of the case, and it took most of the

179

network's remaining funds to pay them in advance. Meanwhile, the Hungarian was organising his private arrangements, too.

Knecht had installed detectives in the lodge of the park across the road from 113 Rue de Lausanne, to watch Radó's flat. Radó, on the alert, noticed them immediately, and was also well aware of the young man on a motorcycle who appeared every time he boarded a tram outside the apartment block, and rode behind it until he alighted. It was time to make a move, before the Swiss police grew tired of waiting and arrested him, too.

It must have seemed quite like old times for the Radós, to be going into hiding again. Radó sent Lène into a clinic, and his younger son and mother-in-law to a *pension* in the mountains. He stayed behind with his elder son and prepared to slip away to the hideout he had already arranged with his friend Dr Bianchi.

Radó's plan required patience and care. His son went in and out of the block quite normally, often riding his bicycle. Each evening and at regular times during the day, Radó took their Alsatian dog for a walk in the park opposite, passing close to the policemen in their lodge, or in the Botanical Gardens just along the road. One night, as darkness was falling Radó emerged from the building with the dog as usual, not wearing a hat or coat in spite of the chill in the air. He strolled briskly to the Botanical Gardens, where the road passed under a railway bridge, and there met his son, who had left the apartment earlier on his bicycle. In the dark under the bridge they changed places. The eighteen-year-old boy emerged with the dog and walked calmly home through the blackout, while Radó rode the bicycle out from the other side of the bridge and pedalled furiously to Dr Bianchi's house in the university quarter of the city.

Bianchi gave Radó a small room to himself, and kept his presence secret. It seemed a reasonably secure hiding place for the time being. But now the problem was how to get the network into action again, for after their first warning to close down temporarily, Centre had begun asking once more for information. Through Hamel's warder, Radó and Foote learned that the Bupo were actively searching for Foote's transmitter in Lausanne. Foote informed Centre of this, but their only response was to order him once more to move house, which was now totally impossible, and until then to send only Lucy's material which they still considered so vital that he must risk everything in order to continue transmitting it.

180

Radó emerged from his hiding place after a few days, to meet Foote in the Park des Eaux-Vives. He made a vague attempt to disguise himself, then took a taxi to the park gates, where Foote was waiting. As he approached him, Foote looked alarmed. The Englishman had seen the taxi driver leave his cab and hurry to a telephone booth. After Radó's disappearance from his flat, Knecht had issued copies of his picture to all taxi drivers in the town, with instructions to call the police if they saw him. Foote realised instantly what had happened, and hustled Radó through the park, away from the entrance where the driver was still standing in the telephone box. On the other side of the park was a restaurant, which backed on to the street. The two agents hurried into the restaurant, passed through the kitchen and walked out through the back door past the astonished staff and into the street beyond.

Swiftly, they exchanged information. Radó gave Foote his new address and told him to contact him when there were urgent messages to be passed. He put Foote in direct touch with Pünter, so that messages from the Pakbo ring would not have to pass through Geneva, but refused to establish a direct link between Foote and Sissy. That would have given the Englishman absolute control over the whole network, including Lucy. What was more, according to Foote, it would have given him and Sissy a chance to compare notes on the money he had supplied to Radó for Sissy's ring, much of which had apparently never reached her.

So Foote travelled from Lausanne to Geneva twice a week to visit Radó in his hideout. He caught trains in the evening so as to arrive at night, then walked through the blacked-out streets for a while before going into a café or restaurant to check that he was not being followed. Finally he took a taxi which he stopped a few blocks away from the Bianchis' home, walking the last few yards again for a final confirmation that no one was tailing him. It was a tiring and complicated procedure, but Radó had lost his nerve and would not venture out.

What worried the Hungarian was the possibility that if he were picked up by the Swiss police they might choose not to imprison him but to expel him from Switzerland – and the Germans were now on every frontier. Whichever way he went, they would be waiting for him. So he continued to lie low, letting Foote take the risks.

On 26th October Foote transmitted a message to Moscow for Radó:

The situation is becoming less and less favourable for continuing our activities. Everything leads us to believe that the Swiss police intend to destroy our network. I propose that we try to make contact with the British and continue our work under a new form of secrecy. I request immediate instructions since the business is urgent.

Searching desperately for some protection, Radó had hit on a bright idea. British Intelligence seemed to enjoy a privileged existence. Therefore, surely, the one place where he would be safe both from the Germans and from the Swiss police would be with British Intelligence.

He asked Pünter to contact the British legation through Salter and ask if they would be prepared to allow him to work from their premises, which were of course protected by diplomatic immunity. In fact the situation bordered on the farcical: Radó was suggesting that he should use the SIS transmitter to send his messages to London first, from where they could be safely relayed direct to Moscow. How Count Vanden Heuvel must have chuckled at the prospect. It would have been the ultimate irony if Ultra Intelligence, which secretly originated from London, had been sent officially via London at the Russians' request. With his tongue pressed very firmly into his cheek, Vanden Heuvel agreed.

But Centre's reply was clear and uncompromising. On 2nd November Radó received this message from them:

Your suggestion that you hide with the British and continue to work from there is absolutely unacceptable. In that case, your network would lose all independence. We understand that you are in a difficult situation and will try to help you. We are retaining a prominent American lawyer who has very good connections in Switzerland. He will certainly be able to help you and all those who are in difficulties. Let us know without delay whether you can still hold on, or whether you can hide somewhere for perhaps two or three months. On receiving your answer we shall arrange for the lawyer. Answer the following questions: who besides yourself in the network is in danger? What is the position of Sissy and Pakbo?

Did the radio operators [the Hamels] receive the text of the indictment? We are now in greater need than ever of co-operation with the Lucy group, and hope this will be possible as soon as your personal situation and that of Jim is cleared. We ask you, dear Dora, to be calm and to do everything that is necessary for your safety and maintaining your ability to work.

Over the next few days, Radó conducted a long wrangle with Centre in a stream of messages which grew more and more frantic. Centre ordered Foote to take over control of the network, and Radó must have felt that his fortunes really had fallen to a low ebb. His only comfort was Lène, who had left the clinic and joined him in his hiding place. No doubt she provided him with added strength which he badly needed. It may have been her idea to give messages to Foote, not in clear but in Radó's own cipher ready for transmission, presumably so that Foote would not be able to read them.

This was a surprise windfall for Treyer and Payot, who were by now busily monitoring everything sent by Foote. They had still made no impression whatsoever on Foote's cipher, so his messages remained secure. Then, suddenly on 11th November, Foote began to send messages in Radó's cipher, which they could read with comparative ease.

Most of these messages referred to the business of working from the British legation. It is evident on reading them now that Radó was concerned with the struggle for control between himself and Foote. He carefully avoids telling the Director that he had not obeyed instructions and put Sissy into direct contact with the Englishman, and that he was searching grimly for a way of holding on to the connection with Lucy. Here are some of the exchanges with Centre as intercepted by both the Swiss and the Germans.

To Director.
In your message received 29th October, you ask Lucy to contact an Allied power in order to be able to continue his work. Lucy refuses to do this because he no longer has a liaison with the British[!] I believed I was acting in your interests in making the same request to the British through Salter, especially as Lucy himself had given this advice. In addition, Salter's request was made without commit-

ment, as though he had been put in touch with them by the Gaullists. Dora.

To Dora.
1.   Your contact with Cartwright [the British military attaché] made without our authorisation, is an unprecedented breach of discipline. Your move was not what we expected. Our evaluation of the situation of your organisation and the prospects of our continued work with Lucy lead us to the conclusion that an official appeal to the British is not necessary. We repeat, it is impossible for us.
2.   You must take immediate steps somehow to undo this unfortunate action and to keep it quiet. At the same time, take care of Jim's security so that the most important information from Lucy can be sent through him. Send an immediate explanation of your incomprehensible actions and suggestions. Director.

To Director.
. . . I see no other possibility of being able to continue working usefully and immediately. Jim is very menaced and dare not work very much, nor meet Sissy often. For these reasons Lucy's important and up-to-the-minute messages are becoming out-of-date. The training of Harry [one of the two potential reserve operators] will take some months yet. I myself am completely paralysed. Only from a building that enjoys diplomatic immunity could I continue to work on the previous scale. I believed I was acting in your best interests when I turned to the British through Salter. Dora.

To Director.
. . . I would organise the work from the British legation in such a manner that the network will keep its autonomy. I insist that this is the only way of transmitting urgent and important information quickly and without interruption. We must make use of Lucy at this time, when she is so very precious to us, or we will lose her not only now but also for the future. Dora.

To Director.
Since there is no immediate way of receiving money from you, the network is also paralysed for lack of funds. Sissy declares that the Lucy group will stop working if payments are interrupted. Lucy has

also declared that there is no sense in his continuing to work for us if his information is not reaching you. Working from the British legation would also solve the money problem, since you would be able to send me money that way.

The American lawyer from the USA will not be able to help here because Switzerland is surrounded by German troops. Edward has the best lawyer in Geneva, Dutoit. The prisoners are held in secrecy and cannot communicate with their lawyer. Dora.

To Director.
1. Maria [Lène] is also severely threatened, Sissy and Pakbo not yet. The prisoners have not yet heard the indictment because the inquiry is not yet completed. The police believe that the operators were working for Britain. That is why the British legation could save them. It is also why I wish to make contact with them. The public know nothing because the censor has forbidden all communication. I do not yet know what they found at Edward's. He had numerous messages in my handwriting and that of Maria and Sissy, and typed on Maria's machine. Also some accounts in my handwriting. Stop. Paul [Böttcher] says his transmitter will soon be finished. Dora.

Radó had done all he could to persuade Centre. But it was not enough. When the Director replied, his message revealed the immense gulf that now existed between the reality of events in Switzerland and Moscow's idea of them.

To Dora.
Re your messages 1 to 5 and the questions posed by Jim. After a profound study of all your messages and a precise analysis of the peculiarities of your affairs, we are inclined to the opinion that the whole of this story – for reasons which are totally incomprehensible to us – has been organised by isolated agents of British Intelligence in Switzerland who apparently have no understanding of the importance of this historic moment for the common cause of the Allied nations. For this reason we are of the opinion that no serious danger threatens you or your people. Knowing your extraordinary ability to make fast and accurate appreciations of political situations, we believe that this time too, in this grave and complicated

situation, you will be able to find the means of getting yourself out and of maintaining, during this historic period of the last days of the war, your important combat position. Director.

As a speech of encouragement from the captain of a ship standing safely on his bridge, to a drowning crew member submerging for the third time in the shark-infested waters overboard, this must surely be unrivalled. But the Director had not finished. He went on immediately to send a message to Foote in his own code, and then got back to normal business with Radó.

To Dora.
Inform immediately the latest state of your personal situation. If you have need of the American lawyer we can certainly find a way of getting him into Switzerland. In addition we are ready to do all we can to help you, but you must try to find a reasonable course and make reasonable propositions. Your interpretation of our proposal that Lucy should approach the British as representing a friendly power is a misunderstanding. Tell Lucy in our name to be calm, that the transmission of his information to us is assured and that his group will most certainly continue to be paid, and at the rate he demands. We are prepared to pay a rich reward for his information. Best wishes. We await your reply. Director.
Why have you started numbering your messages from 1 again?

Poor Radó. He had been reprimanded like an hysterical schoolgirl and told to stop being silly. And now, in spite of all he had said, the Director was totally misreading the situation again, and talking to him in the sort of language one reserves for humouring a tiresome relative. He was even ending his messages with flowery sentiments! It was all too much. Radó gave in. His next messages, which were to be his last, had the ring of pathos about them. They were transmitted by Foote on 18th November.

To Director.
1. To my mind, the whole thing has been an independent action by the Swiss police, who discovered another transmitter at Basle at the same time.
2. During his interrogation Edward was shown a photograph of me

and promised his freedom if he would identify me. He stayed silent.

3. I assure you, especially since your reproach for indiscipline has hit me hard, that in spite of my serious situation I am gripped only by the worry of continuing to work. After what has happened, I shall stay hidden. I make the following proposals: a continuation of our work is now only possible if you accept the risk of Jim going on working. In that case, Sissy and Pakbo can give their important information directly to Jim, and Jim must control station Paul if it is to work at the same time. If this is to be, Paul must transmit part of the information. Jim must control the training of Harry and Roger [the two new recruits – Roger was the girl found by Pünter].

4. I have learned that a man was arrested with Rosie, who was apparently her lover, and about whom I knew nothing.

5. Rosie's lawyer is Dupont of Geneva.

6. I have started a new numbering of messages because I destroyed everything after our misfortune. Thus Paul was not able to receive the last messages.

7. The only way you can help is by introducing Maria and me to an Allied nation before it is too late.

8. At present we have not found an address for the money. We are completely without funds. Dora.

Before a reply could be received, the Lausanne police moved in.

Lieutenant Treyer's radio detection company had pinpointed the third transmitter in Foote's flat at 2 Chemin de Longeraie on 5th November, and had been monitoring his traffic with Centre ever since. By the time Radó's messages of 18th November had been deciphered, the Bupo decided that the game had gone on long enough. Marc Payot had been unable to break Foote's cipher, but the messages which they could read in Radó's suggested that the agents might be preparing to disappear.

At a quarter to one on the morning of 20th November, Foote heard the sound of men in the corridor outside his flat. There could be no doubt who they were, and he swiftly closed and locked the heavy door into his living room, where he was in the process of receiving a message from Centre. As the police began battering at the door, he calmly tore up the few sheets of paper containing messages and enciphering notes, put them into a large ashtray and doused them with lighter fuel.

The whole operation had a touch of the Keystone Kops. The door turned out to be rather stronger than the police had bargained for, but eventually door and frame collapsed under the assaults of two uniformed policemen, who went down with it. Stepping over their recumbent subordinates, Inspectors Pasche and Knecht entered the flat to be greeted by Foote with a broad smile and a welcoming gesture. He sat beside an ashtray in which the last of his papers was just being reduced to ashes.

'Ah, gentlemen,' he said with a casual air. 'Dropped in for a drink? A whisky, perhaps?'

Pasche, a dour Vaudois, glowered. Knecht smiled wryly and gave a Gallic shrug. 'Ah, Mr Foote,' he said, 'it's more serious than than.'

'Oh, very well,' the Englishman replied, not at all put out. 'Later, perhaps.'

Behind him, the radio set still poured out its messages from Moscow. Payot records with admirable precision that it had reached the 244th group of figures, and continued to the end of the message, which totalled 321 groups, without a pause. When it did stop, Treyer took Foote's place at the sending key and tried to start up a *Funkspiel* with Centre. Unfortunately, he did not know Foote's cipher, so had to send in Radó's, which instantly aroused the suspicions of the operators at Centre. They soon noticed the change in technique from Foote's distinctive hand, and tried a few trick questions which naturally caught out the Swiss officer. Nevertheless, the game continued for several days, until Centre grew tired of it and broke off contact.

The two inspectors and their men began a thorough search of the apartment, though the main prize – indeed the only one they were to find apart from Foote's little automatic pistol – was already on view. The radio set was out of its hiding place, and the hide itself, which Foote had built into the ceiling inside a cupboard, was open. Had it been closed, Knecht recalls, there is some doubt that it would ever have been found, so skilfully was the hiding place constructed.

Foote noted that Knecht and Pasche showed commendable intelligence in avoiding booby traps – they made sure he was standing next to any potential danger spot before they tackled it. There were, of course, no dangers and no booby traps, and the police missed the only hidden piece of useful information, though it was right before their eyes. Foote used the hollowed-out battery of a powerful electric torch to store important messages. At that time it contained a list of potential recruits drawn up by Pierre Nicole, which Foote had only partially enciphered. To him, this first 'layer' of enciphering was as easy to read as plain language, and an expert cryptographer such as Payot would have made short work of breaking it. The torch lay on a table in the hall, and Foote was horrified to see one of the policemen pick it up and idly flick the switch. To Foote's relief, he put it down again when it failed to light, and did not investigate it further. The torch was later taken with his other possessions to the jail, where he was able to extract the message and dispose of it in his cell in the classic way – by eating it.

The search did not take long. At about three o'clock in the morning Foote was taken downstairs to a waiting police car. He passed the *concierge* on the way and paused to reassure her that she was not going to be involved in any sort of trouble and should not worry herself about him. With this typical piece of thoughtfulness he left the apartment block and was whisked away to jail. Paul Böttcher's radio set was not ready for operation yet, and he had no ciphers or procedures agreed. The network was now totally cut off from Centre.

When the door of his cell in the Bois-Mermet prison closed behind him, Foote heaved a sigh of relief. For the first time since he had come to Switzerland four years earlier, he could relax, knowing that he was in no danger from anyone except the police – with whom he was soon on friendly terms. He anticipated a long stay in prison, and made sure it was going to be a comfortable one by taking plenty of supplies, including three cases of Scotch whisky, a quantity of preserves to satisfy his sweet tooth, and enough tinned food to last him for a year. As soon as his friends heard where he was, they sent him food parcels filled with his favourite sweets, and he supplemented his diet by arranging for his meals to be sent in from a nearby hotel. He also fixed a regular supply of cigarettes, since he was smoking fifty or sixty a day, and ordered a Spanish dictionary to help improve his knowledge of the language and pass at least some of his time profitably.

With his physical comforts thus taken care of, he could enjoy the entertainment of interrogations with Inspectors Pasche and Knecht

189

and the cryptographer, Marc Payot. From the beginning he made it quite clear to them that he intended to say nothing.

'I warn you in advance,' he told Knecht, 'that everything I'm going to say in reply to your questions will be a lie.'

When he was arrested, Foote was found to have 10,133 francs in a current account at a local bank.

'Where did the money come from?' the police asked.

'I didn't know I had as much as that,' he confessed. 'I'd never counted it.'

The police asked about the 3,255 francs that had been found on him. Where had that come from?

'Heaven knows,' he told them. 'I'd been carrying it around in my pocket for ages.'

They asked about his transmitter. 'A cure for insomnia,' he said. He told them he slept badly and so to fill the long lonely hours had built a kind of machine, amusing himself by tapping away on it at night.

'What about the replies that came back over the machine?'

'Oh, no,' he said. 'No one ever replied.'

When the police asked to which country he sent his messages, and for which country he was working, he replied with great seriousness, 'Guatemala.'

When he had had enough of the game, he would stop.

'I'm ashamed,' he would say, 'really ashamed, to be telling you such bloody stupid stories, especially when you're being so nice to me. When I think how the German or Russian police would react . . . Look, put the typewriter away, forget the questioning, and let's have a nice chat.'

With Scotch and schnapps flowing freely, no wonder Charles Knecht looks back on the interrogations with considerable affection. Knecht is a character himself. A thick-set, heavy man with a face that looks as if it had been whittled rather badly out of apple wood, he is apparently everyone's idea of an amiable, slow-witted peasant. One might wonder how on earth this man could have been responsible for security at so many international conferences. The eyes, however, give him away, for they are alert, amused and foxy.

Knecht had no illusions about Foote. 'He was a professional,' he told us. 'It was a waste of time from the beginning. I could see we weren't going to get anywhere with him, but it was very entertaining. Foote could be very amusing, even in French.'

190

Inspector Pasche, a man of a more puritanical nature, tried a different tack. He told the prisoner sternly that the police knew all about his activities, and that Margrit Bolli and the Hamels had made long statements incriminating him. However, Foote had nothing to worry about from Swiss law, since he had not acted against the interests of Switzerland. All he had to do was to make a complete confession, and he would be released immediately.

Foote had no intention of being released, however. He told Pasche calmly that if he got out of prison too soon then his masters – particularly if they were the Soviet Union, though he did not admit that for a second – would naturally suspect him of betraying their secrets. If, on the other hand, he stuck it out for longer than anyone else – meaning Radó then his masters would be more inclined to trust him as one who had suffered for the Cause. The last thing he wanted to meet in Moscow was a firing squad.

And so he chose to remain inside. This, of course, was no great hardship. On 7th December 1943, Foote wrote to one of his friends, an Irish journalist called Osborne Browne, asking if the head waiter of the Hotel Central had been inquiring about him. He said that he was looking forward to Christmas, having already ordered a duck for Christmas dinner. His only complaint about the prison at this time was that it was too noisy and he often could not sleep. The other inmates would keep pacing up and down their cells, for Bois-Mermet was a remand prison and housed a lot of transient inmates who were not used to captivity. This problem was solved when he was transferred to a quieter cell – in the women's wing.

There was only one interrogation which shook Foote's composure. Marc Payot, the cryptographer, saw Foote many times to question him about his cipher, trying to persuade him to hand over the details. Foote always refused.

'Don't worry,' Payot told him one day, trying to bluff him. 'I know your cipher. I've got it all in here,' he tapped his head, 'right at the tips of my fingers.'

Payot was astonished to see that Foote suddenly went white, though at the time he could not understand why. It was only later, when Foote finally gave him the cipher before leaving Switzerland, that Payot discovered the reason. Foote's cipher was quite different from Rado's, being of the type that is based on a single word of six

191

different letters. In Foote's case, the key word was FINGER. (See Appendix for a copy of Foote's legal deposition to the federal police regarding this cipher.)

Eventually, with the interrogation sessions stopped, Foote became bored with his inactivity. He complained in another letter to Osborne Browne that he felt he had been forgotten by the Swiss authorities. In a letter to a Swiss friend he said, 'I have got nothing to do but talk to myself, but I have given that up because it was becoming a bad habit.'

Early in September 1944, when he had been in prison for ten months, he was visited by a Captain Blazer of the Swiss army legal branch, who tried to start questioning him all over again.

'Are you a gentleman?' Foote asked him when he entered the cell.

Surprised, Blazer said that he considered he was.

'Well, so am I,' declared Foote, 'and I have given my word that I will say nothing. So you would be wasting your time questioning me.'

Blazer, however, was not so easily put off, and persevered.

Foote had a new element to consider: Paris was liberated, the Germans were no longer occupying southern France, and the frontier between France and Switzerland was open again. Foote had become something of an embarrassment to the Swiss authorities, since he was still being held on remand, and they would be delighted to be rid of him. Blazer reminded him that he could be released from jail as soon as he made a confession, adding that he did not even have to mention Soviet Russia. To his delight, Foote agreed, and made a signed statement saying that he had worked as an agent 'for one of the United Nations [sic]'. He wrote a cheque for 2,000 francs for his bail, and on 8th September he was released.

CHAPTER FOURTEEN

Out of the Frying Pan

While Foote was living in Bois-Mermet in considerable comfort, Radó had been in hiding. Ill, cold, often half-starved and worried all the time as to how his Russian masters would react to his flight, Radó lay low. After Foote's arrest it had seemed dangerous to go on living with Dr Bianchi. Too many people knew of this hiding place. In January 1944, therefore, Bianchi found a friend living close by who was prepared to shelter the Radós, and they moved there one night under cover of darkness. Unfortunately, the friend could only offer a tiny, unheated box room, with just enough space for a camp bed, in which Radó and Lène had to stay cooped up. They dared not even move during the mornings, when the charwoman dealt with the rest of the flat, or in the evenings when their host usually had friends in to play bridge. For almost nine months the two Radós never ventured outside the flat, indeed they hardly left their cramped little room. Since they could not use their ration cards, there was rarely enough to eat, either.

It is not surprising that Radó was in no state, physically or psychologically, to stand up to Foote's ruthless manoeuvring when they met again, late in 1944. Many of the Hungarian's subsequent disasters can be blamed on the time he spent in hiding, whereas the Englishman had ten months of comfort in which to plan his strategy.

When he went into prison, Foote already knew that his war was over. The Swiss network now had nothing of real value to give Centre, nothing that could change the course of events. There was no power on earth that could stop the Red Army. In January 1944 they relieved the siege of Leningrad; by April they had entered Romania; in June 350,000 Germans were taken prisoner in the Byelorussian campaign. The Soviet war machine swept onward, westward.

Meanwhile on 4th June, General Mark Clark entered Rome in triumph, and on 6th June Operation Overlord began, and British, French and American troops landed in Normandy. The western Allies and the Russians were heading towards each other, on a collision course. The Cold War was about to begin.

Foote wanted to play his part in that war too. Having spent ten months in prison, he reckoned he had established a certain credit with the Russians. Having heard, no doubt, that Radó was about to surface again, Foote knew that if he was to continue operating as an unofficial British agent, somehow or other he had to deal with the Hungarian, the one man who knew more about him than anyone else in the network, the one man who suspected his real purpose.

Foote went back to his flat in the Chemin de Longeraie, but was not altogether surprised to find that it had been let in his absence. He established himself in the Hotel Central-Bellevue de Lausanne, which had been selected for him by the police, and began to make the rounds again. His old acquaintances were pleased to see him. They still found it hard to believe: had he really been a spy? With many a nod and wink Foote hinted that he had been spying for the British all along; he told no one of his Russian connection.

After a week or two, when he was sure he was not being followed by the police, he went to the various 'places of conspiracy' where he used to meet Sissy, Pierre Nicole and Otto Pünter. Nicole said that Radó and his wife had been smuggled out of Switzerland a few days before and were heading for Paris. Nicole also told him that Radó had left the financial affairs of the network in an appalling mess. He said that Radó owed the Swiss Communist Party some 75,000 Swiss francs, most of which had been borrowed from third parties who were pressing for repayment. What was more the 75,000 francs could not be accounted for. Foote must have smiled to himself at this news. Nicole had put into his hands the perfect means of discrediting his rival.

He met Pünter next, who was keen to get the network going again. Pünter had managed to keep the Pakbo ring intact and operating, and had been collecting information continuously, though he had had no means of passing it to Moscow. The Swiss journalist was, however, in desperate financial straits as he, too, had been providing money for the network, borrowed from various sources in Switzerland. Pünter had raised 65,000 francs himself (as we described in Chapter Nine) as well as being instrumental in helping Radó to borrow a further 300,000 francs from other quarters. It had all been spent.

Pünter had been a good friend to Radó in other ways, too. When the Swiss police took Radó's son in for questioning, they seized the ration cards of the two boys and their grandmother. Later they evicted them from their flat. Pünter used all his influence in high places to have them reinstated, and to prevent their threatened deportation to Germany and Hungary respectively. He also tried, through friends in the federal government, to find a way of getting Radó himself off the hook by legalising his stay in Switzerland, though in this he was unsuccessful.

Pünter had one other piece of interesting information for Foote. He told him that Radó, while still in hiding, had tried to make contact with Centre, via a Chinese attaché in Berne, who was one of Pünter's agents under the code name Polo. The attaché passed the message, in Radó's cipher, to the Chinese government in Chungking. The Chinese foreign ministry handed it in at the Russian embassy there for transmission to Moscow. Centre did not applaud this effort. To them, it was yet another example of Radó's perfidy – he had compromised his cipher again.

Finally, Foote made contact with Sissy, who had been arrested on 19th April, with Böttcher, her daughter Tamara and her cousin Walter Fluckiger. Fluckiger was released the same day, as there was no evidence against him, and shortly afterwards Böttcher was interned until the end of the war, as an illegal immigrant. The others were held in prison until almost the same time as Foote himself was freed. Sissy told him that Rosie and the Hamels had been released in July, but obviously could be of no further use to the network.

Sissy did not, however, tell him that, in spite of the experience of the earlier arrests, she had allowed the police to find incriminating evidence in her flat, including 1,000 messages, in cipher and waiting to be transmitted. They had not found her cipher book, which she had been prudent enough to keep elsewhere, but this hardly mattered for she had kept all the old carbon papers used while typing and enciphering the messages. The police experts had been able to use these to break the cipher. Keeping them seems to have been the careless act of an economical mind, no doubt conditioned by her years of hardship, for the police also found an old shoe box half filled with the worn-down stubs of old pencils.

The evidence found in Sissy's flat provided the final proof needed by the police to identify Taylor and Lucy, code names which by then they knew well. Already, they had their suspicions, having realised the simplicity of most of the code names used by the network – Dora for Radó, Edward for Edmond Hamel, and Maria, her mother's name, for Lène Radó. It had not taken long to guess that Taylor might be simply the English translation of Schneider, and then to note Schneider's regular contacts with Rössler, who lived in Lucerne. In identifying Lucy it helped that some of his messages included material from the files of Swiss Intelligence, particularly one concerning a new Oerlikon gun being manufactured in Switzerland and supplied to Germany. Finding the original message from Lucy, the police were able to establish that it had been typed on the same machine as that used by the Bureau Ha's crack evaluator, Rudolf Rössler.

The pattern was complete. A month after Sissy's arrest, the police picked up Rössler and Schneider, and then Bernhard Mayr von Baldegg. Masson was furious, but the rift between army and police prevented his achieving a great deal and it was nine days before Mayr von Baldegg was released. In spite of added protests from Hausamann, deprived of his evaluator and a principal supplier of information, Rössler was held in prison for 111 days.

Rössler and the other members of the network were not brought to trial until after the war, but Mayr von Baldegg appeared before a military tribunal on 31st May, charged with giving Swiss Intelligence material to foreign powers.

Mayr von Baldegg was charged, in fact, with doing the very job he had been employed by NS1 to do – to play his part in the internal Intelligence mart which operated in Switzerland. He did not deny giving information to representatives of foreign powers, indeed he could hardly attempt to deny it under the circumstances. But he explained that in return he had received information of interest and value to Switzerland. Exchange was no robbery, nor was it treason.

This statement was too much for the judge, Justice Major Gloor of the 8th Division. He asked what kind of information could possibly interest or profit Switzerland. Mayr von Baldegg gently explained the basic facts of military strategy and the Intelligence market. Suppose, he said, that by giving the Radó network an item of Intelligence he could obtain from them details of the whereabouts of a certain German Panzer division, ascertaining whether it was still in Russia or Yugoslavia. Such information could be invaluable to the Swiss, and worth a considerable amount of Intelligence material in exchange.

The judge still failed to understand how such knowledge could profit Switzerland, so Mayr von Baldegg went on to explain, with growing tartness, that if the division were close to the Swiss border, in the Black Forest, for instance, it posed an immediate threat. The Germans could be on Swiss territory in about twenty-four hours, which would give the Swiss military authorities very little time to prepare counter measures. If, on the other hand, the division were in Russia or Yugoslavia, then it would take several days at least to reach Switzerland. To quote a British prime minister, a week is a long time in politics – and in war. The Swiss could mobilise an army in hours.

The judge rather grumpily acknowledged the justice of the defend-ant's case, and dismissed it. Mayr von Baldegg was exonerated and awarded damages of 800 francs. He was delighted.

In addition to giving the authorities the lead which took them to Rössler, Sissy made another serious mistake which aroused the anger of Centre, a mistake brought about by the network's lack of funds following Foote's imprisonment. Moscow's organisation and red tape were so bad that there were no reserve arrangements for making contact after such a disaster. Although there were active links from Moscow through London to the communist members of the French Resistance, some of whom were scarcely a mile away from Sissy's flat, over the border in France, and equally active links with other parts of Europe through the Russian embassy in Stockholm, Sissy had no means of getting in touch with either.

It seems strange that someone as experienced as Sissy, with a French son-in-law and other Frenchmen in her ring, could not have found some way of contacting the Resistance. It has been suggested by more than one expert that her actions were deliberately intended to lead British and Canadian Counter-Intelligence to uncover Soviet espionage activities in Canada, which they did soon afterwards with great success. Whatever the reason, Sissy wrote a letter in thinly veiled language, to her old friend Hermine Rabinovitch at the ILO office in Canada asking her to tell the Russian embassy that she needed $6,700 urgently in order to continue working. She followed this up with a cablegram, then another letter increasing the demand to $10,000, all sent through the open mail and therefore seen by the censors.

Unfortunately, it was some time before her requests were met – partly because Hermine contacted the wrong Russian Intelligence organisation. She got the message to NKGB, as it was then known, the civil Intelligence-gathering and state security outfit, and not to the representative of the GRU, Red Army Intelligence. The NKGB did not want to know about the problems of their rivals, and it took more frantic and revealing messages before the mix-up was sorted out. By that time the Canadians were well informed, and Sissy was in a Swiss jail.

Now, however, Sissy was free again, and ready to begin work once more, as was Pünter. Foote saw his chance. He was the logical choice to be the official resident director – he was Radó's number two, and had already taken over his duties when the Hungarian went into hiding. Telling Nicole to arrange transport for him to Paris, he went to Pünter to collect the accumulated material gathered by his ring and carefully transferred to microfilm. There only remained one source to be checked – Lucy himself.

Rössler had been released on the same day as Foote, and it was decided that he should meet Sissy and the Englishman on 15th December at the Restaurant Bolognese in Kasernenstrasse, Zurich. Foote and Sissy arrived first. Foote had never met the legendary Lucy and was amazed when at last a bespectacled, nondescript little man in his late forties joined them at their table. Rössler handed him a huge file of Intelligence material, saying this was only a fraction of what was available. He could supply much more if only communications were better – he must have some means of contacting Moscow personally.

Events had played into Foote's hands beautifully. He would soon be ready to make his next move.

The magistrate who granted Foote bail released him from prison with official instructions that he was required to stay within the Canton of Vaud and live in a place chosen by the police until brought to trial. Privately, however, he gave the Englishman quite different advice – to get out of Switzerland as quickly as he could. Foote had every intention of doing just that, as soon as he had collected sufficient ammunition for the next round of the game.

By the beginning of November, he was ready, and on the evening of the 7th he kept an appointment with Pierre Nicole at a café near the Swiss frontier on the road to the French town of Annemasse. Nicole was already sitting at a table with two men whom Foote had never seen before. Both were Frenchmen from Annemasse – one was chief of police and the other the president of the committee of liberation. After a glass of wine by way of introduction, Foote gave all the reports, messages, documents and microfilm which he was taking to Paris to the two men, who then left. Foote then took his leave of Pierre Nicole, and calmly passed through the Swiss frontier post on his valid British passport, with no risk.

In no man's-land the two Frenchmen were waiting for him, and they were joined by two young men from the Maquis armed with tommy-guns, who took him past the French frontier guards with a wave of their weapons. A car was waiting to take him directly to Paris with an armed escort for safety, and he enjoyed a comfortable and uneventful ride to the capital, where one of his fellow passengers provided him with a bed for the night.

Immediately after the liberation of Paris in August 1944, the Russians had sent an envoy to reopen the embassy. With him was a separate military mission led by Lieutenant-Colonel Novikov, whom Foote described as 'a tall, fair, flying officer with more than the usual share of Slav charm'. After a good night's sleep and a welcome reminder of French food, Foote set out to find Novikov. It took him a little while, for the embassy itself was in a state of chaos, with hordes of freed Russian prisoners of war milling about inside trying to get themselves repatriated. Foote was, however, eventually directed to the former Lithuanian legation in the Rue Prony, where he found Novikov installed.

At first, Novikov was guarded, fearing that Foote was an *agent provocateur* trying to penetrate the Soviet system. But the Soviet naval attaché from London came in and seemed to know all about Foote, Radó and the Swiss network, and soon established that the big Englishman was indeed a valued and important agent holding the rank of major in the Red Army. It was soon agreed that Foote's material should be sent over the mission's radio to Moscow, using

Novikov's cipher. But since this was designed only for use in Russian, the messages first had to be translated from the French and German in which they were written, before they could be enciphered. This was a long and tedious business, taking the whole of a day and night, but in due course Foote's messages were sent on 11th November. With them went his report that the network was intact and ready to begin work again just as soon as funds and means of communication could be provided.

Novikov told Foote that it would be several days before they could expect a reply, and offered him the hospitality of the mission for that time. The idea of being stuck in a room for a week, while outside there was the whole of Paris waiting to be enjoyed, had no appeal to Foote. He chose to take his chance outside, on his own. He wanted to eat French food and drink French wine again, after his long stay in Switzerland. And, of course, there could be no opportunity of contacting the British from the Russian military mission. Only one element in his scheme was missing. He needed to know what Radó had told the Russians. He asked to be put in touch with him, knowing that he had left Switzerland some weeks earlier and naturally assuming that he would already have checked in. To his surprise, Novikov said he knew nothing of Radó, and had not seen him. Foote shrugged, arranged a rendezvous with the adjutant on the corner of the Rue Prony in a week's time, and set off to enjoy himself.

Radó, in fact, reached Paris on 24th September and had been in touch with Novikov for some time, sending a gloomy report to Centre saying that everything was finished and the situation in Switzerland was hopeless. Every member of the network was known to the police, he had said, and they were all being watched by Counter-Intelligence. The Director in Moscow had been digesting this when Foote's version reached him, presenting an entirely opposite view and even outlining ways in which the network could operate using a transmitter across the border from Geneva in French Annemasse. Foote said that he was ready to operate the set, Pierre Nicole had agreed to organise a safe courier service, and Pünter, Rössler and Sissy were all eager to resume the supply of information which would still be valuable to Russia as the war had, they reckoned, at least several months to run.

Poor Radó knew nothing of Foote's arrival. While the Englishman was enjoying himself, living it up in all the high spots of Paris, ranging from the blackest of black market restaurants to the officers' mess of American army headquarters, Radó and Lène were living in a poor but wildly expensive furnished room. Lène was suffering from chronic bronchitis and Radó had severe rheumatism. They were in no state for optimism.

They had escaped from Switzerland with the help of the doctor who had treated Lène at the clinic. On the night of 16th September he picked them up from their hideout in his car and drove them to the railway station where they hid among the churns on a milk train. The driver took the train past the Swiss frontier guards without stopping, and Radó claims that they were fired on though no one was hit. The French Resistance drove them in a car over the mountains to Annecy, where they stayed for a few days in a villa beside the lake, recuperating and trying to regain strength in their wasted legs. Radó says they almost had to learn to walk again.

From Annecy they moved on to Lyons, where the friendly chief of police provided them with temporary papers, and, finally, they were driven, with an armed escort, to Paris. There, Radó met a few old friends, and learned the sad news that nearly all his relatives had died in Auschwitz concentration camp. Only his sister survived, though he did not know that until several years later.

In spite of their tribulations, however, the Radós were glad to be back in Paris, the city in which they had found refuge after their flight from the Nazis, and where they still had many friends. Lène missed her sons and her mother, and set about seeking permission for them to leave Geneva and join her and Alex. But it was a long and difficult task, particularly for a sick woman. However, Lène Radó was no ordinary woman, and with amazing persistence she finally succeeded in obtaining permission on Christmas Day 1944. By then, however, Radó was already preparing to leave for Moscow.

The decision by the Director to call Radó and Foote to Centre must have come as something of a shock to them both. After the first meeting with Novikov, Foote had gone back to the Soviet military mission, now moved to the former Estonian legation, where there were better facilities for short-wave communication with Moscow. He was asked various test questions set by the Director to prove his identity. When he had answered these satisfactorily, he was told to start working out detailed plans for reactivating the network as he had suggested. Accepted as an honoured agent, he was treated to his first Russian banquet, an enormous dinner liberally washed down with quantities of vodka and wine. He was to discover that Russians are eager to seize any opportunity for such feasting, a characteristic which suited his own tastes to perfection.

Following the banquet, Foote was told to keep in touch by visiting the mission every two or three days under cover of darkness. He spent his time lunching in turn at his favourite restaurant, Chez Mermoz in the Rue de Tremoille, the American officers' mess and the Soviet military mission. Swiss food and drink, even in the French cantons, tend to be rather dull, and Foote must have revelled in the gastronomic delights of Paris, even in wartime. His plans for re-establishing the network with himself at its head were developing nicely, and he was given orders from Moscow to start putting them into operation. He was told that he would shortly be issued with a false Dutch passport and a new cipher. It was a pleasant prospect. Then, on one of his routine visits to the mission, he found Radó sitting in the waiting room.

Foote was surprised, Radó was astonished. He had believed Foote was still locked up in the Bois-Mermet prison. Nevertheless, as Foote recalls, they both acted like the professionals they were and showed no sign of recognition until they were called in to Novikov's room together. There had been a change of plan, Novikov told them. The Director had ordered them both to Moscow. They were booked on the first plane to fly between the French and Russian capitals since before the war. Foote and Radó were to be numbers two and three on the passenger list, travelling like everyone else aboard as returning prisoners of war. Foote was to be given the identity of Alfred Fedorovitch Lapidus, former Estonian national, now a Soviet citizen, deported from Tallin to France by the Germans. Radó was to be known as Ignati Kulichev.

Suddenly it became clear to Foote why they had been kept apart. With their violently differing versions of the situation regarding the network, one of them at least had to be lying. If they had met, there would have been a chance that they might have compared notes and concocted a story which would have protected them both. Foote knew that Radó believed the network was utterly finished, but Radó did not know that Foote had been in touch with all the agents and had

202

made arrangements for it to be resurrected. The showdown was approaching.

To Novikov, the call to Moscow was a splendid excuse for a banquet, and he already had a suitable feast prepared. Foote described the meal as being convivial on the surface but with rather sinister undertones, and says it was the first time he had ever seen Radó affected by alcohol. Radó told him later that it was the first time for many years that he had drunk more than one glass of spirits. With such a handicap he was hardly a match for the English trencherman opposite him, and had all the gaiety of a skeleton at the feast.

The moment of decision had arrived at last. Foote had been presented with the chance of winning the penetration agent's greatest prize, acceptance into the very heart of his target country's Intelligence headquarters. To win the prize, he would have to survive the most rigorous tests and persuade the Director to choose him in preference to the genuine agent. If he failed, he could expect no mercy, even though he had achieved great things for the GRU. Up to now the game had been played according to Swiss rules. Going back to Annemasse as the official resident director of the network would have been simple. There would have been plenty of opportunity for escape if things suddenly got rough. He had been prepared for that. But Moscow . . .? Moscow was something else entirely.

A wiser man would have opted out of the game at that point. It would have been the easiest thing in the world for Foote to have gone home, back to Dansey in London, to claim his reward for a job well done. He could have ended his career in a discreet blaze of glory, and might have been given other jobs suited to his peculiar talents. His brief, after all, had not included journeying into Russia itself.

But Allan Foote was not wise. Having turned his back on the safe, quiet life in 1936, he could not conceive of returning to it. Perhaps his success in Switzerland had gone to his head? Perhaps the lure of adventure was just too strong? Perhaps he simply could not give up the life of clandestinity? He decided to grab the opportunity which had suddenly come his way. We believe he made the decision without consulting his masters in London, and chose to go to Moscow independently, playing it by ear or, in the apt phrase of the period, flying by the seat of his pants. Certainly, he did not make contact with the official British Intelligence representatives in Paris.

It is a pleasing thought, one of the fascinating 'ifs' of contemporary history, that if Foote had presented himself to the British authorities in Paris, he would have been interrogated by Malcolm Muggeridge, then SIS liaison officer to the French Securité Militaire, who was to befriend him in London later. If he had been ordered by his British masters officially to make his way to Moscow, his control officer in London would have been Kim Philby. But Foote chose to let events take their course. He was always something of a maverick.

Foote's fateful decision was entirely in keeping with his character. He had not become a secret agent in the first place for ideology, money or patriotism. He made very little money out of spying, abstract political ideas bored him, and MI5 certainly did not regard him as a patriot when he eventually returned to Britain. But he was a born adventurer, as he had proved in the Spanish civil war.

Foote was a man of paradoxes. He was capable of great violence – both his sister, Margaret, and his old friend Fred Copeman bear this out. He had killed ruthlessly and without thought, but also without enjoyment. He was a man who lived on his adrenalin and on his reflexes, yet – as Pünter and Knecht have pointed out – he was careful and cautious, a thorough planner. Nevertheless the challenge of Moscow was irresistible.

It has become fashionable recently to decry Freudian or psychological explanations of conduct, yet what other means can one use to explain Foote? The product of an unhappy home, rejected by his father, despising his mother, he ran away as soon as he was old enough to get a job. From the age of fourteen he was on his own, coming home only occasionally, mostly to see his younger sister Margaret, to whom he remained devoted all his life.

Apart from the affection and admiration he received from Margaret, Foote was starved of love. Since conventional Freudian theory equates food and love, we should not be surprised that throughout his life he maintained an extraordinary passion, almost amounting to an obsession, for food and drink. His sister recalls that he would eat and drink enormous quantities and could never get enough. Friends in Lausanne remembered his gourmandising there. When he went into prison, he was careful to take a year's supply of canned food and drink, besides making arrangements for meals to be sent in from a hotel. Perhaps it was inevitable that he came to suffer from the spy's occupational illness – stomach ulcers.

Foote was good-looking in his youth. All his life he possessed an irresistible charm. But his sister noticed a physical deterioration in him from the time he left Spain. He began to lose his hair and his figure, and ate and drank more than ever. He was as charming as always, but something had happened inside him during his time at the civil war.

Fred Copeman recalls that anyone in the British battalion of the International Brigade who went on leave to Madrid always consulted Foote about the best brothels. Foote, it seemed, was the expert. Yet once he started to live the double life in earnest, after he went to Switzerland, the only woman who ever figured in his life was Agnes Zimmermann, his fiancée who went mad in the hands of the Gestapo. He would seem to have been able to live without sex – possibly achieving satisfaction and pleasure out of the very act of deception itself. Like the act of sex, this is a peculiar and private experience. With Foote, it had become a passion.

It was this passion, we believe, which made Foote decide to take the opportunity of going to Moscow. He could not bear the thought of a life without deception. He thought that Dansey and British Intelligence would find a way of contacting him there, and if not, then what he learned in Russia would make him invaluable to the Intelligence Service when he returned to London. This belief reveals an extraordinary naïvety – but Foote was never a political animal. A politically conscious man would have thought more seriously about going to Moscow.

The aircraft was supposed to fly back to Russia at the beginning of December, but it did not depart until 6th January. The crew had no wish to leave the delights of Paris which they were sampling for the first time, and made every excuse imaginable to delay their departure, from mechanical faults to illness. But eventually Moscow grew impatient, sent an abrupt and threatening order, and the holiday was over. The passengers, including Foote and Radó, were ushered aboard with their false papers. Only one of them was a genuine ex-prisoner, even though over a million former prisoners in France were begging to be repatriated. Indeed the aircraft had four empty seats.

The journey took several days, with various stops en route, including Marseilles and Castel Benito, where the passengers were entertained in the RAF officers' messes. How Foote must have enjoyed those two nights, revelling in typical RAF mess hospitality and regaling the British officers with wild stories about his supposed imprisonment by the Germans, all told in his idea of an Estonian accent and badly broken English! Each morning he would stagger to the aircraft laden with gifts of whisky, cigarettes and chocolate. If he was venturing into the lions' den, at least he would enjoy himself on the way.

For Radó, the journey was far less happy. He was haunted by visions of what might happen to him in Moscow. Would he be blamed for leaving his post, and for allowing the network under his control to be broken up? How much did the Director know of his mistakes? As the aeoroplane droned steadily on its way, he grew more apprehensive and morose. He and Foote had been forbidden from discussing the network in front of the other passengers, but Foote's joviality and obvious confidence must have spoken volumes to the tortured Hungarian. It was no coincidence that Foote was a skilled card player, excelling at poker and bridge. To Radó it must have seemed as though the man he now realised was his opponent held all the aces.

In Cairo, the next overnight stop, they were accommodated, not in the RAF mess this time, but in the city itself, at the Luna Park hotel. With the chronic shortage of accommodation, it was announced that the travellers would have to share double rooms. Here was Foote's chance. According to his own account, Foote was approached by Radó, who suggested that they should share. We think it far more likely that it was Foote who made the suggestion.

Alone in the hotel bedroom, Radó confided his troubles to Foote. What did the Englishman think Centre would do to him? How much did they know? Foote was sympathetic, and assured Radó that he would do everything he could to help. However . . . he felt he had to warn Radó that he had already told Centre everything: the way in which Radó's cipher book had been found in Rosie's apartment, the accounts books and notes, the fact that a great deal of money was missing, the way that Radó had panicked, everything. Of course, Foote knew that he himself had nothing to worry about. His accounts were impeccable, he had successfully destroyed all his papers, and the Swiss had been unable to break his cipher. He had told the Swiss police and Counter-Espionage absolutely nothing, although he had suffered ten months in jail, while Radó had remained free but inactive. Nevertheless, he would do his best for Radó when the Director cross-examined him about his reports.

Radó shrank, already defeated. But then Foote delivered his master stroke. Things were not so bad, he assured his former chief. He had personally contacted all the important members of the network and everything was ready for work to be resumed. There were no problems that could not be overcome; in fact he had already worked out detailed plans. He had even brought out from Switzerland great quantities of valuable material which Sissy, Pünter and Lucy himself had been keeping safe during the period of inactivity. These were already with Centre, along with Foote's own reports.

It was too much for Radó. Foote had just played a fifth ace. To describe Radó's reaction we cannot improve on Foote's own account of the next few moments. 'There was a long silence after this,' he wrote, 'while Radó sat tapping his fingers on the small hotel table, lost in thought. Then he got up and left the room without a word. I never saw him again. The plane left next morning without him, and his hat, coat and luggage remained in the hotel bedroom uncollected, mute evidence of a spy who had lost his nerve.'

CHAPTER FIFTEEN

Behind the Iron Curtain

The aircraft landed at one of the smaller Moscow airports. Foote was in Russia at last. He was met by Vera, the woman who had been Sonia's predecessor as resident director of the GRU ring in Switzerland, and who had run the network from Moscow throughout the war. She wore the uniform of a major in the Red Army, but was still, at forty, an extremely good-looking woman with raven-black hair.

Vera took Foote to a flat at 29 the 2nd Izvoznia Ulitza, a block which he described as being occupied by the wives of Soviet generals. He was looked after there by a housekeeper, the widow of a lieutenant-colonel in the Red Air Force, and his permanent interpreter-escort-guard, Ivan. This was his home in Moscow for the next eighteen months, and he was settled in with the traditional Russian banquet at which he, Vera and Ivan were the only guests. Next day, while no doubt fighting a massive hangover, he was presented with a typewritten list of questions and a new German typewriter on which to prepare his answers.

This was the beginning of the big test. The questions were searching, and distinctly unfriendly in tone. Until he could convince them otherwise, Centre was regarding him as a possible *agent provocateur* planted on them by the devious British. The vast difference between his and Radó's reports on the affairs in Switzerland had naturally aroused considerable suspicion in Moscow, for Radó had said that the position was hopeless, with everyone compromised, and that they should wait at least two years before trying to form it again.

It was a dangerous situation for Foote, but the sort in which he revelled. He was better prepared than Radó, whose actions – particularly in running away to hide in a Cairo backstreet rather than return to Moscow – hardly inspired the greatest confidence. In addition Foote knew all about Rado's mistakes and misfortunes. In condemning the Hungarian he would automatically improve his own standing. He therefore set out to answer the questions carefully and – as far as was possible – truthfully. Only by telling the exact truth and inventing nothing could he be sure of not making any mistakes. The interrogation was bound to be lengthy. The slightest discrepancy could be fatal.

The process did indeed turn out to be a lengthy one. Each day Vera returned with fresh questions, and each day the questionnaires grew more complex. There were twenty-eight basic questions which were repeated over and over again, while others referred back to answers he had given days or weeks before. Foote never saw his interrogators, only the endless pages of questions which they prepared, but it was obvious that they knew all about the Swiss network.

Radó's disappearance, in fact, worked both for and against Foote. Centre initially blamed it on the British, believing that British agents had assassinated him in Cairo, possibly to clear the way for Foote. As Foote's answers began to satisfy them, however, they decided that perhaps it had been a simple case of defection. They called on the British authorities in Egypt to help find the man they described as a Russian colonel named Ignati Kulichev, who had, they said, deserted in Cairo while being repatriated. Under the terms of the infamous agreement on the return of prisoners of war, which was to cause so much distress elsewhere, the British were bound to find him and hand him over.

Radó had had plenty of practice in hiding during his forty five years, but eventually he was found. At first, he refused to go to Moscow, claiming that he was a Hungarian mapmaker. The Russians, however, were able to point out that his papers, all in perfect order, showed he was Colonel Kulichev, and a Soviet citizen. In the summer of 1945, he was flown to Moscow, to the dreaded Lubianka prison.

Radó and Foote never saw each other face to face again, yet a deadly struggle took place between them as each gave his own version of events in Switzerland. By now, Foote was definitely in the stronger position. Even though there was still suspicion that he might be a British agent, he was not held in a prison cell. Certainly he seems to have been more adept at handling the constant questioning.

After many weeks of searching interrogation, the Director arrived at the flat one evening, accompanied by typical NKVD 'heavies'. It must have been a nerve-racking moment for Foote. He had never met the Director himself before, and did not know his name. He says, however, that he was told the man was a lieutenant-general and one of the few people in Russia who could see Stalin at any time, without an appointment. Oddly, his description does not tally with that of F. F. Kuznetzov given to us by Cecil Barclay. It is possible that Kuznetzov had by then been replaced, or that the man who dealt with Foote occupied a different position in Centre. Foote described the man who visited him as being in his early forties, speaking almost perfect English with some Americanisms, and equally good French and German. With Vera and the heavies, he questioned Foote from six o'clock in the evening until two o'clock the next morning.

They were particularly interested in Pakbo and Lucy. They wanted to know their sources and how the information had reached the network so swiftly. The Director and Vera made it clear that they believed British Intelligence had fed false information into the Swiss network in order to impede the advance of the Red Army. Obviously all military disasters which could have derived from Lucy information were to be laid at the door of the perfidious British.

With the knowledge we have today, it is tempting to wonder how much the Russians actually knew or suspected about Ultra. Certainly, Kim Philby knew of it, though not how the information was given to Russia, and just as certainly Kuznetzov had pointedly asked Cecil Barclay whether Britain had succeeded in breaking the Enigma ciphers. It is possible that in questioning Foote the Russians were trying to discover whether the Swiss network had actually been the medium through which Enigma material had been passed. All this is speculation, however, and had no effect on the outcome of Foote's interrogation.

It was during this questioning that the Director produced a copy of a radio message and asked if Foote remembered sending it. Foote replied that he could not be expected to remember one message among so many. The Director looked stern.

'That message,' he declared, 'cost us 100,000 men at Kharkov and resulted in the Germans reaching Stalingrad. It was sent over your transmitter. After we received this, we could assume that Lucy was a double agent and all his information was false. Only after months of checking did we decide the source was reliable. The information must have been falsified after it left Germany. Perhaps, my dear Jim, you can throw some light on this?'

Foote's reply must have been satisfactory. After retiring with Vera and the heavies to discuss the verdict, the Director returned to announce that Foote had been naïve, but had proved his goodwill. 'You are not to be commended for your actions,' he told him, 'but you are guilty of no crime.'

Foote had passed the test. He was in. He had won the game. Radó had been defeated. At the time, Foote was told that Radó had been executed, a statement no doubt intended to encourage his loyalty. In fact, the little Hungarian was imprisoned in the Lubianka, where he stayed for ten years.

Foote was told to learn Russian as quickly as possible, and that a good job would be found for him. The Director had in mind to appoint Foote as chief of an espionage network in the United States. Following traditional Soviet technique, he was to direct his network from a base outside the target country, in this case from Mexico, where he would live on a false Canadian passport. His months in the Swiss jail improving his Spanish would have been worthwhile.

By now, the war was over. Europe was struggling to come to terms with peace. In Switzerland outstanding matters had still to be cleared up. Justice was to take its course for those members of the network who had not yet been tried.

In Divisional Court 2B at Berne on 22nd October 1945, a trial took place in which the defendants were Rössler, Schneider, Sissy and Böttcher. Only Rössler and Schneider were present, however, for Sissy and Böttcher had both fled the country, Böttcher to Leipzig in the Russian zone of Germany and Sissy to a secret hiding place where she would be safe from the Russians as well as the Swiss. In their absence, the court found them both guilty and sentenced them each to two years' imprisonment.

Rössler was represented by a leading Swiss lawyer, Maître Gerhard Schurch, who had undertaken his defence at the request of his friend Bernhard Mayr von Baldegg. He was charged with having been associated with an illegal Intelligence service operated by a foreign power, i.e. Germany. At the preliminary legal investigation the Swiss Intelligence service had come forward with evidence that Rössler had rendered important services to Switzerland during the war. They declared that he might have believed that as an informant to Swiss Intelligence he was free to pass on to Russia any Intelligence gathered from Germany.

Rössler in his evidence denied he was a communist and sought instead to give the impression that he was a professional spy. He was found guilty. However, under Article 20 of the Swiss Penal Code an accused can be excused punishment at the judge's discretion, if the judge has sufficient reason to believe that he acted in the best interests of the state. The judge did believe it in this case, and Rössler went free.

Schneider was not quite so lucky. He was sentenced to thirty days' imprisonment. He could never understand why he had been punished while Rössler had not.

While his former colleagues in Switzerland were fighting their legal battles, Foote in Moscow was paying a penalty of a different sort for the work he had done during the war. In November 1945 the stresses of the last ten years caught up with him, and he became seriously ill with a duodenal ulcer. The plans for his future had to be shelved while he was taken into the Central Military Hospital for an operation, followed by a period of convalescence at a sanatorium at Bolshova, where he appears to have enjoyed his stay. Playing-cards were illegal at that time in Russia, but Foote had a pack, and spent his time teaching the other patients the elements of gin rummy and stud poker. Since he was an expert card-player, we may assume his convalescence was profitable.

He returned to the flat in the 2nd Izvoznia Ulitza in early 1945, ready to resume his career as an agent – only to find that the job was off. Ironically, the cancellation was at least partly caused by one of his former associates, Sissy. The Soviet spy network in Canada had been broken up by the authorities after the defection of a cipher clerk in the Russian embassy in Ottawa, Igor Gouzenko, who had revealed details of the network in Canada. But the Canadians had already been aware of its existence, having first been alerted by Sissy's appeals for funds. As a result of this affair, Canadian passports were no longer available. Vera and the Director had both been removed from their posts as punishment for allowing the network to be smashed.

Vera was succeeded by Victor, a pleasant character who spoke excellent English and who had some pre-war espionage experience in the USA. Foote does not name the new Director, but says he thought he was probably a Georgian, though he had a rather Mongolian appearance. Foote was not impressed by him. They discussed possible future assignments and the difficulties caused by the passport problem. The day of the forged passport was over with the tightening of controls everywhere. An agent now needed the genuine article, which was never easy to obtain, especially for the USA or Canada. Altogether, Foote felt that Centre's operations were in a bad way and in desperate need of an overhaul and reorganisation. Even so, there was much that would be of interest to London, and he continued to keep his eyes and ears open.

One of the new Director's first acts had been to order the establishment of training schools for Centre agents, and it was decided that Foote should be sent to one of them, a spy school near Sehjodnya, twenty-five miles outside Moscow, to prepare himself for his next assignment. The school was situated in a log house with sixteen rooms, set in five acres of grounds surrounded by a high wooden fence topped with barbed wire. Foote was the first, and, at the time, the only pupil.

Foote described his training as 'fatuous'. He was supposed to receive an intensive course in all the latest developments in espionage – from micro-photography to sabotage, including the manufacture and use of secret inks. He soon realised that he knew considerably more than his instructors. Nevertheless, he stayed at the school from 8th September 1946 until late February or early March 1947.

While at Sehjodnya, Foote was visited several times by Victor and occasionally by the new Director, to discuss plans for setting up an organisation in the USA. However, the problem of obtaining genuine documents still remained, and eventually he was given a different assignment. He was to go to Berlin, as a repatriated German prisoner from Stalingrad, assuming the identity of Albert Müller, born in Riga in 1905 of an English mother and a German father. To explain his accent, he would claim to have been brought up in Spain and to have worked in Egypt and the Far East. As Albert Müller he would acquire papers and a passport, and after establishing his new identity would make his way to Argentina, where he would infiltrate Nazi and pro-Nazi circles.

Such a plan might have been tailor-made for an adventurer like Foote. It even had the added bonus of providing two lines of interest to London. What a hero's welcome he would receive from Dansey when he returned with two such prizes.

Before he left for Berlin, he was given another intensive interrogation by Centre, this time to check his political reliability. Again, he passed the test, and after a final banquet attended by Victor, the new Director and the chief political instructor of Centre, he boarded a plane for Germany. He was now Major Granatov of the Red Army. But they did not trust him to travel alone. He was, as always, accompanied by a 'courier'. Centre were still taking no chances.

In Berlin, as Major Granatov, Foote was given a flat at 12, Grellenstrasse, in the Soviet zone. Then, as Albert Müller, he set off round the municipal offices to acquire documentation. He not only needed to convince the authorities that he was Müller, which turned out to be relatively simple, but also to obtain permission to live in Berlin, which was not. However, in such a situation, Foote was in his element. He was a thoroughly experienced fixer, and with patience and an inexhaustible supply of cigarettes, then a major form of currency in the city, he got his documents.

On 12th April 1947, the day before his forty-second birthday, he was allocated a room in the flat of a Frau Weber at 41 Wisbyerstrasse, Pankow. He transferred his inevitable store of food and cigarettes – some acquired in Berlin and some brought with him from Russia – to his room in Frau Weber's flat. Albert Müller now officially existed; Major Granatov was dead.

All Foote had to do was to bide his time. He had plenty of money, for Centre had given him a year's pay in advance, some 2,000 roubles, the equivalent of £1,200 – a handsome salary in 1947. He could contact Centre in emergency through a Captain Smirnov. In case Centre wanted to contact him, he was to go to Prenzlaver station on the last Sunday of each month, carrying a leather belt in one hand (shades of Geneva!) and his hat in the other. If Centre wished to talk to him, an agent would approach him and say, 'When does the last train go?' Foote's reply to this was to be, 'Tomorrow at 10.00 p.m.' If he wanted to make contact with Centre, he was to put a notice on a particular public notice board reading: 'Wanted. Child's bicycle. A.

Kleber, Muristrasse 12, Berlin/Grunan.' The following day the contact would be at Prenzlaver station to meet him.

Foote never needed to make use of the system, though he did go along to the railway station in case Centre wished to talk to him. He had no difficulty at all in picking out the Russian contact man waiting among the crowds. For three and a half months, he continued to live quietly in Berlin as Müller, patiently building up his cover. Everything went beautifully; the prospects were bright. Yet suddenly, Foote changed his mind. Something happened which made him decide to drop the whole business.

What that something was, we cannot be sure. It was probably a combination of many things. He told Fred Copeman that he had attended a lecture as a Red Army officer, where the truth about Russia's cynical betrayal of the Republicans in the Spanish civil war had been explained in terms of political expediency. This revelation, he said, had made him realise that he no longer wished to go on serving the Soviet Union. It was a neat story, and one which would certainly have appealed to Copeman, but it could never have been more than a cover for his real motives. After all, he had no illusions about Russian behaviour and political morality, had never been a communist himself, and had primarily been serving Britain not Russia – though he could not tell Copeman that.

Two factors, however, changed the odds and put Foote at risk, too much at risk for it to be worth continuing. The first was his health. He had already had an operation in Moscow for a duodenal ulcer, but with his appetite for food and drink, coupled with the strain of his life as a double agent, a recurrence was inevitable. The chance of being caught in the wilds of Argentina with a perforated ulcer could not have been pleasant.

Secondly, Sissy had come out of hiding and returned to Moscow, possibly to stand trial, certainly to be debriefed. Sissy had worked for British Intelligence, and knew how the Swiss network had been used by them. If she did not actually know of Foote's true role, she might well have suspected. Even this was too risky for Foote, for he could not take the chance of someone in Moscow putting two and two together and arriving at the correct answer. When that happened, Albert Müller would not survive long either in Berlin or Argentina.

According to the story he told Copeman, Foote chose a time when he was attending an official meeting, as Major Granatov, close to the border between the Russian and British sectors of Berlin. After the meeting, he went to the toilet, took off his major's uniform jacket and walked calmly out into the street. In the hot sunshine of August 1947 a man in shirtsleeves looked quite unremarkable.

The details of the occasion may have been another bit of romancing for Copeman's benefit. After all, he had abandoned the Major Granatov role months before, and it is hardly likely that Foote would have kept his uniform, or have taken the chance of being seen entering or leaving Soviet military premises when he had taken so much trouble to establish himself as Albert Müller. But that is conjecture. We do know for certain, however, that on 2nd August 1947 he crossed into the British sector of Berlin, stopped the first RAF police patrol he saw and said, 'I am Corporal Foote' – he was never more than AC1: a typical piece of effrontery – 'a deserter from the RAF since 1936. Arrest me.'

Within a very short time, he was handed over to the British security authorities, who asked him to identify himself. At first this seemed a problem, for Foote discovered that Dansey had died two months earlier and the Z Organisation had died with him. Foote needed someone to speak for him.

That night, the telephone rang in Fred Copeman's flat in Lewisham, and a voice said, 'I am speaking from Berlin. Do you know a man called Allan Foote?'

The long adventure was over. Alexander Allan Foote, double agent extraordinary, had finally come in from the cold.

Epilogue

What happens to old spies? Do grateful governments reward them, or are they regarded as embarrassments and quietly tucked away?

On 30th October 1947, after Foote's return to London, the Swiss government finally held the second of its spy trials in the Military Tribunal of the First Division, A, at Lausanne. The accused were Edmond and Olga Hamel, Margrit Bolli (Rosie), Sándor and Hélène Radó, and Alexander Allan Foote. With the Radós and Foote otherwise engaged the proceedings were something of a farce. As Margrit Bolli's lawyer observed, the big game had all escaped and they were left with the small fry.

The presiding judge was Lieutenant-Colonel Roger Corbaz, the lawyer whom Foote had approached about transferring money for the network from the United States. Rössler was one of the witnesses, and at his request Mayr von Baldegg gave evidence on behalf of Hamel.

The result was a foregone conclusion. On the basis of three messages, one of which gave technical details of the new Oerlikon cannon which was manufactured in Switzerland and shipped to Germany, Radó was found guilty of passing Intelligence to a foreign power contrary to the interests of Switzerland. Lène and Foote were also found guilty in their absence. Radó was sentenced to three years in prison, a fine of 10,000 francs, and was forbidden to return to Switzerland for fifteen years. Lène was sentenced to one year's imprisonment and ten years' expulsion. Foote was given two years and six months in prison, a fine of 8,000 francs and fifteen years' expulsion. His transmitter and cash, including the money he had in his bank account, were confiscated. Since the Swiss police held his money, and his bank account had been frozen at the time of arrest,

Foote was the only one of the three major agents to suffer materially as a result of the trial. He lost all the money he had in Switzerland.

The Hamels and Margrit Bolli were also found guilty. Edmond Hamel was sentenced to one year in prison, less three months of the time he had already spent in detention when he was arrested, although the prosecutor had asked for six months to be deducted. He was also fined 1,000 francs and everything seized during the raid on the villa in the Route de Florissant was confiscated. Olga Hamel was sentenced to seven months in prison, less three months already served, although the prosecutor had asked for five months to be deducted. Margrit Bolli was sentenced to ten months in prison, minus the 272 days she had spent in preventive detention, and fined 500 francs. The prosecutor had demanded only a fine of 200 francs. After the trial, the prosecutor, Major Pierre Loew, remarked to Hamel that it was the first time since the beginning of the war that a court had inflicted heavier penalties than the prosecution had demanded.

At the end of their sentences the three returned to normal private life. All three are still alive and well in Switzerland. Hamel still runs his radio shop in Geneva, though he and his wife were divorced a few years ago. Margrit Bolli married and is now a prosperous and highly respectable bourgeois matron who refuses to be reminded of her exploits during the war.

When Foote gave himself up to the RAF patrol, he had every reason to feel confident of his reception. The British Intelligence services would surely welcome him with open arms. He had done everything his masters had asked of him – and more. Indeed, one could argue that he had proved to be one of the most successful British agents of the war. Not only had he provided one of the channels by which relevant Ultra information could be fed to the Russians, but as second-in-command of the Swiss network he had been in a position to ensure a degree of protection for this highly sensitive material.

As far as future operations were concerned – and at this time Foote seems to have had no doubt that he had a future in the service – he was in a unique position. He had recently undergone training at a Soviet spy school, and for two years had been in regular contact with senior officers of the GRU. There could be few British agents with more extensive and up-to-date information on the latest techniques of

Soviet espionage, and fewer still who were personally acquainted with the administrators and planners of future enemy Intelligence operations.

Foote confidently awaited his reward. But none came: none was ever to come. It is unlikely that he was naïve enough to expect instant gratitude, but he must have been surprised to discover that he was actively under suspicion himself. It is a truism of espionage – a remark that was frequently made to us while we were researching this book – that a double agent can never be trusted, even by his own side. The very fact of 'going double' inevitably involves compromises that might later be difficult to justify to one's real masters. In order to receive one must first give; in order to earn loyalty one must be seen to demonstrate loyalty – particularly to one's false masters. By the very nature of the game he has chosen to play the double agent struggles in a morass of compromises that would require the moral rigour of a St Thomas Aquinas to weigh in the scales. The successful double agent is he who is seen to balance accounts in favour of his real masters, or at least balance them in such a way that those masters believe them to be in their favour. This surely Foote had done.

Yet he was held by MI5 for two and a half months: a month in Germany and six weeks in a flat in Hammersmith. During this time he was permitted to make one outside contact: he was allowed to see his sister, Margaret. She found it an unnerving experience. She was called to meet him in London, in a room in an anonymous building near Victoria Station. They were left alone, so that they could speak privately. But as they embraced her brother whispered to her to be careful what she said, because 'they' were listening. This upset her, and she recalls a stilted, nightmarish conversation. Obviously Margaret had inherited none of her brother's flair for clandestinity.

One of the many intriguing questions about this whole episode is why Foote was held by MI5 at all. MI5 is the Security Service; MI6 is the Secret Intelligence Service. Granted he was not one of that department's official agents, but since 1936 he had been working for them, albeit indirectly, via the Z Organisation. Surely someone at MI6 must have known enough about his background and career to have spoken up for him? Dansey, of course, was dead, but Count Vanden Heuvel was working as an attaché in Rome and Victor Farrell was still very much alive. Perhaps they were not consulted.

Ten weeks is a curious length of time to hold a man like Foote. As a rule it takes months to debrief anyone adequately – particularly a man with Foote's unique and detailed knowledge. By comparison, the Russians held Kim Philby incommunicado for at least seven months while they debriefed him, and West German Intelligence is reported to have taken a full twelve months to debrief a recent KGB defector.

In a statement, dated 3rd November 1955, Foote says, 'I announced myself to British Intelligence in West Berlin, and subsequently in Hannover made a report to a certain Mr— who, I understood, had flown from London to interview me. Mr— adopted a rather un-friendly and sceptical attitude towards me and more or less limited himself to taking down notes of statements I had volunteered . . . little interest was evinced in what I had to say or what I had learned . . . During the interview I reported the names of two of my former colleagues, "John" and "Sonia" [i.e. Len and Ruth Brewer, alias Ruth Kuczynski, alias Ursula-Maria Hamburger, alias Ursula-Maria Schultz], who since 1941 had been living in England . . . '

Later in London he met one of Sonia's sisters who had not yet heard of his defection. She confided to him that on the very day the Brewers (more likely just Ruth) were due to go to an important secret rend-ezvous the police had come to question them and had searched their home on the pretext that the marriage was illegal (sic), whereupon both Len and Sonia fled to East Germany.

This is partially confirmed by Sonia herself in her book, *Sonia's Rapport*, which was published late in 1977 in East Germany, where it became a best seller. Her version differs only slightly from Foote's, which was admittedly secondhand.

According to Sonia, she and Len were living at their cottage at Great Rollright, near Chipping Norton, in the Cotswolds, when in August or September 1947 (i.e. within a week or two of Foote's 'defection'), two men came to the door. Their first words were ob-viously intended to startle her into some kind of revelation. They began by informing her that they were from MI5 and that they knew she had been a Russian agent.

Since there is evidence to suggest that at the time Sonia was running Klaus Fuchs, the atom spy, the visitation must have come as a horrible shock. However, her reaction was totally English – she invited the men in for a cup of tea!

The men went on to reassure her that they knew she was no longer active, having become disillusioned with the Soviet cause as a result of the Russo-Finnish war. They knew she was now a loyal British citizen: that was why they had come to ask for her co-operation. They began to question her about her activities in Switzerland. But Sonia refused to answer. She admitted that she was disillusioned with communism, but this did not mean that she was prepared to work against the cause. She also insisted that her activities prior to her acquiring English citizenship by her marriage to Len were none of MI5's business.

The men then demanded to speak to Len who was working in the garden. But his reaction was identical to his wife's. He refused to talk about Allan Foote and Switzerland and refused to co-operate on the grounds that he was an ex-, not an anti-communist.

The men from MI5 went away, apparently convinced by the story. There was no subsequent surveillance. Nevertheless Sonia realised that her work in Britain was over and she made plans to escape to East Germany.

Such is Sonia's account of the events.

It seems reasonable to assume that the visit from MI5 (not the police, but the confusion is not important) was the direct result of Foote's disclosures of the Brewers' activities to British Intelligence in August 1947. It is curious, however, that afterwards there seems to have been no further official interest in the household at Great Rollright. As Foote rightly observes: 'If [the Brewers] had been put under lengthy surveillance, instead of being alerted by precipitous . . . action, their contacts with sources of information in this country would ultimately have been disclosed. . .'

Not surprisingly, in his later years Foote became obsessed with the idea that there were traitors somewhere in the upper reaches of both Secret Services. 'If I at the time of my defection,' he complained, 'had been persuaded to continue my work with the Soviets, very possibly the latter would now be in possession of facts and information about [Red Army Intelligence] activities which at present they do not have.' With increasing desperation he attempted to bring his complaints to the notice of those in authority. He wrote letters to several Conservative MPs. At one stage he even demanded that a committee of Privy Councillors should examine the reasons why British Intelligence had failed to make use of the information he had brought back from Russia. But, alas, no one paid any attention. He was ignored.

Today, with the hindsight of revelations arising from Andrew

Boyle's book, *The Climate of Treason*, it is tempting to see the hand of the Cambridge *apparatchiks* behind both the failure of the authorities to arrest Sonia and Foote's later troubles. We now know that by the end of the war both MI5 and MI6 had been penetrated by the Soviets at a very high level; by Blunt and Philby, to name but two. It seems likely that there were traitors able to nullify any compromising stories that the returned double agent might be able to tell. Who was responsible for Foote's professional demise and his later hounding by MI5, we do not know. Yet someone somewhere effectively blocked all his efforts to make the authorities listen to what he had to say, and indeed went to considerable lengths to make his life intolerable thereafter.

Their task was made much easier thanks to that peculiarly British phenomenon, more evident in 1947 than now – snobbery. Foote was not a Fellow of Kings or Trinity. He was the son of a failed poultry farmer and had himself been a corn merchant. He had little schooling and spoke with a broad North Country accent. He was certainly not the product of a good public school or a fashionable regiment or an Oxbridge college, and he had not even held a commission in the RAF. He was a maverick. He was an adventurer. Above all, he was not of the Establishment, and the Establishment was in a mood to crucify him.

When he was turned loose, Foote was still immensely confident about his future. If British Intelligence did not want him, he had plans to cash in on his experiences, and he wrote to tell his friend Osborne Browne that he had negotiated a deal with a publisher, Museum Press, to write his memoirs. He had high hopes of an American sale, and signed a contract to deliver a manuscript of some 80,000 to 100,000 words by the end of March 1948. He was also offered work as a co-writer of an anti-communist film, but he turned this down.

With the confiscation of his money in Switzerland, he was now almost penniless, and the resulting worry caused his ulcer to flare up again. Nevertheless, in order to live, he found a job with an insurance company. The job lasted only three months before he was fired – he had done very little insurance work, spending his days writing his book instead.

The book, however, was not a success, for which he blamed MI5. 'They mutilated my book,' he told Professor David Dallin in 1953. He said that MI5 had cut the most interesting parts and inserted things that were simply not true, without asking his permission, or indeed informing him. If the book had been a success, he had intended to leave London to take up farming. He was at that time living in a tiny sixth-floor room in a small hotel in Clifton Gardens, Maida Vale, where he was to stay for the remaining years of his life. It was there that Charles Knecht found him when he visited London on business in 1949.

Knecht was horrified at the conditions in which his old adversary was living and invited him to share his hotel suite during the week or ten days he was staying in London. The two men spent a week or so drinking and talking about old times, busily trying to pump each other. Knecht learned a little more, particularly about Foote's Russian experiences, and still recalls the week with great pleasure.

'Foote,' he told us, 'always was good company, and he was at the top of his form '

Eventually Foote became an executive officer in the Ministry of Agriculture and Fisheries. It was a safe position, from which he could never be fired, and where 'they' could still keep an eye on him. And there was a pension at the end. But whatever the intention, it was an act of cruelty – like putting an eagle into a grasshopper's cage. Foote was a man who lived on his reflexes, a cool, cautious man of action. Someone in the Intelligence Establishment condemned him to a life of form-filling and pen-pushing. It is small wonder that he did not live long.

Foote kept in touch with his sister and her young family, spending many weekends at their cottage in Sussex, where he enjoyed pottering in the garden. He stayed on at his hotel in Clifton Gardens, partly because it seemed pointless to move and partly because there were several excellent card-players in residence. He played bridge almost every night.

It was about this time that he met Malcolm Muggeridge, who has recorded the meeting in the second volume of his autobiography, *Chronicles of Wasted Time*:

He was working as a clerk in the Ministry of Agriculture and Fisheries, then located in Regent's Park near where I was living. He used to drop in for a chat on his way home: a large stolid-looking Yorkshireman, who could be very funny about his time in the

USSR and the training in espionage methods that he was given . . . No one could have been less like the popular idea of a secret agent – he was much more like an insurance agent, or possibly a professional cricketer – but he had developed a taste for clandestinity, and found his overt life with Ag and Fish very tedious.

For some years Foote nursed the belief that British Intelligence would call on him again. But he was too well known. He had been 'burned': his face was now familiar to every counter-intelligence officer in the western world. He was not even called upon by British Intelligence to advise or lecture. He was simply left to rot, and rot he did with the help of alcohol – which inflamed his ulcer, so that he drank even more to deaden the pain.

Why did Foote submit to this treatment? He was still only in his early forties, a man of intelligence and charm, who spoke four languages and had more than his fair share of initiative. He also had considerable commercial experience from his early years. One would have thought a man like that could easily have found employment as – at least – an overseas sales representative. Instead Foote meekly bowed to the will of MI5 and the Ministry of Agriculture. There can only be one explanation: MI5 had something on him, something that put him forever in their power. It is difficult to imagine what it might be, though we believe that whatever it was arose from events subsequent to his arrival in this country. Foote's degeneration, both physical and in morale, can be seen in the photographs. Compare the one of Foote taken at his peak in 1942 or '43, wearing a hat and looking like a big-time gangster, and the pathetic ruin photographed by *Der Spiegel* in 1955. This was the period dominated by the Burgess, MacLean and Philby scandals, but there is no proof that Foote ever met them or even knew of their existence. And in any case Foote would never have been an easy man to intimidate. Yet Malcolm Muggeridge told us that Foote was a broken man when he knew him. He was frightened of MI5, though what hold they had over him Muggeridge never discovered. When we approached MI5, we were informed that they were not prepared to discuss Foote.

Foote rarely complained of his treatment – certainly not to his sister. However, when David Dallin and his wife Leila interviewed him at the end of October 1953, they found him bitter about British

Intelligence. The British did not trust him and would not give him a decent job, he said.

At the beginning of 1956 it looked as though his luck was about to improve, when he was offered a lecture tour of America speaking on the subject of espionage. Even though McCarthyism was at its height, when anyone with the remotest link with communism was shunned, if not banned, the Americans were willing to allow in a man who, on face value at least, had been a Soviet agent for eleven years. Presumably, someone in the British Establishment was prepared to vouch for him, and to give the assurances necessary to obtain an American visa. Perhaps it was the same unknown person who made it possible for him to be given a job in the Civil Service, which also had the most stringent rules about security clearances for any officials. Perhaps, after all, there was someone who knew about him, and cared just a little.

Foote was very excited at the prospect of touring America, but by then his health was causing him great problems. He suffered considerable pain from his ulcer, and vomited back almost everything he ate or drank. He could not possibly contemplate a lecture tour in such a condition, and his sister persuaded him to go into hospital first for an operation. Foote agreed. In typical style, he was determined to enjoy everything that America had to offer, including food and drink. Towards the end of July, he entered University College Hospital in Gower Street, London.

When his sisters visited him there, they found him in good spirits, and looking forward to the American trip. But the operation was not a success. The surgeon took Margaret and her husband aside and told them there was little he could do for Foote. Already half his stomach was missing, and the condition was now inoperable. He had only months to live.

Foote's condition deteriorated rapidly in hospital. On 31st July, Margaret and Foote's other sister were sent for. They found their brother lying in bed with dressings and tubes attached to his abdomen, obviously in a poor state. The doctors were not hopeful, and gave them a room next to Foote's, where they could spend the night. Foote's last words to them, as he looked down at the dressings on his stomach, were, 'This is no damn good.'

In the early hours of 1st August 1956, he calmly and deliberately tore off his dressings, and died. His death certificate gave the cause of death as 'acute peritonitis due to perforated duodenum (operation partial gastrectomy)'. There was no inquest. He was fifty-one years old.

Rudolf Rössler survived for two years longer than Foote. By the time he died he had been turned into a legendary figure as Lucy the great master spy. While Ultra was still secret, the British were quite happy to allow the cover story of Rössler's mythical informers in the German high command to blossom, for there were other countries still using Enigma ciphers and the SIS wanted to go on reading their signals, unsuspected. Consequently, they were delighted to encourage the legend in the post-war years. Unfortunately, such a legend can create disastrous consequences, particularly if the man concerned comes to believe in it himself.

The post-war years were not kind to Rössler. He was beset by business worries as his publishing house, Vita Nova, began to wither in the bitter wind of competition from a reviving Germany. In November 1949 he brought out a new monthly magazine called *Extempore*, which was devoted to providing an independent information service on international political and economic affairs, unpolluted by propaganda. Only five issues were published before it was banned by the Swiss government.

With his publishing house failing fast and his magazine banned, Rössler saw that he would soon be left without a voice to speak effectively to the spirit of Germany, a spirit which, he believed, desperately needed his moral guidance. He was appalled at the new German democracy led by Adenauer, watching in horror as former Nazis emerged like bugs from the woodwork to take up their places in industry, commerce and even government, as if the crusade against fascism had never been. In dire need of money to finance Vita Nova and continue his personal campaign, Rössler turned to the legend of Lucy and his old friend Xaver Schnieper for help.

Schnieper had moved much further left after the war. He had joined the editorial staff of *Vorwärts*, a communist paper, and in 1945 had become president of the Lucerne branch of the Swiss Communist Party, though he was expelled a year later after a financial scandal. He was then offered a job with Caritas, a large Catholic charity, which sent him to work in Prague from December 1947 until February 1948.

Epilogue

The Czech connection seemed too good to miss. The communists had still not seized power, and Rössler foresaw that Czech Intelligence might be interested in his valuable services, since they knew of him already. In fact Karel Sedlacek, the former Uncle Tom, was now installed as an attaché in the Czech legation in Berne, and it was therefore a simple matter to make contact.

For the next few months Rössler and Schnieper worked happily for Prague, with Rössler making political, economic and military assessments of the situation in West Germany, based on his own knowledge and a vast library of press cuttings, and Schnieper typing and posting them off, and making contacts. The Czechs were duly grateful, and paid well. Rössler took seventy-five to eighty per cent of the proceeds, Schnieper the remainder. It was a good and lucrative system, but it was brought to an abrupt halt in October 1948 when the communists took over in Czechoslovakia.

In 1950 Schnieper visited Prague again, and was contacted by the reorganised Czech Intelligence, who invited him and Rössler to work for them once more. By this time, espionage and counter-espionage techniques had become more sophisticated. Schnieper was urged to invest some of his own money in photographic equipment suitable for microphotography. The two men started operations again – with Schnieper sending Rössler's evaluations on microfilm to Prague, though on one occasion he took undeveloped film with him on a business trip to Vienna and handed it over to a Czech agent there.

Everything was soon running smoothly, and the two men worked hard. There was only one problem – the Czechs did not pay. Perhaps this was an endemic weakness in any communist Intelligence organisation, bearing in mind the Soviet record with the Swiss network during the war. In spite of his assertions that he was working for his principles and ideals. Rössler wanted money, too. Just as, in the war, he had threatened to stop supplying the network unless regular payments were made, now, in 1951, he stopped sending material to Prague.

On 22nd April 1952, Rössler and Schnieper received an undated, unsigned letter from Berne. Inside the envelope was a suitcase key, a left luggage slip and a letter which simply read, 'Go and get it. This is from your very good friend Konrad [their new Czech contact man].' Schnieper took the slip to the station, where he collected a suitcase – which they found contained 3,000 francs in notes. It was the beginning of the final phase of the Rössler saga. They were in business again.

During 1952 the method of sending the material was changed. The new way was for the film to be sent to an agent in Germany, hidden in parcels of food. This was simple enough, and continued to work well until early 1953, when Schnieper was away and Rössler himself had to do the posting. He bought a jar of honey and a jar of figs, placed microfilm inside each, and sent them separately to the usual address: Josef Rudolf, Linienstrasse 106, Dusseldorf. But Rössler made a mistake – exactly what, we do not know – perhaps he was supposed to mark the parcels in some special way, or maybe he wrongly addressed them. The parcels were returned to the sender whose name and address were written on them, Herr Heinrich Schwarz of Zurich. But Herr Schwarz did not exist – he was an invention of Rössler and Schnieper. When the Swiss Post Office found they had two similar parcels sent by the same non-existent person, someone became curious. The parcels were opened, and the jar of figs and the jar of honey examined. Inside were the two microfilms, one concerning Allied airfields in West Germany, the other concerning the transfer of American officers with Korean combat experience to units in West Germany.

The Bupo investigation did not take long. The two Lucerners may already have been under suspicion. They were arrested in March 1953. When Inspector Maurer went to arrest Rössler and to search his house, he found him in despair, sitting in the kitchen with his head in his hands. He had every reason to be worried, for he knew that if he were found guilty he might well be deported to Germany, where there were many who regarded him as a traitor to the Fatherland. Indeed, we have been told that both the American and German governments brought pressure to bear on Switzerland to deport him. On the other hand, Swiss Intelligence did not want Rössler brought to trial, but were overruled by the Bupo.

The trial itself came as a complete anti-climax, interesting mostly for its brevity and for what did not emerge in the evidence presented by the prosecutors. It began in Lucerne on Monday 2nd November, and judgement was given on the Thursday morning.

Rössler and Schnieper were charged with operating from Swiss territory an espionage or Intelligence ring dedicated to the service of a foreign power (Czechoslovakia) and against the interests of other foreign powers (named as West Germany, the USA, Great Britain, France and Denmark). The first day was taken up with the statement of the prosecution case, the facts of which were not contested, except in a few minor details. The two accused admitted sending between 110 and 160 Intelligence reports to the Czechs between 1947 and 1953. They also admitted receiving in return between 33,000 and 48,000 francs (about £4,000 at the rate of exchange then existing). Presumably the difference of 15,000 francs between the two figures represented running costs and expenses.

Only three witnesses were called: Inspector Otto Maurer of the Bundespolizei, Father Otto Karrer, a Jesuit priest who appeared as a character witness for Rössler, and Dr von Sergesser, a former member of the *Entscheidung* group before the war, as a character witness for Schnieper.

The defence was ingenious and seemingly incontrovertible. Rössler and Schnieper admitted sending reports to the Czechs, but denied operating an espionage ring. All the reports, they said, were compiled by Rössler from material which had been freely and openly published in newspapers and magazines in Germany, Switzerland, America, and other countries. Rössler, the human computer, had simply analysed and evaluated some 20,000 press cuttings – an activity, it was argued, which could not be described as espionage by any stretch of the imagination. The prosecution were unable to present any evidence to contradict this, suggesting only that the Czechs were preparing to use the two agents in some future operation, and for this reason were prepared to pay handsomely for information which any good pressing cuttings agency could have provided at a fraction of the cost. What they did not appreciate was that the Czechs were paying for Rössler's evaluations, in which he was highly skilled.

On Thursday 5th November, the court handed down its verdict. The accused were both found guilty. Rössler was sentenced to one year's imprisonment, less the 242 days he had already spent in detention, Schnieper to nine months, less the 242 days. They were ordered to pay the costs of the case, with Rössler bearing three-fifths of the total, and Rössler's collection of press cuttings was confiscated. The tribunal also made the extraordinary ruling that 'the systematic collecting of press cuttings can be considered as espionage', a judgement which not unnaturally disturbed the foreign press community in Switzerland, who, like any journalists, relied on press cuttings for much of their work. Were they to be regarded as spies from now on?

Federal sources soothed their worries. The Swiss government had had enough of Rudolf Rössler, and the trial had been in the nature of a warning. He had not been deported, and his sentence, effectively only four months' imprisonment, was lenient. But it had been made clear to him that the government, careful of its neutrality more than ever in the difficult days of the Cold War, would no longer tolerate his activities on Swiss soil.

Rössler was crushed by the verdict. His health had never been good, he was still racked with asthma, and now he was deeply disillusioned. He continued working in Lucerne, just managing to keep his publishing house alive, but the spark had gone. It was as though some delicate but vital part of the mechanism had been broken. Gradually, he declined.

In October 1958, Rudolf Rössler, evaluator extraordinary, human computer, tragic incompetent of the world of espionage, died from his final attack of asthma. The funeral was attended only by his wife and a few friends and colleagues, including Xaver Schnieper and Bernhard Mayr von Baldegg. He was buried in the neat little cemetery at Kriens, a suburb of Lucerne, not far from where Schnieper now lives and works as a journalist and Mayr von Baldegg still practises as a successful lawyer. A small stone marks his grave. On it are carved simply the words: 'Rudolf Rössler 1897–1958'.

His wife, Olga, returned to West Germany, where she still lives, uneasily, near Augsburg. Most of his other colleagues, collaborators and contacts are now dead. Schneider and Hausamann died in their native Switzerland; Sedlacek in London in 1967; and Sissy in East Berlin in 1975. Only Böttcher survives, living in Leipzig still, in East Germany, where until recently he was assistant to the editor-in-chief of the party newspaper, the *Leipziger Volkszeitung*.

Sonia and John – Ruth and Len Brewer – are still alive and happily married, living in semi-retirement near the Baltic Sea in the East German state of Mecklenburg. At the age of seventy-two, Sonia is still a colonel in the Red Army and both she and Len have been decorated (she holds two Orders of the Red Banner and a medal as a fighter against fascism). Her memoirs have become a best-selling book – at the time of writing, sales had passed 350,000 and a further edition of 50,000 was being printed – and after appearances on East

German television she also threatens to become something of a celebrity.

To survive in the field, a spy needs a rare combination of luck and good judgement. To survive in retirement he needs the same combination, but to an even greater degree. Foote and Rössler survived the war but became victims of the peace. Otto Pünter and Sándor Radó, on the other hand, revealed a truly remarkable ability to survive under any circumstances. Both, of course, had already had successful careers before they came to espionage, Radó as a distinguished geographer and Pünter as a journalist. When there was no longer any call on their unique talents in the espionage field, they were able to take up their previous careers again without apparent difficulty.

Pünter's post-war career provides a remarkable demonstration of what native Swiss shrewdness, good sense and discretion, as well as considerable talent, can achieve. To begin with, he was never brought to trial. When we spoke to him in Berne, we asked why he had never even been arrested, and he grinned like a wayward elf.

'I asked the chief of federal police that myself,' he replied. 'He told me it would be embarrassing for the Bupo to arrest me. Why? Because I would be on oath if I were tried. The president of the court would ask me where I was on such and such a day and whom I was with – and I would have to answer "At police headquarters" or "In such and such a café, talking to the chief of federal police".'

The Bupo preferred not to put one of their own informants on trial, particularly one with powerful friends in the Swiss Socialist Party and in the trade union movement, and one who knew so much about their own operations. He could also have proved, as did Mayr von Baldegg, that his espionage activities were in Switzerland's interest and against her possible enemies. It must be remembered, too, that a number of highly-placed Swiss, such as Pilet-Golaz, the federal president in the early part of the war, had been either pro-Nazi, or, through fear of German power, 'adjustors' sympathetic to the Nazi cause. To have indicted Pünter and not the sympathisers of the losing side would have courted severe political and social repercussions inside Switzerland.

After the war, Pünter sensibly continued to preserve his close links with the Swiss Socialist Party, the trade unions, and the federal police.

He continued as a journalist, before becoming head of press relations for Swiss television, a post he held for about ten years. He also became a local magistrate in Berne.

Werner Rings, a television producer and commentator who wrote a thirteen-part series on Switzerland and the war, shown on Swiss and German television in 1973, told us a story which illustrates both the degree of security under which Pünter and the others worked during the war, and the curiously provincial air of the network's operations. Rings had arranged to meet Bernhard Mayr von Baldegg for Sunday lunch at a country restaurant, to discuss Mayr von Baldegg's appearance in the programmes. Before the lawyer arrived, Pünter and his wife entered the restaurant purely by chance, greeted Rings, whom Pünter knew through his work in television, and sat at a table on the other side of the room. When Mayr von Baldegg arrived, Rings went across to the Pünters' table and asked Otto Pünter if he would like to meet 'Louise', having asked the lawyer if he would like to meet 'Pakbo'. Marta Pünter was not pleased – she thought Rings wanted her husband to meet an old girl-friend! But Pünter and Mayr von Baldegg were both delighted. Throughout the war they had communicated regularly, but only through cut-outs. They had not met face to face until then, some twenty-eight years after the war had ended.

Today, Otto Pünter lives with his wife in retirement in Berne, a neat, balding man who looks much younger than his eighty years. It is typical of the man that he has just finished writing his memoirs – not of his espionage career but of his experiences as an international journalist. Pünter is living proof of what a spy can achieve if he operates from his native heath and wins the protection of a powerful political movement and of the police. He is a classic example of the spy as patriot.

Radó, on the other hand, represents the spy as the politically-committed man, a communist whose commitment has not wavered even after ten years in a Soviet prison. All that he will say about his imprisonment is that he was 'one of the victims of the cult of personality', a victim of the Stalinist era.

He emerged in 1955 not, as one might have thought, as a 'non-person', politically suspect and doomed to suffer in a sectarian limbo for the rest of his life, but almost in triumph. In fact, he appears to have been reinstated into the groves of academe with what, for the communist world, amounts to quite extraordinary dispatch.

As soon as he was released, he returned to Hungary, for the first time since 1919, where he was joined by Lène, who had been living in France while he served his sentence, unhappy and unwell. They enjoyed a brief Indian summer together until she died tragically on 1st September 1958. Her ashes repose in a tomb in Budapest donated by the People's Republic of Hungary, on which the inscription proudly describes her as a founder member of the German Communist Party.

Since his wife's death, Radó has gone from strength to strength. He has been politically rehabilitated by the Hungarian Communist Party, and honours have been showered on him, as if to make amends for all his years of suffering. Today, Professor Sándor Radó, Doctor of Science, Doctor of Economics, Fellow of the Royal Geographical Society, President of the Hungarian Geographical Society, Co-president of the Hungarian Society of Geodesy and Cartography, lives in Budapest and works from the Hungarian Office of Lands and Mapping. He still travels extensively. Even at the age of eighty-one he can be described as 'a man of tremendous vitality, radiating shrewdness, knowledge of the world and good humour'.

In a letter to us recently, he wrote, 'I consider my activity during the years of the second world war as an episode of my life which made me put aside my vocation as scientist, because I felt it my highest duty to fight the dangers of Hitlerism with all the possible means at my disposal.'

Through the strange, complex, mixed-up means of his secret network in Switzerland, he can be said to have achieved his aim, and done his duty. He can now also be said to have had the last laugh over his former colleague and arch-rival, Alexander Allan Foote.

APPENDIX

Foot's Deposition on his Cipher

1. The code I used for all my dealings with Moscow had been handed to me by Sonia at the end of 1940. It was based on the word FINGER in the following way:

00	3	6	40	8	9
F	I	N	G	E	R
1	03	06	41	44	47
A	B	C	D	H	J
01	04	07	7	45	48
K	L	M	O	P	Q
2	5	08	42	46	49
S	T	U	V	W	X
02	05	09	43		
Y	Z	SIGNAL			

2. As can be seen, all the letters not appearing in 'Finger' are written in alphabetical order in horizontal lines under this word. The numbers 1 to 9 with the exception of 4 are substituted for the letters ASITNOER. The numbers follow each other vertically beginning top left. The 'signal' (01) shows a change in the message of the text in letters to a text in numbers (see below). In this case each figure is repeated three times.

JIM	(Key Group)	.TH	EQU	ICK
47307	77109	43544	84808	30601
21320		64302	67861	13067

BROW	N FO	XJU	M P	SO VE
03974	66007	49470	80745	27428
43206				
46170				

R LAZ	Y D	OG	NR.SIG.	1 3
90410	50241	74143	69430	91113
			31206	
			90636	

6		(Key Group)		
33666	43434	21665	34343	77989

3. All the messages I sent had the name 'JIM' at the beginning of them. All messages addressed to me from Moscow had 'JIM' as well but were signed 'DIRECTOR'.

4. The key cipher book that I used from March 1941 till July 1943 was *Statistical Handbook of Foreign Trade for 1938* published by HMSO and Sonia had used it before me. From July 1943 till my arrest I was using *Swiss Handbook of Trade Statistics for* 1939.

5. This book supplied the numbers which were added to a coded text in order to finish the message.

6. The numbers taken from the cipher book began with the third figure of numbers in the chosen column, eg:

			Col. 3			
3rd	39460	1321	94320	7302	43671	94306
figure	3462	3061	4321	3206	4302	67861
	13067	43206	42861	43261	67801	13467

21320, 64302 etc. etc. These numbers were added to the coded text in the fashion illustrated on page 1. In order to let the recipients of the message know what numbers were taken from the cipher book a key group was established thus:

*Page**	*Col.*	*Line*
68	3	02

*NB. Where the page number was above 99, the first figure was omitted, for we used to begin with the encipherment of a message at the point in the cipher book where we had finished the preceding message.

We used to add to these figures a group of 5 constant figures which, in my case, from March 1941 to the end of 1942 [?] was the number 73737, as well as the 5th group of the coded text and its final numbers, thus:

68302	—	page, column, line
73737	—	constant number
46170	—	5th group, etc.
77109 total	—	key group.

This group of numbers was inserted between the 1st and 2nd group of the coded text in the way shown on page 1. (For the most part I used the 5th group in my coded messages, but from time to time on orders from Moscow other groups of figures were used, for example the 6th or the 7th group, etc.)

7. A similar group was made up with the help of a group at the end of the message, with the exception of the 5th group at the beginning of the coded text, and this key group was added between the 2nd last and the last group in the line. (See page 1.).

68302	—	page, column line
73737	—	constant group
90636	—	5th group before the
21665		end of the message

6. A final group was added to the finished message, for example:

Groups*	Message No.	Date
19	36	2

These numbers were added to the 1st group of the telegram.

19362
68627
77989

*NB. In a case where the message contained more than 99 groups and the number of the message was above 99, we only took the two last figures of these numbers to form this group, in all cases we only used the last figure of the date.

Bibliography

Published sources used in the preparation of this book include the following.

Pierre Accoce and Pierre Quet, *The Lucy Ring*, W. H. Allen, London, 1967

Restmir Amort and I. M. Jedlicka, *The Canaris File*, Allan Wingate, 1974

Drago Arsenijevic, *Genève Appelle Moscou*, Robert Laffont, Paris, 1969

Lord Avon (Anthony Eden), *The Reckoning*, Cassell, London, 1965

Bernard Barbey, *Aller et Retour*, Neuchâtel, 1967

Bernard Barbey, *P.C. du Général 1940–1945*, Neuchâtel, 1947

Patrick Beesley, *Very Special Intelligence*, Hamish Hamilton, London, 1977

Edgar Bonjour, *Geschichte der Schweitzerischen Neutralität*, Basle, 1946

Andrew Boyle, *The Climate of Treason*, Hutchinson, London, 1979

Vincent Brome, *The International Brigades*, Heinemann, London, 1965

J. R. M. Butler and J. M. A. Dwyer, *Grand Strategy (History of the Second World War)*, H.M.S.O., London, 1964

Paul Carrell, *Scorched Earth* (Vol. 2), Harrap, London, 1970

Paul Carrell, *Hitler's War on Russia*, Harrap, London, 1964

Vasily Ivanovich Chuikov, *The Beginning of the Road*, MacGibbon & Kee, London, 1963

Winston S. Churchill, *Great War Speeches*, Transworld Publishers, London, 1957

Winston S. Churchill, *The Second World War*, Cassell, London, 1948–1954

Alan Clark, *Barbarossa*, Hutchinson, London, 1965

David Dallin, *Soviet Espionage*, Yale University Press, New Haven, 1955

David Dilks (editor), *Diaries of Sir Alexander Cadogan*, Cassell, London, 1971

Allen Dulles, *The Secret Surrender*, Weidenfeld & Nicolson, London, 1967

Allen Dulles, *Germany's Underground*, Macmillan, New York, 1947

239

Allen Dulles, *The Craft of Intelligence*, Weidenfeld & Nicolson, London, 1963

Kurt Emmeneger, *QN wusste Bescheid*, Zurich, 1965

John Erickson, *The Soviet High Command*, Macmillan, London, 1962

John Erickson, *The Road to Stalingrad: Stalin's War with Germany*, Weidenfeld & Nicolson, London, 1975

Wilhelm F. Flicke, *Spionagegruppe Rote Kapelle*, Kreuzlingen, 1954

Wilhelm F. Flicke, *Agenten funken nach Moscow*, Munich, 1954

Alexander Allan Foote, *Handbook for Spies*, Museum Press, London, 1949, 1953

Noble Frankland and Christopher Dowling (editors), *Decisive Battles of the Twentieth Century*, Sidgwick & Jackson, London, 1976

Reinhard Gehlen, *The Gehlen Memoirs*, Collins, London, 1972

Józef Garliński, *Intercept. The Enigma War*, K. M. Dent, London, 1979

Franz Halder, *Kriegstagebuch*, Stuttgart, 1962

History of the Great Fatherland War of the Soviet Union, Moscow, 1961

Heinz Höhne, *Codeword: Direktor*, Frankfurt, 1970

Robert Jaquillard, *La Chasse aux Espions en Suisse*, Lausanne, 1947

R. V. Jones, *Most Secret War*, Hamish Hamilton, London, 1978

David Kahn, *The Codebreakers*, Macmillan, London, 1967

Willhelm Keitel, *Memoirs*, William Kimber, London, 1965

David Kelly, *The Ruling Few*, Hollis & Carter, London, 1952

Jon Kimche, *Spying for Peace*, Weidenfeld & Nicolson, London, 1961

Arthur Koestler, *The Invisible Writing*, Hutchinson, London, 1969

Steven Kolkowicz, *The Soviet Military and the Communist Party*, Princeton University Press, Princeton, 1967

Kriegstagebuch des Oberkommando der Wehrmacht, Frankfurt

Hans Rudolf Kurz, *Die Schweiz im zweiten Weltkrieg*, Thoune, 1959

Hans Rudolf Kurz, *Nachrichten-Zentrum Schweiz*, Frauenfeld, 1972

Ronald Lewin, *Ultra Goes to War*, Hutchinson, London, 1978

Sir John Garnett Lomax, *The Diplomatic Smuggler*, Arthur Barker, London, 1965

Ivan Maisky, *Memoirs of a Soviet Ambassador*, Hutchinson, London, 1967

Fritz Erich von Manstein, *Lost Victories*, Methuen, London, 1958

Alphons Matt, *Zwischen allen Fronten*, Verlag Huber, Frauenfeld Stuttgart, 1969

F. W. von Mellenthin, *Panzer Battles*, Cassell, London, 1955

Frantisek Moravec, *Master of Spies*, Bodley Head, London, 1975

Malcolm Muggeridge, *Chronicles of Wasted Time* (Vol. 2), Collins, London, 1973

Kim Philby, *My Secret War*, MacGibbon & Kee, London, 1968

Otto Pünter, *Guerre Secrète en Pays Neutre*, Lausanne, 1967

Bibliography

Sándor Radó, *Sous le Pseudonym Dora (Dora Jelenti)*, Paris, 1972

Alan Reid, *A Concise Encyclopedia of the Second World War*, Osprey, London, 1974

Werner Rings, *La Suisse et la Guerre*, Lausanne, 1975

Report of the Royal Commission (Canadian) on Espionage, Ottawa

Walter Schellenberg, *Memoirs*, André Deutsch, London, 1956

Wilhelm (Ritter) von Schramm, *Verrat im Zweiten Weltkrieg*, Dusseldorf, 1967

Patrick Seale and Maureen McConville, *Philby, the Long Road to Moscow*, Hamish Hamilton, London, 1971

Albert Seaton, *The Russo-German War*, Arthur Barker, London, 1971

Albert Seaton, *Stalin as Warlord*, Batsford, London, 1976

Ronald Sydney Seth, *Forty Years of Soviet Spying*, Cassell, London, 1954

Hugh Trevor-Roper, *The Philby Affair*, William Kimber, London, 1967

Walter Warlimont, *Inside Hitler's Headquarters*, Weidenfeld & Nicolson, London, 1964

Ruth Werner, *Sonja's Rapport*, Verlag Neues Leben, East Berlin, 1977

Charles Whiting, *The Battle for Twelveland*, Leo Cooper, London, 1975

F. W. Winterbotham, *The Ultra Secret*, Weidenfeld & Nicolson, London, 1974

Georgii K. Zhukov, *Memoirs*, Jonathan Cape, London, 1970

Newspapers and Magazines

Basler Nachrichten, 3rd March, 1949

Construire, April, 1972

Feuille d'Avis de Lausanne, 29th March, 1972

Gazette de Lausanne, 2nd, 4th, 17th February, 2nd March 1949, 3rd November, 1954

Journal de Genève, 26th January, 1963

Neue Zürcher Zeitung, 2nd November, 1953, 22nd December, 1967

Der Spiegel, February–March, 1954, 16th January, 1967

Television

Swiss Television Service: Round Table Discussion programmes, 15th and 22nd May, 1966

The Principal Spies and their Code Names

RADÓ NETWORK:

Sándor Radó = 'Dora' and 'Albert'
Lène Radó = 'Maria'
Edmond Hamel = 'Edward'
Olga Hamel = 'Maude'
Margrit Bolli = 'Rosie'

FOOTE'S NETWORK:

Allan Foote = 'Jim'
Max Habijanic = 'Max The Cobbler'
Anna Müller
Agnes Zimmermann = 'Mikki'

DÜBENDORFER'S NETWORK:

Rachel Dübendorfer = 'Sissy'
Christian Schneider = 'Taylor'
Paul Böttcher = 'Paul'
Walter Fluckiger = 'Brant'

PÜNTER'S NETWORK:

Otto Pünter = 'Pakbo'
Léon Sousse = 'Salter'
Georges Blun = 'Long'
Ernst Lemner = 'Agnes'

Rudolf Rössler = 'Lucy'

Ruth Kuczynski = 'Sonia'

Bernhard Mayr von Baldegg = 'Louise'
George Wilmer = 'Lorenz'
Joanna Wilmer = 'Laura'

Victor Sukulov = 'Kent'

Len Brewer = 'Jack'

Abbreviations and Glossary

ABWEHR	German Military Intelligence
BUPO	Bundespolizei (Swiss Federal police)
BUREAU HA	Bureau Hausamann
CENTRE	Intelligence HQ, Moscow
GESTAPO	Geheime Staatspolizei (Secret State Police)
GRU	Glavnoye Razoedyvatelnoye Upravlenie (Chief Intelligence Directorate/Red Army Intelligence)
ILO	International Labour Office
JIC	Joint Intelligence Committee
KGB	Komitet Gosudarstvennoi Bezopasnosti (Russian Committee of State Security)
NKVD	Narodny Kommissariat Vnutrennich Dyel (People's Commissariat For International Affairs)
NS1	Swiss Military Intelligence Centre
RSHA	Reichssicherheitshauptamt (Reich Security Headquarters)
SA	Sturmabteilung (Storm Troopers)
SD	Sicherheitsdienst (Security Service/SS Counter-Intelligence)
SOE	Special Operations Executive
SS	Schutzstaffel (Protection Squad)
STAVKA	Soviet General Staff
V-MANN	Vertrauenamann (trusty)

Index

247